Sport Foundations for Elementary Physical Education

A Tactical Games Approach

Stephen A. Mitchell, PhD

Judith L. Oslin, PhD

Kent State University

Linda L. Griffin, PhD

University of Massachusetts, Amherst

Human Kinetics

Library of Congress Cataloging-in-Publication Data

Mitchell, Stephen A., 1959-
   Sport foundations for elementary physical education : a tactical games
approach / Stephen A. Mitchell, Judith L. Oslin, Linda L. Griffin.
      p. cm.
Includes bibliographical references (p.   ).
   ISBN 0-7360-3851-5 (Soft Cover)
   1. Physical education for children--Curricula. 2. Sports--Study and
teaching (Elementary)--Curricula. I. Oslin, Judith L., 1950- II.
Griffin, Linda L., 1954- III. Title.
   GV443 .M565 2003
   372.86--dc21
                                    2002153007
ISBN: 0-7360-3851-5

Acquisitions Editor: Scott Wikgren; **Developmental Editor:** Tom McGeary; **Assistant Editor:** Kathleen D. Bernard; **Copyeditor:** NOVA Graphic Services; **Proofreader:** Erin Cler; **Permission Manager:** Dalene Reeder; **Graphic Designer:** Nancy Rasmus; **Graphic Artist:** Kathleen Boudreau-Fuoss; **Photo Manager:** Leslie A. Woodrum; **Cover Designer:** Jack W. Davis; **Photographer (cover):** Corbis; **Photographer (interior):** © Human Kinetics; **Art Manager:** Kelly Hendren; **Illustrator:** Brian McElwain; **Printer:** Versa Press

Printed in the United States of America   10   9   8   7   6   5   4   3   2   1

Human Kinetics
Web site: www.HumanKinetics.com

United States: Human Kinetics
P.O. Box 5076, Champaign, IL 61825-5076
800-747-4457
e-mail: humank@hkusa.com

Canada: Human Kinetics
475 Devonshire Road Unit 100, Windsor, ON N8Y 2L5
800-465-7301 (in Canada only)
e-mail: orders@hkcanada.com

Europe: Human Kinetics
107 Bradford Road, Stanningley, Leeds LS28 6AT, United Kingdom
+44 (0) 113 255 5665
e-mail: hk@hkeurope.com

Australia: Human Kinetics, 57A Price Avenue, Lower Mitcham, South Australia 5062
08 8277 1555
e-mail: liahka@senet.com.au

New Zealand: Human Kinetics
P.O. Box 105-231, Auckland Central
09-523-3462
e-mail: hkp@ihug.co.nz

To my wife, Carolyn,
and children, Katie and Matthew,
all enthusiastic games players.

Steve Mitchell

To my parents, Betty and Irv,
for their unconditional love and support.

Judy Oslin

To my Dad (Maurice "Moe" Griffin),
who was my first sport teacher and hero,
for believing in me
and teaching me to follow my dreams.
I am forever grateful.

Linda Griffin

contents

preface

The tactical games approach to teaching sport has increased considerably in popularity since we wrote our initial book, *Teaching Sport Concepts and Skills: A Tactical Games Approach,* in 1997. We received plenty of positive and encouraging feedback on that book from physical education teachers in the field. That book was the first, and is still the only, available textbook providing teachers with a complete rationale for teaching games and sport tactically and including practical materials to assist in planning games lessons, units, and curricula. To those teachers who provided us with valuable feedback, we thank you!

However, some of you at the elementary level have posed pertinent questions and expressed some frustrations. Your comments have included the following: "I really like this method of games teaching, but the beginning lessons seem a bit difficult for my students." "I need to try and adapt this further for my younger students." And "Please write a new book to help us make the most out of this approach with elementary students." We have written *Sport Foundations for Elementary Physical Education: A Tactical Games Approach* in response to these comments, and it is our way of saying, "This is a great way to teach games and sport at the elementary level—and here's how!"

This new book focuses on teaching the tactical concepts and associated decision-making processes, movements, and skills of sport at a level that is sufficiently simplified for the elementary student beginning at approximately the second-grade level. Those of you familiar with our first book will notice some improvements and evolution in our tactical games approach over the past several years. This book has several features:

- It has expanded game lesson formats.
- It is organized by game category instead of by individual games.
- It introduces a thematic approach to aid learning transfer.
- It discusses assessment in four learning outcome domains.
- It considers "curriculum building."

The practical materials in the book have been field tested at various elementary grade levels (beginning at the second grade), and for this we are very grateful to the physical education teachers of the Kent City Schools, particularly Linda Clemens at Davey Elementary School, Ann Wood at Walls Elementary School, Barb Vasbinder at Franklin Elementary School, and Shawn Bates at Longcoy Elementary School.

These and other physical educators who have employed a tactical approach have noted many reasons for its effectiveness in helping students learn to play games:

- Modified game play provides a developmentally appropriate environment for student learning. Changes to equipment, playing areas, and game conditions enable young children to play games that suit their needs.

- Increased time spent in game play provides a more enjoyable and motivational experience for young learners. They will not need to ask the all-too-common question, "When are we going to play a game?"

- The approach enables young learners to see the links between the skills they practice and the application of those skills to game situations.

- In the lessons, students learn to appreciate the value of skill practice. Early game play and discussion demonstrate the need for skill practice; later game play allows the application and performance of learned skills in the game. This makes for a more motivational environment during skill practice.

• The tactical components of one game can transfer to the learning of another, tactically similar game. Team handball, soccer, ultimate Frisbee, and floor hockey are tactically similar games despite using different skills and equipment, so an understanding of one should help in the performance of another. As an example, during the early stages of a second-grade invasion games unit, students were playing a modified game of team handball. When a girl whose play indicated a good understanding of supporting movements was asked by the teacher, "How did you know that was a good place to move to?" she replied simply, "I play soccer!"

If a tactical games approach is new to you, read on without concern. We will review its essential components to familiarize you with (or let you review) tactical language and thinking. After this, we consider issues of particular concern to the elementary school environment and provide lesson outlines so that you can begin thinking and teaching games using a tactical approach. Then we show how to assess learning and develop a curriculum for a tactical games approach. Good luck!

PART I

A Tactical Games Approach

chapter 1

Introduction

In writing this book, we seek to provide a useful resource for those teachers familiar with using tactical approaches to games teaching but who need additional resources specific to the elementary level. We also hope to provide a guide for elementary physical educators seeking to change the way they think about and teach games. Chapter 2 begins with an explanation, or review for those of you with tactical games experience, of the concepts underlying a tactical games approach; we also outline how a thematic approach can be adopted at the elementary level to provide a broad sport foundation for the novice learner. The four game categories (invasion games, net/wall games, striking/fielding games, and target games) are

then broken down into their tactical components through the development of tactical frameworks, and these components are sequenced for developmentally appropriate instruction in the form of levels of game complexity.

Chapter 3 addresses issues that arise in using a tactical approach, with its multiple small-sided games, at the elementary level. These issues include the need to prepare students for a tactical games approach by training them to play small-sided games, teaching appropriate sport behavior, teaching gymnasium rules and routines, developing teams, and establishing student roles and responsibilities.

Chapters 4 through 7 provide frame-works, game complexity levels, and sample lesson outlines for the four game categories. Each chapter also provides suggestions for equipment and playing area modifications, progressions to teaching the game, and conditioning or modifying games to make tactical thinking more likely. An important aspect of the thematic approach that we advocate at the elementary level is that the same lesson can apply to numerous games with just a change in skill focus (if this makes you curious, read on). This applies particularly to invasion games; chapter 4 suggests teaching cues for numerous skills within various invasion games.

Lessons in chapters 4 through 7 follow a tactical format that begins with a developmentally appropriate game form, which is a game modified to suit the students, and the learning objective for the lesson. Game play is followed by skill or movement practice tasks designed to help enhance later game performance. We also suggest task extensions for these practices that will challenge all students and provide questions you might ask to prompt students' thinking and to help them develop an awareness of the need for skill practice. Each lesson ends with game play to apply the skills and movements practiced. The lessons provided are only outlines, which we encourage you to modify as appropriate to meet your own needs and to suit your environment.

In chapter 8, we address the important issue of assessing student learning. After presenting our four main beliefs about assessment, we discuss four domains of assessment and suggest types of assessment tools to measure student learning in each domain. The chapter also emphasizes the degree to which a tactical games approach addresses the National Association of Sport and Physical Education content standards

(NASPE, 1995) for the physically educated person.

Finally, chapter 9 discusses the tactical games curriculum. We link the elementary and secondary levels and suggest how a tactical games curriculum can span the K through 12 physical education curriculum. To conclude, the chapter suggests how a tactical games approach can be broadened and considered as a curriculum model, and we discuss aspects of this model.

We thank the elementary teachers with whom we have worked. Many of our ideas come from their input or from the opportunity to put our ideas into practice in their gymnasiums. They have rethought, and are continually rethinking, their own games teaching, and we encourage you to begin or continue to do the same. Using this book as a resource, you are in a position to provide greater depth of games learning than might previously have been achieved by elementary students. This increased depth will result in your students experiencing similarities among games that will aid them in transferring learning from one situation to another, enabling you as the teacher to build game understanding and performance more quickly and effectively.

This book will provide food for thought and a challenge for many of you—it will encourage you to begin to change the way you think about and conduct games teaching. Nothing in the book is cast in stone, and we encourage you to adapt the content ideas presented in chapters 4 through 7 as necessary but within the tactical format to ensure the optimal teaching environment for yourself and the optimal learning environment for your students.

chapter 2

A Tactical Games Approach at the Elementary Level

Elementary physical education curricula typically introduce sport and games content at the second- or third-grade level. This introduction usually takes the form of teaching and learning manipulative skills through drill-type activities, as lead-up activities to game play, which will come later. In fact, we have heard some physical educators express the opinion that children as young as second grade are not capable of game play and should be restricted to skill practice only. Needless to say, we disagree with this viewpoint and argue that it is the responsibility of the teacher to modify the game so that young students can play. These modifications involve changes to game goals, equipment, team size, scoring, and playing areas.

Tactical Games

In this chapter, we discuss several important aspects of the tactical games approach. First, we describe the key features of a tactical games approach; second, we explain the thematic approach that we advocate at the elementary level.

Clarifying Terms: Tactics and Strategy

Teachers have often asked us what we mean by the term *tactical* or have asked us to differentiate between *tactics* and *strategy*, two terms that are often—but incorrectly—used interchangeably. The terms originated in military usage. *Strategy* is the military science of large-scale operations involving attempts to engage the enemy under the most advantageous conditions, whereas *tactics* is the short-range maneuvering and arranging of troops and equipment in action to achieve overall outcome. In line with this distinction, most authors who address the concept of game tactics do so with reference to problems that arise during game play. For example, Gréhaigne and Godbout (1995) define tactics as "an adaptation to opposition," meaning what players should do to respond, offensively and defensively, to the changing demands of a game in progress. For example, novice soccer players playing as defenders will stay in front of their own goal even when the ball has moved to the far end of the field. A more appropriate response to the movement of the ball in this case would be for defending players to move up the field, to at least the halfway line.

Similarly, Bunker and Thorpe (1982), in their original Teaching Games for Understanding model, aimed for a higher degree of "tactical awareness" in the learner, meaning an increased understanding of what to do during game play situations. This recognizes that decision-making capacities are particularly important during game play, but that execution of appropriate decisions might be limited by physical capabilities. Research does suggest that novice students will acquire cognitive understanding (i.e., knowledge) more easily than physical skills (French & Thomas, 1987). For example, in early net games learning, a novice tennis player might be able to see the value of pushing the opponent toward the back of the court, but she may lack the skill (i.e., the ball-striking abilities) to achieve this outcome.

Our use of the term *tactical* refers to the problems players need to solve to be successful in game play. In this sense, it corresponds quite closely to Bunker and Thorpe's notion of "what to do." Every game has two overall goals: to score and to prevent scoring by opponents.

Players and teams must also pursue a third goal: They must be able to start and restart play in such a way that they retain an advantage. For the purposes of game analysis and content planning, we identify specific "tactical problems" that players and teams must solve to score, to prevent scoring, and to restart play. For example, a soccer team must decide how to retain possession of the ball to score, how to defend space to prevent scoring, and how to keep the ball when taking a throw-in or corner kick.

We see the relationship between strategy and tactics as follows: Strategy is the overall game plan and, as such, is the sum of tactics used. One team's strategy (such as in soccer) might rely heavily on a possession game (i.e., a lot of passing) and a low-pressure defense, whereas another team might emphasize a more direct attacking style of play (more dribbling and perhaps longer passing) and a high-pressure defense. Other than to differentiate between *tactics* and *strategy*, we will not use the latter term in this book.

Our tactical games approach has three important features: a tactical classification system for games; the effects of conditioned games (i.e., games modified by simple rule changes that place students in problem-solving situations) on tactics, movements, and skills used to play the game; and the identification of tactical problems.

Classifying Games

Following a classification system proposed by Almond (1986), our tactical games approach classifies games by conditions, goals, and tactics. For example, invasion games (soccer and hockey) have similar ways of solving the fundamental tactical goals of scoring, preventing scoring, and starting and restarting play, so they are grouped together. In both soccer and hockey, the main tactical problems for the offense are keeping possession of the ball and attacking the goal. Badminton, tennis, and racquetball are also similar tactically, so they are classified as net/wall games. The other categories of games with similar problems, and therefore tactics, are striking/fielding games and target games. The complete games classification system is shown in table 2.1.

The defining features of each game category follow. In each game category, the rules and

Table 2.1 A Tactical Games Classification System

Invasion	Net/Wall	Striking/Fielding	Target
Basketball (FT)	**Net**	Baseball	Golf
Netball (FT)	Badminton (I)	Softball	Croquet
Team handball (FT)	Tennis (I)	Kickball	Bowling
Soccer (FT)	Table tennis (I)	Rounders	Lawn bowls
Hockey (FT)	Pickleball (I)	Cricket	Pool
Lacrosse (FT)	Volleyball (H)		Billiards
Water polo (FT)			Snooker
Speedball (FT/OET)	**Wall**		
Rugby (OET)	Racquetball (I)		
Football (OET)	Squash (I)		
Ultimate Frisbee (OET)	Handball (H)		
	Fives (H)		

FT = Fixed target, OET = Open-ended target, I = Implement, H = Hand target.

Adapted, by permission, from L. Almond, 1986, Reflecting on themes: A games classification. In *Rethinking games teaching*, edited by R. Thorpe, D. Bunker, and L. Almond (Loughborough University), 71-72.

conditions of play are similar. Players are faced with similar goals to accomplish, similar problems to solve, and similar decisions to make both offensively and defensively. These decisions lead to skill execution or movement without the ball.

Invasion games. Teams score by moving a ball (or other projectile) into another team's territory and either shooting into a fixed target (a goal or basket) or moving the projectile across an open-ended target (i.e., across a line). Players must usually decide among passing, shooting, or dribbling options when in possession of the ball and positioning possibilities when not in possession. To prevent scoring, one team must stop the other from bringing the ball into its territory and succeeding in scoring attempts. Decisions about whom and where to guard are important. Solving these offensive and defensive problems will require similar tactics, even though many of the skills used will be quite different. Although players must understand the need to shoot if they are to score in both floor hockey and team handball, the skills used to shoot in these two games, striking and throwing, respectively, are very different. In both, play restarts when the projectile is put into play from out-of-bounds or because of a rule violation.

Net/wall games. Teams or individual players score by hitting a ball into a court space with sufficient accuracy and power that opponents cannot hit it back before it bounces once (as in badminton or volleyball) or twice (as in tennis or racquetball). Players make important decisions based on their own strengths and weaknesses and on the positioning of opponents. These decisions often result in choices about the power and placement of shots. To prevent scoring, players and teams must return the ball before it bounces once or twice. Play restarts with a service of some kind.

Striking/fielding games. In games such as baseball, kickball, and cricket, players on the batting team must strike or kick a ball with sufficient accuracy and power that it will elude players on the fielding team and give time for the hitter to run between two points (bases or wickets). To avoid fielders, players again make decisions about the power and placement of shots, often resulting in the use of various techniques. To prevent scoring in striking/fielding games, the fielding team's members must position themselves so that they can gather or catch a hit ball and throw it to the base or wicket (to which the hitter is running) before the hitter reaches this base or wicket. In making defensive decisions, players choose where to position themselves initially and where to throw once the ball is fielded. Play is initiated by a ball being delivered, in bent- or straight-arm fashion, to a batter.

Target games. Players score by reaching a target with a ball by either throwing or striking the ball. In some target games, such as golf and lane bowling, players are unopposed, whereas in others, such as lawn bowls and croquet, players are opposed because they are allowed to block or hit their opponent's ball. In opposed target games, players seek to prevent scoring by hitting the opponent's ball to place it in a disadvantageous position relative to the target. Players must decide about equipment (as in golf) or about the power and placement of shots. Play is initiated individually at a player's turn.

Teaching Tactical Games

Here we address some important points to consider in using a tactical games approach. An understanding of game conditions, tactical problems, and teaching during game play will help you in implementing the approach.

Game Conditions

Regardless of the game (or game category from table 2.1) being taught, selection of teaching content is driven by the conditions the teacher imposes on the game. Note that by *game* we mean a competitive situation in which there are two approximately equal teams, each of which has an opportunity to score (rather than a "gamelike" practice situation such as a 3 v 1

ball possession activity). A tactical approach views games teaching this way:

**Game conditions → Tactical goal →
Tactical problems → Movements and skills**

If you consider teaching and learning games in this way, changes to the game conditions will affect the tactical problems and ultimately the movements and skills used in the game. Table 2.2 provides a soccer example.

In table 2.2, notice how a change in the game conditions affects the goal, tactics, and movements and skills of the game. In game 1, teams score by passing the ball among team members for an uninterrupted four passes. This objective emphasizes the tactical problem of keeping possession of the ball, to be solved by using the skills of passing and receiving and by supporting the player who is in possession of the ball. In game 2, players score by shooting into the opponent's goal, forcing players to solve the tactical problem of attacking a goal. They need to be able to shoot the ball to be successful in this game. Finally, in game 3, players score by passing the ball to a teammate positioned permanently behind an end line (along which she can move). The size of the playing area will also affect tactics and the skills and movements used. Using a larger field or court will lead to the need for longer passes and more sophisticated receiving skills. The point here is that you as a

---

Table 2.2   Effects of Game Conditions on Teaching Content

Game conditions	Game goal (offense)	Tactical problem	Decision/Skill/Movement
Game 1 4 v 4 (small-field) possession game 4 passes = a goal	To score by keeping the ball	Keep possession	Decision: where and when to pass Skill: short possession passes, receiving on the ground Movement: support—players position to receive a pass
Game 2 4 v 4 (small-field) game Ball in goal = 1 point	To score by shooting the ball into the opponent's goal	Attack the goal	Decision: when to shoot and where to aim Skill: shooting on the ground
Game 3 4 v 4 (small-field) game Passing to a target player = 1 point	To score by passing the ball to a target player positioned behind an end line	Attack the goal	Decision: passing between defenders Skill: penetrating passes, use of target player Movement: support—target player positions to receive a pass

teacher can influence students' use of skills during game play by instituting simple changes in the game conditions. Remember:

**Game conditions → Tactical goal →
Tactical problems → Movements and skills**

Tactical Problems of Game Play

Each game category is defined by the tactical problems associated with scoring and preventing scoring (the overall goals of game play). These tactical problems are solved by the use of particular off-the-ball movements (when players don't have the ball) and on-the-ball skills (when players have the ball). For example, in invasion games, the tactical problems associated with scoring include keeping possession of the ball, penetrating the defense and attacking the goal, and transitioning from defense to offense, whereas the tactical problems associated with preventing scoring include defend-

ing space, defending the goal, and winning the ball. During any particular tactical games lesson, a skilled teacher will modify the game in order to make players focus on solutions to a particular tactical problem. Once players see the need to practice skills to help solve tactical problems (often prompted by the teacher's questions), the teacher introduces practice tasks designed to enhance skill development. After skill practice, players return to game play to see if game performance has improved as a result of skill practice, so content for a typical tactical games lesson would be planned using a similar format to that presented in figure 2.1. Major components of the plan are in bold, followed by points for the teacher to consider. Chapters 4 through 7 contain many completed tactical game lessons.

For some teachers, the unusual feature of this planning format is that a lesson begins with game play. In fact, we are often asked why this is

---

Game _____ Lesson # _____ Grade level _____

TACTICAL PROBLEM: What is the tactical problem being addressed during the lesson?

LESSON FOCUS: What is the focus of the lesson, in terms of how the tactical problem will be solved?

OBJECTIVE: What are the major cognitive and psychomotor learning objectives for the lesson?

1. GAME 1:	What is the modified game being played?
Conditions:	What conditions will you put on the game to ensure that students have to solve the tactical problem?
Goal:	What performance goal will you give to the students for the game?
Questions:	After this initial game play, what are the questions you might need to ask (and what answers do you anticipate) to help students focus on the tactical problem and its solution?
2. PRACTICE TASK:	What skill practice is appropriate to help students develop a solution to the tactical problem when they return to game play?
Goal:	What performance goal will you give to the students for the skill practice?
Cues:	What teaching cues will you use to assist the learner in skill acquisition?
Extension:	How might you extend the skill practice to make it more challenging, or easier, for students of varying abilities?
3. GAME 2:	What is an appropriate modified game to help students apply newly learned skills to solve the tactical problem during game play?
Conditions:	What conditions will you put on the game to ensure that students use the skills learned to address the tactical problem?
Goal:	What performance goal will you give the students for the game?
4. CLOSURE:	What would make an appropriate closure or discussion for the end of the lesson?

Figure 2.1   Planning format for a tactical games lesson.

the case. The reason is this: The first game sets up the problem to be solved and, in doing so, helps the learner see the need for particular movements or skills as solutions to the problem and to appreciate the value of practicing these skills. Remember it this way:

**The game sets the problem;
the skill practice solves the problem.**

The first game and the subsequent skill practice(s) are linked by a brief question and answer period to establish the need for the skill practice. During the second game, the learner finds out how well the solutions (movements or skills) solve the problem.

A key goal for you as the teacher is to facilitate critical thinking by asking questions designed to make students think about possible solutions to the tactical problem presented by the game. An ideal time for this is after the first game, although questioning can and should be done throughout the lesson. Developing good questions is a teaching skill; we have suggested some appropriate questions in chapters 4 through 7, but do not feel limited by these. You will develop additional questions for your own use. The following suggestions might help you in the process. Your questions should do the following:

- Relate to the goal of the game.
- Ask students what to do in a particular situation.
- Ask students why one solution is better than another.
- Be open-ended (if you do not have a particular answer in mind).
- Force choice ("Is this solution or that solution better?") if you do have a particular answer in mind.

During game 1 or game 2, conditions might be applied to ensure that players address the tactical problem that is central to the lesson, though it is wise to try to ensure a period of condition-free play in the second game during which you can encourage players to solve problems on their own, without being forced to do so by the externally imposed conditions. Devising conditions for games is addressed specifically in chapters 4 through 7. It is also important to set goals for each game and practice task as a means of communicating desired performance to your students. These goals become a means of accountability for you and a measuring stick for student learning.

Teaching During Game Play

Many of our beginning teachers feel unsure of themselves while game play is in progress, and they often ask, *What should I be doing?* or *How can I teach during game play?* Frequent and focused game play is essential for students to develop effective decision-making capabilities, and, given the amount of time students spend engaged in game play when learning by a tactical approach, it is appropriate to mention teaching strategies for "teaching within the game." First, it is important to observe your students in game play once they have begun. As you observe, ask yourself the following questions:

"What is happening in the game(s)?"

"Is this what I want?"

"What changes do I need to make to help students play more effectively? Do I need to change the conditions?"

During game play, two important strategies for teaching within the game are freezing the game and reconstruction and rehearsal (which usually follow freezing the game).

Freezing the game. Use freezing the game (stopping game play) to point out (in a constructive manner) appropriate, or perhaps inappropriate, performance. Bear in mind the students need a prearranged signal for freezing, and you should stop game play immediately when you see a particular situation occur. It is also important that players freeze immediately in place so that the context of a situation is not lost.

Reconstruction and rehearsal. Having frozen a game, you can now use the process of reconstruction to identify what happened and demonstrate appropriate game performance or critique inappropriate performance. If reconstruction is used for critique, then rehearsal can follow to facilitate learning of appropriate performance, taking a "this is what should happen" approach. Reconstruction and rehearsal is potentially useful for teaching decision making, a critical component of game performance which should be taught during game lessons. To many teachers, this is synonymous with coaching. Indeed, teachers at our workshops have often said things such as, "I do this [reconstruction and rehearsal] all the time when I coach, but it never crossed my mind to do it during PE classes as well." We encourage you to teach decision making in your instruction.

A Thematic Approach to Games Teaching

In our book *Teaching Sport Concepts and Skills,* we describe a tactical games approach according to specific sports. In this section we describe the thematic tactical games approach we advocate for teaching in elementary grades. Other teaching approaches, such as the skill themes approach advocated by Graham, Holt/ Hale, and Parker (2001), suggest that student learning is best accomplished when different content is collapsed into themes to emphasize common components. Similarly, for elementary grades, we advocate teaching not discrete games, such as soccer, volleyball, and softball, but instead teaching units of invasion games, net/wall games, striking/fielding games, and target games centered on specified tactical problems. For example, in teaching invasion games such as soccer, hockey, and basketball, you might teach young students to keep possession of a ball by passing, receiving, and supporting. Depending on the length of your instructional unit, time spent on invasion games might also include the learning of shooting techniques. In this way, students learn to solve the tactical problems of invasion games play rather than looking only at the skills of a specific game in isolation.

This approach is intended to develop more knowledgeable and adaptable game players at the elementary level—players who can switch easily among different invasion games or among different net games and retain a degree of understanding of game play that transfers from one game to another. For example, because of the similarity among invasion games, students should be able to move from soccer to hockey and retain a degree of understanding of game tactics.

This thematic approach will be a different way of thinking for many teachers, who will voice concern about the lack of time for skill development in any one activity. Our response is simple: Because of the large amount of practice time required for skill development, competence is rarely (and proficiency is almost never) achieved in elementary games teaching and learning. Regardless of the approach used, there is insufficient curriculum time for skill learning to occur, but some depth of tactical learning is both possible and desirable.

The development of instructional materials for such a thematic approach requires that you first identify the tactical problems to be addressed in elementary games teaching and then appropriately sequence instruction related to these tactical problems. Our attempt to do this takes the form of tactical frameworks and levels of game complexity.

Tactical Frameworks

Games should be broken down into tactical problems. Solutions to these problems will be in the form of (1) decisions to be made, (2) off-the-ball movements, and (3) selection and execution of on-the-ball skills. These solutions represent the content of games instruction at the elementary level. We recommend the development of frameworks similar to that for invasion games presented in table 2.3, which shows a tactical framework for invasion games. This framework provides the scope of content for teaching invasion games at the elementary level by breaking down invasion games according to the problems associated with scoring, preventing scoring, and starting or restarting play. The levels of "game complexity" provided in the subsequent section provide an appropriate sequence for this content. Taken together, the framework and levels of game complexity provide developmentally appropriate scope and sequence of invasion games content for elementary children. Ideally, game play should be of no larger than 3 v 3 players at first, progressing to a maximum of 6 v 6 players in games such as soccer and hockey.

Levels of Game Complexity

Tactical content should be sequenced in order to make games instruction developmentally appropriate. We recommend identifying levels of game complexity for each games category.

Table 2.3 A Tactical Framework for Content for Teaching Invasion Games

	Decisions	
Tactical goals and problems	**Movements (off-the-ball)**	**Skills (on-the-ball)**
Offense and scoring		
Keeping possession of the ball	Supporting the ball carrier When to pass	Passing and receiving the ball
Penetrating the defense and attacking the goal	Using a target forward When to shoot and dribble	Moving with the ball Shooting Faking
Transition	Moving to space—when and where to move	Quick passing
Defense and preventing scoring		
Defending space	Guarding and marking Footwork Pressuring the ball carrier	
Defending the goal	Goalkeeping—positioning Rebounding—boxing out	Goalkeeping—stopping and distributing the ball Rebounding—taking the ball
Winning the ball		Tackling and stealing the ball
Starting and restarting play		
Beginning the game	Positioning	Initiating play
Restarting from the sideline	Supporting positions	Putting the ball in play
Restarting from the end line	Supporting positions	Putting the ball in play
Restarting from violations	Supporting positions	Putting the ball in play

These levels will include the learning of concepts, movements, and skills across a variety of games. So at level I you might teach your students to keep possession of a ball by passing, receiving, and supporting in soccer, hockey, and basketball. Depending on the length of time spent on invasion games, level I might also include the learning of shooting techniques in these games. Table 2.4 presents three possible levels of complexity for invasion games, on which the development of unit and lesson plans can be based. Notice that we advocate beginning invasion games play with no more than three players per team. This limit allows for some decision making (*Should I pass to player A or player B?*) but does not force a vast range of possibilities. We have even found two-a-side games to be effective because this situation decreases the passing options, forcing players to make straightforward decisions (*Do I pass to my teammate, shoot, or dribble?*). Such a limit represents decreased complexity in the early stages of invasion games learning. Table 2.4 shows how game

complexity can increase as students progress through levels II and III. Transition is a more complex tactical problem and is addressed only at level III.

Using a tactical games approach, you can plan instructional units that enable students to learn to address similar tactical problems across a variety of invasion games. Looking at table 2.4, you can see that students' initial exposure to invasion games might address the concepts of possession, penetration, defending space, and simple starts and restarts while they play a small, conditioned version (2 v 2 or 3 v 3) of any invasion game. Although the game can be changed at any time (because the problems addressed are similar, regardless of the game being played), the skills taught would be different. For example, skills needed to keep possession in soccer are different from those needed in basketball and hockey. However, the key to this approach is that, by learning the same concepts, students will more quickly understand what needs to be done to play invasion games successfully.

Table 2.4   Levels of Game Complexity for Invasion Games

Tactical goals and problems	Level of game complexity		
	Level I **Three-a-side maximum**	**Level II** **Four-a-side maximum**	**Level III** **Six-a-side maximum**
Offense and scoring			
Keeping possession	Pass, receive, footwork When to pass	Pass, receive, footwork Support	
Penetration and attack	Shooting, moving with the ball (dribbling) When to dribble and shoot	Shooting, feinting	Using a target forward Shooting, faking, change of speed, moving with the ball
Transition			Moving to space, quick passing
Defense and preventing scoring			
Defending space		Guarding or marking, pressure	Clearing the ball, quick outlet pass
Defending the goal		Goalkeeper positioning	Goalkeeper shot stopping and distribution, rebounding
Winning the ball			Tackling and stealing the ball
Starting and restarting play			
Beginning the game	Initiating play	Positioning in a triangle	
Restarting from the sideline and end line	Putting ball in play	Positioning	Quick restarts
Restarting from violations	Putting ball in play	Positioning	Quick restarts

Summary

To conclude this chapter, we will summarize the essentials of using a thematic approach to teaching tactical games. These essentials can be summarized in the following seven points:

1. The tactical games approach is a teaching method. (It can also be viewed as a curriculum model, which is discussed in chapter 9.) It is a problem-solving approach for games teaching that improves knowledge of games and game performance, and it is motivational because the student does the following:
   - Spends plenty of time in game play.
   - Sees the value of skill practice before engaging in it.
   - Discovers tactical similarities among different games.

2. A tactical games approach classifies games according to their tactical similarities: invasion games, net/wall games, striking/fielding games, and target games.

3. At the elementary level, we advocate a thematic approach in which game instruction is focused on the preceding classification rather than on specific games so that students come to understand game similarities.

4. Within each of the categories, games can be broken down into tactical problems, which become the focus of planning and instruction.

5. Players learn to solve tactical problems during game play by making decisions: using movements when they don't have the ball (off-the-ball) and using skills when they do have the ball (on-the-ball).

6. After identifying tactical problems and their solutions, learning solutions can be sequenced progressively from simple to complex. At higher levels of development

(perhaps at fifth grade rather than third grade), a teacher should plan to teach game play involving more complex tactical problems and solutions.

7. A tactical games approach lesson uses the following format:

    a. The lesson begins with a conditioned game that requires students to think about the tactical problem. The game is set up to present a problem and to make students think about what they need to do to solve the problem. A brief question and answer segment leads students to identify possible solutions (involving movements and skills) to the tactical problem.

    b. Students then practice the movements and skills needed to solve the tactical problem. Task extensions are planned and used as appropriate.

    c. The lesson finishes with a second game in which the students apply newly learned movements and skills.

    d. Verbal closure reinforces understanding of the problem and its solution.

chapter 3

Preparing Students for a Tactical Games Approach

This chapter describes how to prepare young students to adapt to a tactical games approach to teaching. These young learners will need to be well trained so that they can undertake independent activity. You should make no assumptions about how they understand your expectations. You should be prepared to direct activities, such as warming up and stretching in the early lessons, and to demonstrate and set up game play. A tactical approach requires that elementary students engage in game play independently in small groups; this requirement is a different way of learning for most elementary

students. An additional concern for most elementary teachers is the time factor. Many elementary physical education teachers have back-to-back classes approximately 30 to 40 minutes long. When one class is finished, the next class is already lined up at the door ready to enter the gymnasium—a scenario familiar to many of you who teach in elementary schools—and a first-grade class might be followed by a fourth-grade and then a third-grade class, making it virtually impossible to set up equipment and leave it for three classes in a row. The time factor is particularly problematic for games teaching, in which equipment setup is crucial. Especially specific to a tactical games approach is the problem of fitting the game–skill practice–game format into a 30- to 40-minute time period. The use of multiple small-sided games requires considerable coordination and training of students; setting up the multiple games could be time consuming if teachers are not well organized.

This chapter provides suggestions to ease the transition to a tactical approach and to enable both teachers and students to manage a new environment for teaching and learning.

Training Students to Play Small-Sided Games

This section outlines procedures for training elementary students, as young as second grade, to play small-sided (usually modified or conditioned) games independently. In particular, young learners must learn simple rule structures and to respect the game play of other games on adjacent courts or fields, particularly when a ball enters another court. Second-grade students have shown their ability to adhere to two simple rules:

1. When your ball rolls into another game, wait at the edge of that court or field for the ball to be returned to you (move around the outside of the gymnasium if necessary).

2. When a ball rolls into your game from another game, stop it and roll it back to that game (or to the nearest sideline if the other game is too far away).

Simple though they seem, these rules must be taught and reinforced in the early stages of games teaching, when multiple games are being played. We and other teachers at the elementary level have found young learners more than able to restrain themselves from rushing onto another court to retrieve a ball and also able to resist the temptation to kick or throw away a ball that has come into their game from another game. Once again, teach and reinforce these rules.

An additional challenge lies in having elementary students learn and understand the court or field boundaries. We advise assigning students to permanent courts or fields to aid in this learning. For example, in figure 3.1 the gymnasium is divided into four courts for invasion

games teaching, presumably by taped lines on the floor, each of which is numbered. Play is conducted across the width of the gymnasium so that each court is longer than it is wide, and teams (which remain the same throughout a games unit) are permanently assigned to a home court for entry into the gymnasium and warm-up activities. This organization facilitates a smooth and active start to lessons, with students knowing where to go immediately upon entry into the gymnasium. Preset warm-up activities enable teams to enter the gym and begin activity immediately and independently. Attendance taking is usually unnecessary at the elementary level, but if required, this can be done while students are warming up. Learners at the second-grade level can work independently in this way if organized and taught to do so. We stress that you can and should teach routines, rules, warm-up procedures, and other aspects of management in much the same way as you

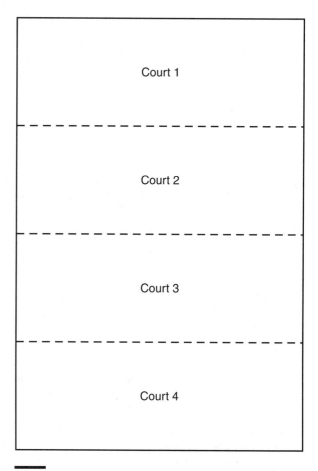

Figure 3.1 Permanent court or field assignment for invasion games.

might teach other lesson content. Provide plenty of opportunities for students to practice routines and give appropriate feedback and praise for successful implementation.

Figure 3.2 illustrates possible setups for net games. In figure 3.2a, the gymnasium is divided into halves, with an equal number of court spaces (6) in each half, providing 12 small courts. Nets are spread across each half of the gymnasium, providing multiple playing areas for net games. Note that in the early stages of net games learning (perhaps at second grade), you may decide to work without nets and instead might use cones, ropes, or simply a line over which the ball must cross. This makes court setup easier for younger children. Figure 3.2b shows the nets set up over the length of the gymnasium, creating multiple court spaces, in this case four courts, across the gymnasium.

Field arrangements for striking/fielding games can also be accomplished in such a way as to ensure that young learners receive maximum opportunity for involvement in game play. Of course, for this to occur, teachers must dispense with the traditional single game approach, in which players receive very little ball contact, either in the form of batting or fielding. Figure 3.3 illustrates a triangular setup; three games back to back and a "safety zone" in the middle for batting teams is ideal. In this setup, batting teams are always hitting away from each other. Each field might be split in half so that even smaller spaces can be used for 2 v 2 or 3 v 3 games, as will be illustrated in chapter 6 on striking/fielding games.

Teaching Appropriate Sport Behavior

In most second- or third-grade classes, several children will have gained youth sport experience through programs run by the local parks and recreation department or perhaps by the

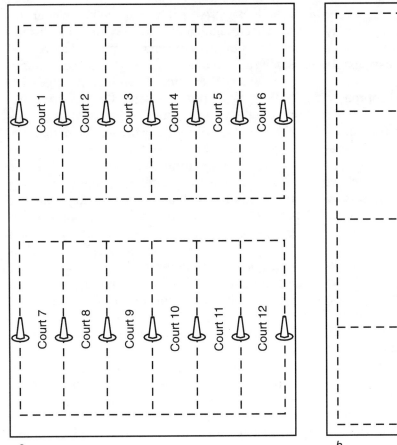
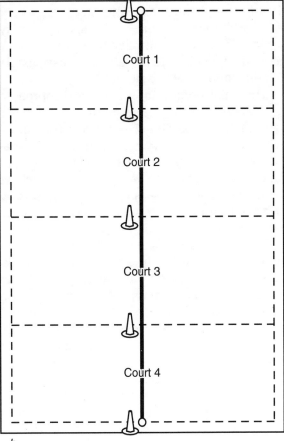

Figure 3.2 *(a)* Split gymnasium for net games and *(b)* lengthwise net arrangement.

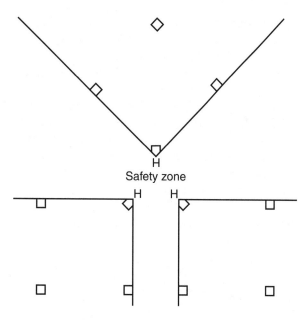

Figure 3.3 Multiple striking/fielding game-playing areas.

YMCA or YWCA. However, these programs are administered and coached by adults, often with lower coach-to-player ratios than the 1:20 or 1:30 facing physical education teachers every day. Additionally, these programs often play large-sided games controlled by an adult, alleviating the need for the players to be responsible for the conduct of the game.

The small-sided nature of a tactical approach, combined with the higher number of students per teacher, makes it necessary for students to learn to organize their own game play cooperatively so that they are able to play a purposeful game. In the following paragraphs, we suggest organizational strategies to accomplish this by describing appropriate sport behavior in a constructive manner.

The organization of teams and assignment of simple roles and responsibilities can facilitate learning game play and appropriate sport behavior. In this section, we advocate the use of the Sport Education curriculum model (Siedentop, 1994) to provide mechanisms for team, equipment, and game organization, as a means of developing appropriate sport behaviors. Several features of the Sport Education model help students develop into competent, literate, and enthusiastic sports persons. Rather than describe these features in depth, we will briefly describe the way we have used the Sport Education model to facilitate use of a tactical

approach to games instruction at the elementary level.

Figure 3.4 is the team contract we presented to a class of fourth-grade students at the beginning of a team handball "season." Each student accepted responsibility for one of the roles on the contract and signed his name next to that role to confirm a willingness to carry out the necessary responsibilities. Once responsibilities were defined, it became much easier for these fourth-grade students to enter the gymnasium and begin play immediately. Each team was assigned a "home court," to which they would go upon entering the gym. The equipment manager would distribute vests of the appropriate color and set up goals, while the coach went to the "coaches' corner" to read the starting activity (game) from the chalkboard. The administrator took attendance, and warm-up and stretching began under the direction of the athletic trainer. Teams remained the same throughout the season with 2 v 2 games played within the team and 4 v 4 games between teams. Likewise, following class demonstrations, skill practices were organized at the home court by the coach, eliminating the need for time-consuming transitions to alternative playing areas and saving any confusion on the part of the students as to where they should conduct practices.

With each student aware of her responsibilities to the team, lessons began and ran to conclusion smoothly and in a time-efficient manner. The teacher informed the coaches of small changes, eliminating the need to gather the class together to communicate information. In this team handball unit, students kept track of win-loss records and fair play points (awarded by the teacher) to decide on a regular season champion prior to commencing "play-offs." Several good discussions took place within and among teams concerning individual members' responsibilities and the importance of ensuring that those responsibilities were met. Sport behavior was also discussed, and the importance of fair play and effective leadership by coaches became apparent. Disputes were resolved by a "do-over," and teachers stressed the value of shaking hands and congratulating your opponents on a well-played game.

We gave a simpler version of the contract, called an "agreement," to a second-grade class; the only defined role was that of equipment

TEAM CONTRACT

Class_____ Semester_____ Sport_____

Team name _____

The team members and especially the coaches are to be good examples to their teams in these ways:

I. Fair play—Know and play by class and game rules.

II. Hard work—Practice and work your hardest to be a good team player. Congratulate your teammates and opponents on playing well, not only on winning. Shake hands.

III. Cooperation—Whenever possible, team decisions should be made by all team members together.

IV. Respect—for classmates, teachers, equipment.

V. Positive attitude—Work hard to encourage team members to be positive.

VI. Responsibility—Help in lesson organization by carrying out your role.

We will do our best to carry out our roles and to cooperate and work as a team under the leadership of our coach.

TEAM MEMBERS' SIGNATURES

_____ (Coach—organize practices)

_____ (Athletic trainer—organize warm-up and stretching)

_____ (Equipment manager—give out and collect equipment)

_____ (Reporter—sports reporting)

* Do your best   *** Play by the rules**   *** Congratulate your opponents**

* Play fair   *** Encourage your teammates**   *** Have fun!**

Figure 3.4 Sample team contract.

From *Sport Foundations for Elementary Physical Education* by Stephen Mitchell, Judith Oslin, and Linda Griffin, 2003, Champaign, IL: Human Kinetics.

manager, which was shared on a rotational basis. With this second-grade class, the Sport Education model was limited to maintaining the same teams and home courts throughout the season, ensuring that these young learners understood their own boundaries of play.

Teaching Rules and Routines

In this section we suggest some simple rules and routines that will be helpful in making tactical games lessons run smoothly within the short time frame (30 to 40 minutes) available to the elementary physical education teacher.

Entry Into the Gymnasium (or Playing Field) and Equipment Management

Routines have an enormous impact on effective use of time in physical education. We see many classes that begin with the students sitting in squads, on spots, or in a circle so that attendance can be taken and the teacher can explain what will happen and distribute equipment. We advocate routines that allow for a more active start to a lesson, in which students enter the gymnasium and begin activity immediately, organizing their own equipment. We have already provided one example of a fourth-grade routine in this chapter (see the Sport Education example mentioned previously), but perhaps an additional example will serve to illustrate the value of time-efficient routines for gymnasium entry.

Consider a second-grade class of 24 students involved in net games play, in which they are learning the tactics, skills, and movements of a modified net game against an opponent (singles play) in a designated playing area. Rather than use a net in the early stages of play, they engage in a simple throw-and-catch game across a line (or perhaps across a jump rope laid flat on the floor), which enables students to work on tactical aspects of play without having to worry about having to clear the height of a net. The game also uses a mandatory "one bounce within the boundary" rule (i.e., the ball must bounce once on the opposite side of the "net"). Assuming that equipment is not left out by the previous class (because this class might have been kindergartners or fifth graders, who are learning something different), the teacher's first task involves setting up 12 playing areas and getting play started as quickly as possible. Obviously, it is not time effective for the teacher to set up all the playing areas; she needs a simple system for the students to follow so that they can set up their own playing areas. Using the available gymnasium floor lines, it is easy for the students to set up playing areas such as those in figure 3.2a. Students enter the gymnasium and, in their established pairs, set up the court by taking cones from a predetermined location and placing them in the appropriate place. It is important to use small pieces of colored floor tape to guide students in placing the cones in the right position. Court setup can be accomplished independently by one player, while the opponent can locate the ball to be used. Play can begin immediately after the court is set up.

Restart Rules

Games have natural breaks in play (frequent during the early stages of learning), so students must learn how to initiate their own game play and how to restart play when a natural break occurs, such as the ball going out-of-bounds or into the net. First, experienced players know that when one team causes a ball to go out-of-bounds in an invasion game, the game is restarted at the sideline by the other team.

This concept will need to be taught to young novice players and frequent reminders provided until the rule is understood. As a principle, it is best to adapt restart rules to increase the likelihood that a team passing the ball into play can do so successfully so that the game can restart without the ball going immediately out-of-bounds again. You might stipulate that any defender must be at least one arm's length back from the player taking the in-bounds pass, or you might use a rule that the first pass into play is "free" (i.e., cannot be intercepted) but that it must go backward (i.e., toward the passer's own goal).

In a game such as soccer, where a ball is thrown into play and must be controlled with the feet, we recommend use of a free "kick-in," which makes it easier for the ball to be controlled by a receiving player. Options for restarting after a goal is scored can also vary between a restart at the center (as in soccer) to a restart from the goal line (as in basketball). The advantage of using a restart from the goal line in all invasion games teaching is that it speeds up play; players will learn to restart more quickly and make an effective transition from defense to offense before the opposing team recovers. The advantage of a restart at the center of the court or field is that it enables a team who has conceded a goal to restart from farther up the court or field. The choice will be yours and it may depend on characteristics and preferences of your students.

Similarly, some sensible principles will help with efficient restarts in net games. First, at the early stages of learning net games, all starts and restarts (i.e., "service") should take the form of an underhand toss or in volleyball a "rainbow" toss. This provides a ball that is easier for the opponent to receive and therefore increases the likelihood of a longer rally or point being played. Second, service should alternate every point so that no single player can dominate a game (or be dominated) by having a strong (or weak) service. Third, in games where rules state that scoring is only done by the serving player or team, as in badminton or volleyball (or elementary modifications of them), a "rally scoring" system can be used where points can be scored on either team's serve. Again, this rule provides more scoring opportunities for novice learners.

Defense Rules

The intensity of defense, particularly in invasion games, is often a hindrance to offensive performance. (We hear you saying, "As it is supposed to be!"). Although high-intensity defense is necessary for effective game play, it also makes it less likely that decision-making capacity and motor skill performance will develop. We advocate the teaching and use of a graded system of defense, beginning with cold defense and moving through warm and hot defense. Cold defense is obviously the easiest type of defense to play against. In skill practice and game situations, this amounts to defenders simply being obstacles for players to have to pass or move around. Defenders can neither intercept passes nor knock balls from their opponents' hands when playing cold defense, making it somewhat inappropriate for game play situations.

On the other hand, warm defense is ideal for game play situations with novice players because it allows players to intercept passes but not knock the ball out of an opponent's hands or tackle an opponent. In warm defense, a defender must stay one arm's length away from the player in possession of the ball, providing some space and time for decision making and skill execution. Warm defense also provides an appropriate extension of skill practice tasks that begin with cold defense to facilitate skill performance. Hot defense is recommended as a progression once decision making and skill learning have taken place. Players are permitted to intercept passes and to tackle in hot defense, the latter having implications for the teaching of appropriate sport behavior as outlined previously in this chapter.

Getting Started

A few comments about getting started with a tactical games approach are in order, echoing advice we always give at in-service workshops and the suggestions we gave in *Teaching Sport Concepts and Skills.* Here are four suggestions.

First, *choose one class and make it a class with which you have good rapport, with students who will be adaptable to a new way of doing things.* The student takes on more responsibility for her own learning in a tactical games approach, making it important that a class be self-directed in the early stages as you familiarize yourself with the new teaching method.

Second, *select a game or game category with which you are comfortable, so that you can be confident that you have a high degree of content knowledge.* Familiarity with the content will enable you to adapt to a new teaching method free of concerns about developing teaching content that is appropriate to the level of the learner.

Third, *be prepared to let go of tasks such as equipment management, and learn to approach your teaching from a question-driven perspective.* This approach will help you to allow students some input to their learning and will enable you to produce thinking games players in your classes.

Finally, *find company.* Work with others who are inclined to think the same way. Share your ideas with other elementary teachers in your and other districts and discuss tactical games teaching with physical educators at the secondary level, some of whom may already use this approach. Good luck!

PART II

Lesson Plans
for Elementary Games Teaching

chapter 4

Sport Foundations for Invasion Games

Invasion games, with numerous simple and complex decision-making challenges, provide the early learner with more freedom of movement than other game types and with the opportunity to interact with peers in a socially oriented team environment. These features make invasion games wonderful vehicles for high levels of activity and for the achievement of psychomotor, cognitive, behavioral and social, and affective learning outcomes.

Modifications for Invasion Games

In the following sections, we suggest modifications (or conditions) for teaching invasion games. These modifications are intended to ensure a developmentally appropriate progression of learning and an environment conducive to understanding invasion game play.

Equipment and Playing Areas

As a rule of thumb, early invasion game experiences should be of the throw-and-catch variety, such as a simple version of team handball, because this type of game incorporates manipulative skills that young elementary school students (again, we are thinking of second grade as a starting point) are able to perform in both practice and game situations played in confined space, as is typically the case in the average elementary school gymnasium. Medium-sized sponge balls (about 8–9 inches, or 20–22 centimeters, in diameter) work well for the throw-and-catch game because they are big enough to facilitate catching, small enough to not hinder throwing, and soft enough that no one will get hurt when hit with the ball. Several sizes of balls, as well as of Frisbees™, made from foam are commercially available, and these should be in every elementary school physical educator's equipment storeroom.

In early throw-and-catch games, it is wise to eliminate movements with the ball, such as running or dribbling, so that passing, receiving, shooting, and movement by supporting teammates become the focus of the game. Allowing young players to move with the ball will lead to either excessive physical contact or to players simply running or dribbling down the court with their heads down. Once students start to become more competitive with each other, it is also wise to restrict defense to intercept passes only. You could call this *arm's length defense* or alternately, to distinguish among different levels of defensive intensity, *warm defense,* as described in chapter 3. Again, this suggests that *cold defense* will involve very low defensive intensity (probably in skill practice situations), whereas *hot defense* conditions will allow players to knock the ball out of their opponents' hands.

Once students are accustomed to playing a simple throw-and-catch invasion game, teachers might progress to a different game that uses similar skills or perhaps to one that uses different skills but emphasizes similar tactical problems. By choosing a game that requires different skills, you emphasize the transfer of tactical understanding. The game can only require skills that young players are able to perform, such as a modified floor hockey game, perhaps "pillow

polo," using sponge balls of varying sizes (depending on the students' ability to strike the ball) and commercially available pillow polo sticks, which have a Styrofoam head. At this point, the new game will allow students to move with the ball by dribbling, opening up a range of new offensive possibilities as players penetrate the defense with the ball. It will, of course, be important to revisit the rules regarding balls intruding onto neighboring courts because control of the ball will be more difficult with the stick and the ball will therefore go out-of-bounds more frequently. It will be difficult to eliminate dribbling in games such as soccer and hockey, and increased movement will increase demands on the available space, suggesting that these games should be played outdoors where possible. Also, outdoor surfaces, particularly grass, slow the movement of the ball, making skill execution easier.

Notice that in the level I invasion game lessons, the first four lessons emphasize keeping possession in team handball—a throw-and-catch game requiring lower levels of skill. Once students are comfortable playing these games independently, the remaining lessons rotate team handball with pillow polo while focusing on the tactical problem of attacking the goal. Addressing the same tactical problem reinforces players' tactical understanding of game play; it reintroduces tactical problems in different invasion games to provide depth of tactical learning and transfer of tactical learning from one game to another. As students become more independent games players, it will even be possible to switch the equipment during a lesson so that more than one game is played addressing a particular tactical concept. Switching equipment during a lesson is more likely to be possible with level II or III learners than with those at level I. Where more space is available, in larger gymnasiums or outside areas, it will be possible to expand the range of invasion games played to include games such as soccer, in which the ball travels farther and faster and in which more time is needed to execute difficult ball control skills.

Game Conditions

A critical aspect of a tactical approach to teaching games is the use of game conditions to increase the likelihood that players will have to think about ways to overcome a problem and execute skills appropriately. Creating and designing game conditions really involves little more than the teacher applying simple rule modifications and adjusting any or all of the goal of the game, the scoring system, playing areas, and equipment so that players are faced with a problem that must be solved through the application of particular movements and skills. Think of yourselves as "architects of task design." Consider these examples:

1. In a situation in which you want players to think about how to keep the ball as a team by supporting the player in possession, it makes sense to play a possession game with the goal of completing a certain number of consecutive passes in order to score a point. Restricted movement for the player with the ball will also encourage supporting players to move to a space where they can receive a pass.

2. Conditions related to defense, in addition to the use of cold, warm, or hot defense, can have a valuable effect on offensive play. For example, in basketball, you might want players (probably older elementary students) to think about and execute shots from outside the shooting key as a prelude to practicing jump shots in a skill practice setting. By establishing the condition that the defending team must stay inside the key, it becomes less likely that the offensive team will try to shoot from close to the basket and more likely that they will shoot from outside, where they have space and time.

3. When you add direction to the game by moving from the possession game to a game that involves shooting into a goal (see the following section), you will see some players who attempt to shoot from a long distance. This cuts down on team play and eliminates some of the passing, receiving, and supporting work previously practiced. It is tempting to insert a condition that forces players to pass a certain number of times (say three times) before any team member can shoot, but this might have two unintended and negative effects:

- First, it might actually penalize players who get the ball into a shooting position with one or two excellent passes to players who are supporting effectively. Not being allowed to shoot in this case can become frustrating for players.

- Second, those quick-witted players seeking to take advantage of the condition might simply make three very quick, short passes before one of them takes a long shot anyway.

Rather than a three-pass condition, it is probably better to stipulate an area of the court or field from where players must shoot in order to score, ensuring that the team must work together to get the ball to this area. To prevent an excessive number of long shots, it might be best to stipulate that teams must get the ball across midcourt (at the halfway line) or perhaps into the offensive third of the court or field before taking a shot.

The previous examples illustrate the simplicity of setting game conditions. As the teacher, you should ask yourself the following two questions: *What do I want my students to think about and do in this game?* and *How do I design the game to make this happen?* Although this may be a different way of thinking for many of you (at least perhaps initially), the more game conditions you devise, the easier it becomes to develop conditions that will make students think about solving particular problems through the use of specific skills. Remember, the conditions of the game set the problem to be solved and help students see value in the use of particular skills before these skills are then isolated for practice.

Progressions for Teaching Invasion Game Play

We and our colleagues in elementary schools have frequently raised the issue of the starting point and progressions for learning game play. Specifically, we have asked the following two questions:

1. What type of invasion game provides the easiest introduction for the elementary school student?

2. What types of invasion games best enable students to make progress and develop their understanding of game playing to a more mature level?

The following suggestions represent our thinking concerning these two questions.

Possession Games

A 2 v 2 or 3 v 3 possession (keepaway) game is a sensible game form when you are beginning to teach the invasion game. Be aware that 3 v 3 is more complex than 2 v 2 because the extra player on each team provides an additional passing option. Early lessons in this chapter use a 3 v 3 format, but this format could be changed to 2 v 2 if simplification is necessary. The choice of game (i.e., two- or three-a-side) may also be determined by class numbers, gymnasium size, and available equipment. Regardless of team size, it should be possible to fit several small-sided possession games into a normal-sized elementary school gymnasium (assuming a class size of about 24 students). Figure 4.1 shows six games of 2 v 2 in a gymnasium, whereas figure 4.2 shows four games of 3 v 3. Floor tape can easily be used to mark playing areas for either format.

The benefit of the possession game is that young learners do not have to concern them-

selves with direction. They can simply move anywhere on the court and count the number of passes the team makes. You might notice any or all of the following things occurring early on in the students' learning of possession games:

1. Some players (say at the second-grade level) might be reluctant to play against the other team to the point that they will stand and watch while opponents pass the ball back and forth. If this is the case, you will probably need to encourage them to try and "get" (intercept) the other team's passes.

2. Players will stand still, hold out their hands, and yell, "Throw it here!" Assuming that the other team has responded to your previous (if necessary) prompts to intercept passes, the stationary player on the first team is very easy to guard simply because she is static. You will need to encourage these players to move into open space.

3. Not only will players stand still and expect to receive a pass, but they will also stand

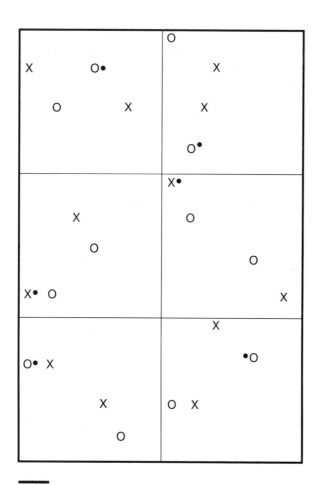

Figure 4.1   A gym floor layout for 2 v 2 invasion games.

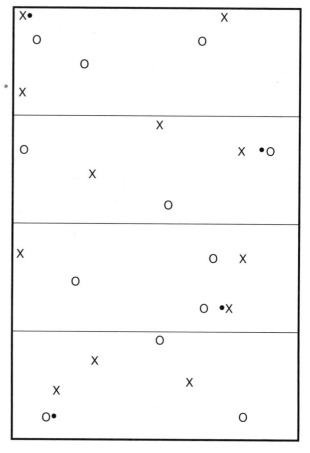

Figure 4.2   A gym floor layout for 3 v 3 invasion games.

close to the player who has the ball, which sometimes happens because teachers have, perhaps rightly, suggested that short passes will work better than long ones. This proximity makes the game very congested and decreases the likelihood of completed passes because the poor use of space decreases the amount of time available to players. Try suggesting to players that they will actually be more helpful to a teammate who has the ball by moving away from him into open space. Be aware that some may take this as meaning "go to the next county" and move out of accurate passing range, so you will probably need to demonstrate appropriate distances.

4. You will often notice that the player with the ball will take a long time to decide to pass to an open teammate. This can cause frustration because by the time the player in possession makes the pass, defenders have moved to guard the previously open player. Remember that speed of thought in game play is developmental in the same way that motor skill is. It is only by being put in these decision-making situations that young games players will develop the ability to make appropriate decisions with sufficient speed to allow for effective implementation. Occasional freezing and reconstructing of game situations to demonstrate appropriate decisions will be a useful teaching strategy.

5. You might notice that the player with the ball often goes unguarded. This actually represents some intelligent thinking on the part of novice players, which we have seen in students as young as second grade. It is an acknowledgment that the player with the ball cannot move (as per the rules you have established) and is, therefore, not a threat. What you will see in this case is an effective double teaming of the other player (in a 2 v 2 game). This makes it very difficult for a team to keep possession of the ball, and the situation might require some intervention from the teacher. Try any or all of the following: Require one-to-one guarding, encourage a lot of movement from the supporting player to make double teaming harder, and allow the player with the ball to take three steps while in possession.

6. Remember that you will have to teach start and restart rules, particularly for the out-of-bounds balls.

Games to a Goal

The best way to increase the complexity of invasion game play for young learners is to place a goal (using a pair of cones) at each end of the court or field and tell one team to try to throw the ball through one goal and the other team to throw the ball through the other goal. Some words of caution here:

1. Some young learners will need several reminders of the goal into which they are attempting to score.

2. It is best to restrict movement with the ball to either one step or, to prevent arguments, to no movement at all.

3. Insist that the ball must be traveling downward (unless it has bounced first) as it goes between the cones and that it must go cleanly through the cones (i.e., if the ball hits the cone, it does not count).

4. Remember to specify warm defense and to teach restarts for out-of-bounds balls.

At first, it is best to restrict the width of the goal (to about 6–8 feet, or 1.8–2.4 meters) so that a goalkeeper is not necessary. This goal size keeps all players active and involved in the decision-making aspects of the game. As game-playing proficiency improves, it becomes appropriate to widen the goal (12–16 feet, or 3.7–4.9 meters) and include a goalkeeper. A goalkeeper creates a greater challenge for shooting accuracy and, as a by-product, is a useful strategy for taking a player out of field play to provide more space for field players to play the game. Again, some words of advice: First, make sure that the ball being used is sufficiently soft so that it will not hurt a goalkeeper on contact; second, for safety reasons, specify a line past which no player other than the goalkeeper can move (some teachers tape a goalie's box on the floor); and third, rotate the goalkeeper frequently.

Games to a Target Player

Moving on a little in complexity, all invasion games require that teams penetrate the opponent's defense in order to make progress toward the goal. A useful way of teaching penetration is to position a target player in the other team's half of the field or court and try to reach this player with an early pass. This is a good way of moving the ball forward quickly to transition from defense to offense. In soccer, this player is actually referred to as a *target player,* whereas basketball uses the term *post player.* Regardless of the term used (we will use *target player*), the incorporation of the target player into a small-sided game is a useful way to teach penetration by encouraging players to look for gaps in the opposing team's defense through which to pass to the target player, thereby penetrating the defense. In the 3 v 3 game, a team scores by getting the ball to its target player (OT or XT), as shown in figure 4.3.

The following are points to be aware of in target player games:

1. Players need to be reminded that the target player is replacing the goal, the purpose of the game being no longer to shoot through the goal but to *pass to their own*

target player, who is positioned behind an end line in the offensive end.

2. Target players will have an initial tendency to stand still (which will not help their teammates reach them with a pass) and will need to be reminded that they can move at any time, anywhere along the end line to help open up gaps through which teammates can pass.

3. It will be important to emphasize appropriate restarts after a team has reached the target player (target players must give the ball back to the other team after a score so that play changes direction).

Games to an End Zone

Some invasion games, such as American football, rugby, and ultimate Frisbee involve scoring in an end zone. These games represent increased complexity because players must carry the ball (or Frisbee) into the end zone or receive it inside. Again, these games can easily be played using gymnasium lines and modified equipment. This type of game is also useful for emphasizing moving with the ball. If dribbling in soccer or basketball is the focus of instruction, it might be appropriate to have players score by dribbling the ball under control across the end line and into the end zone. Again, restarts (giving the ball back to the other team after a score) will need to be reviewed to prevent a team from simply moving in and out of the end zone with the ball, claiming to have scored each time. In addition, safety must be stressed in games such as ultimate Frisbee and football, in which players might be running forward but looking back to receive a pass.

Scope and Sequence

In developing the content suggestions for this and the next three chapters, we have asked ourselves the following three questions:

1. What are the problems or concepts of invasion games that can be realistically addressed at the elementary level? (That is, how much can elementary students understand about game play?)

2. How are these problems solved by movements that occur without the ball (off-the-

Figure 4.3 Court or field layouts for 3 v 3 invasion game with target players. XT and OT are target players positioned in their respective end zones.

ball) and skills that are performed with the ball (on-the-ball)?

3. How can this content be sequenced in levels so that young learners can play a developmentally appropriate game at each level?

Note that in addressing the third question, we are suggesting a different approach to the development of the games curriculum. At the beginning of a typical games unit of instruction, teachers normally ask themselves, *What skills shall I teach?* Here, we advocate a different question, *How do I want (or how can I expect) the game to look at the end of this unit?* This question places a different emphasis on the development and sequencing of content because all content is chosen with the idea of enhancing the overall quality of game performance at each level rather than of enhancing skill alone.

The tactical framework for invasion games was presented in table 2.3, whereas table 2.4 sequenced this content into three levels of game complexity to allow for developmentally appropriate instruction. Note that in table 2.3 the scope of content is restricted to that which is essential for a modified version of any invasion game. Players must understand and be able to keep possession of the ball if their team is to be successful offensively and must then turn this possession into offense by attempting to penetrate the opposing team's defense and attack the goal. Frequent changes of possession will be the norm at the elementary level, and an understanding of how to turn defense into offense (transition) will also be beneficial. More advanced tactical aspects of offensive team play, such as creating and using space, are not as appropriate for the elementary level because they are needed less in the small-sided game. For defense, players will need to know how to defend space, defend the goal, and win the ball back when it has been lost. The decisions, movements (without the ball) and skills (with the ball) suggested as means of addressing the tactical problems are rudimentary and appropriate for the elementary level. Table 2.4 suggests that the game will look different at successive levels by virtue of the number of players on each team and the increased complexity of decisions, movements, and skills anticipated as solutions to tactical problems.

Invasion Game Lessons

The following sections provide sample lesson outlines for invasion games at game complexity levels I, II, and III. Lessons are intended to provide a progression of tactical and skills learning and, as such, are sequential.

Level I

Level I lessons (second and third grade) focus on a game of three-a-side, beginning with a simple throw-and-catch version of team handball. Tactical problems addressed are limited to keeping possession, penetration and attack, and starting and restarting play. These are the essentials of invasion game play for the novice. There are several points to note as you explore these lessons:

- Modified equipment, particularly more appropriate types of balls, will enable young learners to play games more effectively.
- Changing from one game (team handball) to another (pillow polo) will reinforce the similarities among invasion games.
- Only a limited number of teaching cues are suggested, providing the learner with just the essential input to assist in skill acquisition, thereby preventing information overload.
- Restarts, such as they are taught at this level, would be addressed primarily during game play as these situations arise. In particular, there will be numerous opportunities to address restarts from a ball out-of-bounds.
- Some prior teaching and learning of the fundamental manipulative skills of throwing and catching is assumed.
- Notice that here, and in chapters 5 to 7, the first lesson (or sometimes two lessons) at each game complexity level is given over to organizing teams, assigning courts, and teaching students how to play the game. This involves teaching simple procedures, as outlined in chapter 3, to ensure that future lessons run smoothly. A lesson on these organizational matters will save time over the course of an instructional unit or season.

LESSON 1

TACTICAL PROBLEM: Playing the game and keeping possession.

GAME: Team handball using a volleyball-sized sponge ball (8 to 9 inches in diameter).

LESSON FOCUS: Court and team organization and passing.

OBJECTIVE: Students will learn court spaces and complete successful passes that enable them to play a "keepaway" game within a specified court.

1. **START-UP:** Designation and familiarization (as warm-up) of court spaces (1 through 4).

   Mark the lines with floor tape and label the courts. Have students jog to the appropriate court when that court number is called; frequent changes to the court number called make this an active warm-up. Exercises can be put in at particular stopping points in the warm-up.

   Players form or are assigned to teams of three, and they choose or are assigned to home courts. Each team gets half a court as "home court" (figure 4.4).

2. **PRACTICE TASK:** Triangle passing.

   Condition: Do not move with the ball.

   Goal: 10, 15, or 20 consecutive passes without dropping the ball.

   Extension: Pass and move to another space on your court.

   (If students' ability warrants it):
   Play 2 v 1 with a goal of eight passes in a row, then switch (defender must go to the ball). Cold (standing) going to warm (arm's length) defense.

3. **GAME:** (if time permits) 3 v 3 possession game (four passes in a row is 1 point).

   Conditions: Do not move with the ball.

   Use a warm defense (start to teach this in game play).

   Use a throw-in from the out-of-bounds line for a ball that is out-of-bounds.

   Goal: Keep the ball.

4. **CLOSURE:** Questions and discussion on court spaces.

   Q. What is an effective way to keep the ball away from another player in a game?
   A. Pass it to a teammate and then move to space.

   Note: Next lesson starts with pass and move or 2 v 1 at home court.

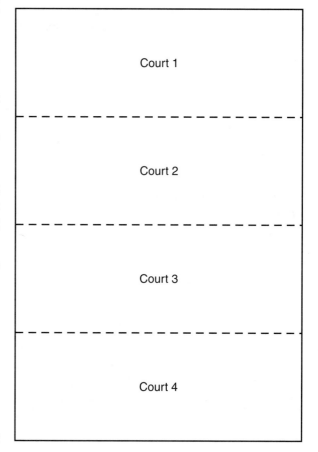

| Court 1 |
| Court 2 |
| Court 3 |
| Court 4 |

Figure 4.4

LESSON 2

TACTICAL PROBLEM: Playing the game and keeping possession.

GAME: Team handball (sponge ball).

LESSON FOCUS: Passing and moving in a 3 v 3 game.

OBJECTIVE: In a 3 v 3 game students will pass the ball to keep it away from the other team.

1. **GAME 1:** Pass and move or 2 v 1 at home court.

   Conditions: Defender must try to get the ball.

   Use warm (arm's length) defense; do not slap the ball out of hands.

   Goal: Four passes in a row.

2. **GAME 2:** 3 v 3 possession game (four passes in a row is 1 point).

   Conditions: Do not move with the ball.

   Use a warm defense.

   Use the usual boundaries and restart rules.

   Goal: Keep the ball.

3. **CLOSURE:** Questions and discussion on boundaries and etiquette.

   Ask team members to describe how they work to keep the ball.

   Note: Next lesson starts with 3 v 3 possession game.

LESSON 3

TACTICAL PROBLEM: Playing the game and keeping possession.

GAME: Team handball (sponge ball).

LESSON FOCUS: Passing and moving in a 3 v 3 game.

OBJECTIVE: In a 3 v 3 game students will keep the ball away from the other team by effective passing and moving.

1. **GAME 1:** 3 v 3 possession game (four passes in a row is 1 point).

   Conditions: Do not move with the ball.

   Use a warm defense.

   Use the usual boundaries and restart rules.

   Goal: Keep the ball.

   Questions:

   Q. Where do your passes have to go so that your team can keep the ball?
   A. To a teammate.

   Q. Are two-handed passes better than one-handed passes to make sure the ball gets to a teammate? Why?
   A. Yes, because you can get it to your teammate more easily (more accurately).

   Q. When are one-handed passes better?
   A. When you have to throw a long way.

2. **PRACTICE TASK:** Triangle passing using a two-handed chest pass.

   Goal: 10 passes in a row around the triangle (passes should go straight to the receiver).

   Cues: Chest pass:

   > Ball to the chest.
   >
   > Step and push away.
   >
   > Point fingers at the receiver.
   >
   > Receiving:
   >
   > Watch the ball.
   >
   > Move in front of the ball.
   >
   > Keep hands out.
   >
   > Put fingers up for high catch, down for low catch.
   >
   > Throw pass:
   >
   > Take the ball back with elbow bent.
   >
   > Step with the opposite foot.
   >
   > Throw to your receiver.

   Extensions: One-handed throw pass.

   > Pass and move 2 v 1.

   Question:

   Q. How and where should you move?
   A. Quickly to space.

3. **GAME 2:** Same as game 1.

   Goal: Keep the ball as long as possible by making good passes to teammates.

4. **CLOSURE:** Questions and discussion on boundaries and etiquette. Questions and discussion on good passing (which pass to use) and moving in game play.

LESSON 4

TACTICAL PROBLEMS: Playing the game, keeping possession to make forward progress, and attacking the goal.

GAME: Team handball (sponge ball).

LESSON FOCUS: Passing and moving forward in a 3 v 3 game.

OBJECTIVES: In a 3 v 3 game students will keep the ball and move it forward to score in the goal as a team. They will work on timing the pass to beat a defender (passing at the right time).

1. **GAME 1:** 2 v 1 at home court.

   Conditions: Defender must try to get the ball.

   > Use a warm (arm's length) defense.

   Goal: Eight passes in a row.

   Question:

   Q. When is a good time to pass?
   A. As the defender comes toward you. (Set up a demonstration of this: Teacher is the defender approaching a player with the ball. Have players say "now" at the point when the player should give the pass to a supporting teammate.)

2. **GAME 2:** 3 v 3 to small goal (1 point per score).

   Conditions: Do not move with the ball.

   Shoot from outside a designated point or line.

   Shoot down to score. A hit cone is no goal.

   Use a warm defense.

   Usual boundaries and restart rules apply.

   Goal: To move the ball forward as a team and score in the goal with a downward shot.

   Cues: Pass as the defender comes toward you.

   Pass the ball ahead of the receiver.

   Extension: Widen the goal and put one player from each team in goal.

3. **CLOSURE:** Questions and discussion on determining the right time to pass the ball in a game.

   Note: Next lesson starts with game 2.

   Note: Now that a game is being played, it is appropriate to change to a different invasion game by simply changing the equipment. To this point players have become accustomed to playing small-sided games in defined spaces and are able to start, restart, and play independently; and they have learned that it is important to keep the ball. Now they are asked to move the ball forward to get into position to score. Students can address this problem in more than one invasion game, and it would now make sense to begin discussing similarities among games. Lessons will now progress to address the problem of attacking and will alternate between two invasion games, but bear in mind that these lessons can really be used with any invasion game.

LESSON 5

TACTICAL PROBLEM: Keeping the ball and attacking.

GAME: Pillow polo (pillow polo sticks and 6-inch foam or gator balls).

LESSON FOCUS: Dribbling and stick control.

OBJECTIVE: In a 3 v 3 game students will move the ball forward by dribbling under control with the stick. (*Note:* This is a difficult skill, made more difficult by the pressure of a game situation. It may require two lessons of practice time, hence several practice task extensions.)

1. **GAME 1:** 3 v 3 to goal with goalkeeper.

   Conditions: Always keep sticks below knee height.

   Players can move with the ball.

   Goalkeeper can save with feet or stick.

   Only the goalkeeper is allowed inside the goal box or line.

   Goal: Get the ball forward and score.

   Questions:

   Q. How can you get the ball forward (other than passing, as you did before in handball)?
   A. Run with the ball (dribble).

   Q. When should you dribble?
   A. When you have space in front of you.

2. **PRACTICE TASK:** Whole class dribbling.

   Conditions: One ball per person.

   Free dribbling in the gym.

   Avoid hitting anyone else's ball.

   Goals: Control the ball.

   Evade opponents.

   Cues: Keep hands apart on the stick.

   Push the ball forward (don't hit it).

   Keep the ball close.

   Push the ball left and right.

   Look up so that you don't hit others.

   Extensions: Stop ball on the whistle by putting the stick on top of ball (demonstrate control).

   Avoid the teacher (who is a tackler) as you go around.

   Decrease the playing area; this makes evasion harder.

   Dribble and try to push others' balls away.

3. **GAME 2:** Same as game 1.

4. **CLOSURE:** Question and discussion on keeping ball from opponent.

   Q. If an opponent is trying to get the ball from you, how else can you move it forward?
   A. By passing next time.

LESSON 6

TACTICAL PROBLEM: Keeping the ball and attacking.

GAME: Team handball (sponge ball).

LESSON FOCUS: Moving forward to support the passer.

OBJECTIVE: In a 3 v 3 game students will keep the ball and attack goal by moving forward to support the player with the ball.

1. **GAME 1:** 3 v 3 to goal.

   Conditions: Do not move with the ball.

   Use a warm defense (arm's length).

   Goal: Move when you don't have the ball.

   Questions:

   Q. What should you do after you have passed the ball?
   A. Move.

   Q. Where to (in which direction)?
   A. Forward.

   Q. Why forward?
   A. To get closer to the goal to shoot.

   Q. How should you move (quickly or slowly)?
   A. Quickly.

2. **PRACTICE TASK:** Team practice in which players pass and move up and down home court (figure 4.5).

 Goal: Three passes between the team to get the ball to the other end of their home court.

 Conditions: Do not move with the ball.

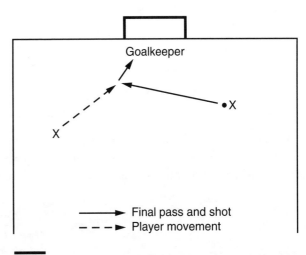

 Pass and move to end of home court.

 Pass and move back to goal before shooting past the goalkeeper (of the three team members, one is goalkeeper while the other two are the passer or shooter).

 Cues: Pass and move forward into space.

 Receive and pass quickly.

 Pass ahead of the receiver (lead the receiver).

 Extension: Four passes using faster passing and faster movement.

3. **GAME 2:** Same as game 1.

Figure 4.5

4. **CLOSURE:** Questions and discussion on where to move after passing. Support discussion with demonstrations and examples.

LESSON 7

TACTICAL PROBLEM: Keeping the ball and attacking.

GAME: Pillow polo (pillow polo sticks and 6-inch foam balls).

LESSON FOCUS: Passing and receiving.

OBJECTIVE: In a 3 v 3 game students will move the ball forward by dribbling, passing, and receiving.

1. **GAME 1:** 3 v 3 to goal with goalkeeper.

 Conditions: Sticks are always below knee height.

 Players can move with the ball (dribble).

 Goalkeeper can save with feet or stick.

 Only the goalkeeper is allowed inside the goal box or line.

 Goal: Get the ball forward and score.

 Question:

 Q. It is hard to dribble if someone is trying to get the ball away from you. How else can you get the ball forward as a team?
 A. Pass it.

2. **PRACTICE TASK:** Pairs passing.

 Conditions: With a partner and one ball:

 Stand about 5 yards apart and pass back and forth.

 Move around the gym together passing the ball back and forth between you (all pairs working at the same time).

 Goal: Make every pass go to your partner.

Cues: Passing:

Step and push to your partner.

Push the ball ahead of your partner (lead your partner).

Receiving:

Put your stick behind the ball.

Push the ball to get it ready for your next pass.

3. **GAME 2:** Same as game 1.

Goal: Good passing and dribbling to keep the ball and get it forward.

4. **CLOSURE:** Question and discussion on where to pass the ball.

Q. Where should you pass the ball if you are moving forward with a teammate?
A. Ahead of that teammate.

LESSON 8

TACTICAL PROBLEM: Attacking.

GAME: Team handball.

LESSON FOCUS: Shooting.

OBJECTIVE: In a 3 v 3 game students will shoot the ball down into the goal when the opportunity arises.

1. **GAME 1:** 3 v 3 to goal with goalkeeper.

Conditions: Do not move with the ball.

Use a warm defense (arm's length).

Goal: Shoot when possible.

Questions:

Q. What should you do if you are open in front of the goal?
A. Shoot.

Q. Should you shoot up or down? Why?
A. Down. It is harder for the goalkeeper to save the ball if it is low.

2. **PRACTICE TASK:** Team shooting practice with a passer, a shooter, and a goalkeeper. Rotate.

Conditions: Two players passing between each other make three to four passes and take a shot.

Alternate shots.

Goal: All shots go down at the goal.

Cue: Step and shoot down.

Extensions: Pass quickly to confuse the goalkeeper.

Fake a shot and pass or shoot.

3. **GAME 2:** Same as game 1.

4. **CLOSURE:** Questions and discussion on attempting goals.

Q. What do you do when you have the ball in front of the goal?
A. Shoot!

Q. How can you confuse the goalkeeper?
A. Fake.

LESSON 9

TACTICAL PROBLEM: Attacking.

GAME: Pillow polo (pillow polo sticks and 6-inch foam balls).

LESSON FOCUS: Shooting (wrist shot).

OBJECTIVE: In a 3 v 3 game students will shoot at the goal when they have the opportunity.

1. **GAME 1:** 3 v 3 to goal with goalkeeper.

   Conditions: Keep stick below knee height.

   Players can move with the ball.

   Goalkeeper can save with feet or stick.

   Only the goalkeeper is allowed inside the goal box or line.

   Goal: Get the ball forward and score.

   Questions:

   Q. When you get close to the goal what should you try to do?
   A. Score.

   Q. What do you have to do to score? What do we call it?
   A. Shoot.

2. **PRACTICE TASK:** Whole class dribbling and shooting.

   Conditions: One ball per person.

   Free dribbling and shooting in the gym. Dribble and shoot into any goal (these are set up already on each home court).

   After scoring in one goal you must dribble to another for your next shot.

   Goal: Score as many goals as you can.

   Cues: Hands apart on the stick.

   Push the ball ahead.

   Push and flick the wrists.

   Extensions: Put in goalkeepers.

   How many goals can you score in 30 seconds?

   Note: Player cannot shoot into the same goal twice in a row.

3. **GAME 2:** Same as game 1.

4. **CLOSURE:** Question and discussion on attempting goals.

   Q. What do you do when you get close to the goal?
   A. Shoot.

LESSON 10

TACTICAL PROBLEM: Attacking.

GAME: Pillow polo (pillow polo sticks and 6-inch foam balls).

LESSON FOCUS: Shooting after a pass.

OBJECTIVE: In a 3 v 3 game students will shoot after receiving a pass close to the goal.

1. **GAME 1:** 3 v 3 to goal with goalkeeper.

    Conditions: Keep stick below knee height.

    Players can move with the ball.

    Goalkeeper can save with feet or stick.

    Only the goalkeeper is allowed inside the goal box or line.

    Goal: Get the ball forward by passing and score.

    Question:

    Q. If you receive a pass close to the goal what should you do?
    A. Shoot the ball.

2. **PRACTICE TASK:** Whole class passing and shooting.

    Conditions: One ball per pair.

    Free passing and shooting in the gym. Pass and move around the gym and shoot into any goal.

    After scoring in one goal, you and your partner must pass and move to another for your next shot.

    Goal: Score as many goals as you can.

    Cues: Keep hands apart on the stick.

    Pass the ball ahead of your partner.

    Receive and push ahead to get ready for the shot.

    Extensions: Put in goalkeepers.

    See how many goals you and your partner can score in 30 seconds.

3. **GAME 2:** Same as game 1.

4. **CLOSURE:** Question and discussion on attempting goals.

    Q. What do you do when you receive a pass close to goal?
    A. Shoot.

Level II

Level II (third and fourth grades) invasion games are suitable for players who have experienced the content covered in level I, understanding that they may have acquired these skills in or outside of physical education. Lessons at level II focus on more sophisticated means of keeping possession and attacking the goal, and introduce aspects of defense and goalkeeping and some formal teaching of restarts. Assuming a wider range of skill among students, it would be more reasonable at this level to vary the game being taught to reinforce to students the essential similarities of invasion games. For those of you who wish to experience this flexibility by changing the game occasionally, we challenge you to teach the same game for no more than two consecutive lessons and also to change equipment, and therefore the game played (for example, changing from team handball to ultimate Frisbee), midway through a lesson. You might be impressed at the student's ability to transfer an understanding of one invasion game to performance in another. For those of you who wish to err on the side of caution and maintain a more traditional approach of teaching a single game "unit," the lessons are written in as flexible a manner as possible so that, with a change in equipment and teaching cues during skill practice, lessons can apply to any invasion game you are teaching for a complete unit. For example, if your preference is for basketball, lessons 1–8 can still apply, with some revision to allow for different types of passes (although these would be very similar to handball) and shots (which might not be so similar). We advocate organization of permanent teams on which players have defined roles and responsibilities, as outlined in chapter 3.

LESSON 1

TACTICAL PROBLEM: Keeping the ball.

GAME: 2 v 2 team handball (gator balls).

LESSON FOCUS: Court and team organization and the possession game (review of level I).

OBJECTIVE: Students will recognize court spaces and complete successful passes within specified courts (1 to 3).

1. **START-UP:** Designation and familiarization (as warm-up) of court spaces (1 to 3). Players form or are assigned to teams of four and choose or are assigned to a home court.

2. **GAME:** 2 v 2 possession at home court (see figure 4.1).

   Conditions: One step only with the ball.

   Warm defense (arm's length).

   Five passes in a row equal 1 point.

   Goals: 5 points per team.

   Completion of contract (see figure 3.4). Responsibilities: Coach, equipment manager, trainer, reporter.

3. **CLOSURE:** Questions and discussion on boundaries and responsibilities. Questions and discussion (with coaches only) on fairness of teams (for example, are the teams equal in playing ability?).

   Note: Next lesson starts with 2 v 2 at home court.

LESSON 2

TACTICAL PROBLEM: Playing the 4 v 4 game, keeping possession, and attacking the goal.

GAME: Team handball.

LESSON FOCUS: Passing and receiving in a 4 v 4 game.

OBJECTIVE: In a 4 v 4 game students will keep the ball and move it forward to score as a team in the goal or end zone.

1. **GAME 1:** 2 v 2 at home court.

   Conditions: Take only one step.

   Use warm defense (arm's length).

   Five passes in a row equal 1 point.

   Goal: 5 points per team.

   Questions:

   Q. What are the best types of passes to make to keep the ball?
   A. Quick, chest, bounce.

   Q. How should you catch the ball—by putting the hands out or by bringing the ball in?
   A. Hands out.

   Q. Why?
   A. You can pass it again much faster that way.

2. **PRACTICE TASK:** Practice passing and receiving in pairs with the goal of 10, 15, or 20 consecutive passes.

   Cues: Pass:

   > Step to your target.
   >
   > Push the ball away.
   >
   > Use a firm pass.
   >
   > Receive:
   >
   > Show a "target hand."
   >
   > Put hands out to receive.
   >
   > "Give" a little to absorb the force.
   >
   > Use a quick pass back.

   Extension: Pass and move to lead the receiver.

3. **GAME 2:** 4 v 4 to end zone (1 point per score).

   Conditions: Use one step only.

   > Use a warm defense.
   >
   > Use the usual boundaries and restart rules.

   Goal: 5 points per team.

   Extension: Play to target player.

4. **CLOSURE:** Questions and discussion on boundaries and etiquette.

   Note: This lesson can be done with any invasion game: ultimate Frisbee, floor hockey, ultimate football, soccer, speedball. Answers to questions might be different, as will teaching cues. The next two lessons show how the pass and receive theme might be addressed in ultimate Frisbee.

LESSON 3

TACTICAL PROBLEM: Keeping possession and attacking.

GAME: Ultimate Frisbee (sponge Frisbees).

LESSON FOCUS: Passing the Frisbee backhand.

OBJECTIVE: In a 4 v 4 game students will pass accurately using short passes with a backhand technique.

1. **GAME 1:** 4 v 4 to end zone.

   Conditions: Do not move with the Frisbee.

   > Score in end zone.
   >
   > Use warm (arm's length) defense.
   >
   > Dropped or knocked-down Frisbee is a turnover.

   Goal: Move Frisbee forward and score in end zone.

   Questions:

   Q. What type of pass do you need in this game (long or short)?
   A. Short.

   Q. Why?
   A. Because it is hard to throw the Frisbee a long way.

2. **PRACTICE TASK:** Triangle passing (demonstrate backhand pass).

   Goal: 10 passes without dropping the Frisbee.

   Cues: Thumb on top, fingers underneath.

   Step with the same foot as the hand you are throwing with.

   Reach across your body.

   Throw to your target.

   Let go level with your front foot.

   Extension: Pass and move.

3. **GAME 2:** Same as game 1.

   Goal: Use short backhand passes and forward supporting movements to space to score.

4. **CLOSURE:** Question and discussion on types of passes. Review cues.

   Q. Are long or short passes best?
   A. Short ones are more accurate.

LESSON 4

TACTICAL PROBLEM: Keeping possession and attacking.

GAME: Ultimate Frisbee (sponge Frisbees).

LESSON FOCUS: Catching the Frisbee with two hands.

OBJECTIVE: In a 4 v 4 game students will catch the Frisbee efficiently to move forward.

1. **GAME 1:** 4 v 4 to end zone.

   Conditions: Do not move with the Frisbee.

   Score in end zone.

   Use arm's length defense.

   Dropped or knocked-down Frisbee is a turnover.

   Goal: Move Frisbee forward and score in end zone.

   Questions:

   Q. How should you catch the Frisbee (one or two hands)?
   A. Two.
   Q. Why?
   A. Because it is easier and safer (but it is quicker with one hand).

2. **PRACTICE TASK:** Triangle passing (demonstrate backhand pass).

   Goal: 10 passes without dropping the Frisbee.

   Cues: Move into line.

   Keep thumbs down to catch high Frisbee.

   Keep thumbs up to catch low Frisbee.

   Use a quick pass to your target.

   Extensions: Pass to receiver's side to make her move and catch.

   Use one-handed catches for speed.

3. **GAME 2:** Same as game 1.

   Goal: Use short backhand passes, safe catches, and good moves to space to score.

4. **CLOSURE:** Question and discussion on types of catches. Review cues.

   Q. Are one- or two-handed catches better?
   A. Depends on whether you need or want safety or speed!

LESSON 5

TACTICAL PROBLEM: Keeping possession and attacking.

GAME: Team handball.

LESSON FOCUS: Passing quickly in a 4 v 4 game.

OBJECTIVE: In a 4 v 4 game students will keep the ball and move it forward by passing to open players quickly after receiving the ball.

1. **GAME 1:** 4 v 4 to goal.

   Conditions: Take only one step.

   Use a warm defense (arm's length).

   Goal: Find open players to pass to.

   Questions:

   Q. When you catch the ball, what should you do?
   A. Pass it.

   Q. When should you pass it? (Or how should you pass?)
   A. Right away (quickly).

2. **PRACTICE TASK:**

   Practice pressure passing and catching in a triangle. One passer and two feeders rotate after 30 seconds. A passes to B, who passes back to A, who then passes to C, who passes back to A, who passes to B, and so on. D is coach (figure 4.6).

   Goal: No dropped passes in 30 seconds.

   Cues: Receiving:

   Put two hands out, spread fingers.

   Thumbs down for high ball.

   Thumbs up for low ball.

   Passing:

   Step to your target and pass immediately.

   Extensions: Most passes you can do in 30 seconds.

   Feeders move toward goal after feed and receive a return pass from A (this extension requires two balls: one for B and one for C). Reverse the direction.

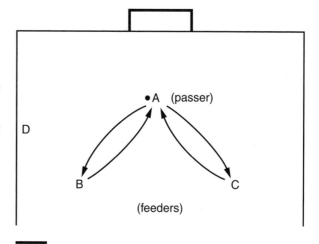

Figure 4.6

3. **GAME 2:** Same as game 1.

    Note: If it becomes necessary to spread out the 4 v 4 game, have students choose to be defender (must stay in own half), two middle players (can go anywhere), and forward (must stay in opposing half).

4. **CLOSURE:** Questions and discussion about passing.

    Q. What is important about your passing in the game?
    A. Do it quickly.

    Q. Why?
    A. To move the ball over space faster.

    Note: Have students do practice task from this lesson to warm up next time.

LESSON 6

TACTICAL PROBLEM: Playing the 4 v 4 game and keeping possession.

GAME: Team handball.

LESSON FOCUS: Moving and supporting in a 4 v 4 game and timing the pass.

OBJECTIVE: In a 4 v 4 game students will keep the ball and move it forward to score as a team in the goal or end zone.

1. **GAME 1:** 2 v 2 at home court.

    Conditions: Take only one step.

    Use warm defense (arm's length).

    Five passes in a row equal 1 point.

    Goal: 5 points per team.

    Questions:

    Q. How can your teammates help you keep the ball and get it forward?
    A. Move to places to receive a pass from me.

    Q. Like where?
    A. Away from opponents and ahead of me.

    Q. When should you pass?
    A. As soon as my teammate is free and there is a passing lane.

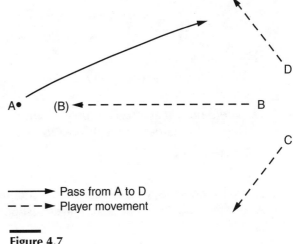

Pass from A to D
Player movement

Figure 4.7

2. **PRACTICE TASK:**

    Player A has the ball and says "go." Players C and D can move to a supporting position. Player A must time the pass so that it is given when the passing lane is open. Player B (the defender) advances toward player A and tries to block the pass to C or D. Restart after C or D receives the ball. Rotate roles every turn. In figure 4.7, player A has passed to player D.

    Cues: Supporting teammates (C and D) move quickly from behind the defender (player B).

    Passer (A) passes when the lane is open.

    Extension: 3 v 1 up to 6 passes.

3.   **GAME 2:** 4 v 4 to end zone (1 point per score).

Conditions: Take only one step.

Use a warm defense.

Goal: 5 points per team.

Extension: Play to target player (a permanent end zone player).

4.   **CLOSURE:** Questions and discussion on supporting movements, boundaries, and etiquette.

Note: This lesson can be done with any invasion game: ultimate Frisbee, floor hockey, ultimate football, soccer, and speedball. Answers to questions would be similar among these games, though teaching cues would differ because different skills are taught.

LESSON 7

TACTICAL PROBLEM: Attacking.

GAME: Team handball.

LESSON FOCUS: Receiving and shooting quickly and accurately.

OBJECTIVE: Players will transition to shoot, and shoot accurately, after receiving a pass.

1.   **GAME 1:** 4 v 4 to goal (with goalkeeper).

Conditions: Three steps with the ball.

Use a warm defense (arm's length).

To score, players shoot downward from outside shooting line or goal box.

Questions:

Q. What should you do if you receive a pass close to the goal?
A. Shoot.

Q. Where do you aim (up or down)? Why?
A. Down. It is harder for goalkeeper to save.

2.   **PRACTICE TASK:**

Shooter A passes to feeder F, who passes the ball across to shooter A, who has advanced. Shooter A receives and shoots at goal. Player B shoots next (figure 4.8).

Cue: Pass, move, receive, step, and shoot downward.

Extensions: Feed from other side.

Fake a shot before the actual shot.

Jump and shoot.

3.   **GAME 2:** Same as game 1.

4.   **CLOSURE:** Questions and discussion on shooting.

Q. When is the right time to shoot?
A. As soon as you get the chance.

Q. Where do you aim the shot?
A. Down, to make it harder for the goalkeeper.

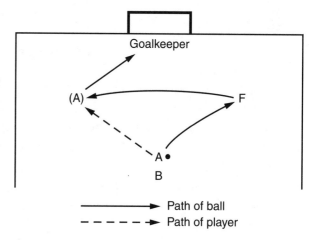

Figure 4.8

LESSON 8

TACTICAL PROBLEM: Defending space in the game.

GAME: Ultimate Frisbee.

LESSON FOCUS: Marking and guarding players.

OBJECTIVE: Students will guard an opposing player in open play to make it difficult for that player to find space to receive a pass.

1. **GAME 1:** 4 v 4 to end zone.

   Conditions: Take only one step.

   Use a warm defense (arm's length) on player in possession.

   Use the usual boundaries and restart rules: Dropped or knocked-down Frisbee is a turnover.

   Goal: Get close to an opponent when the other team has the Frisbee.

   Questions:

   Q. What is it called when you get close to an opponent?
   A. Guarding.

   Q. Where should you stand to guard your opponent?
   A. Between your opponent and your end zone (set up demonstration of this) where you can see both your opponent and the Frisbee.

2. **GAME 2:** 4 v 4 to target player.

   Conditions: Same as game 1.

   Goal: Appropriate guarding position.

   Questions:

   Q. What should you do when your opponent gets the Frisbee?
   A. Get closer to him (pressure).

   Q. What should you do when your opponent gets closer to the end zone?
   A. Get closer to him.

   Q. How should you stand? Why?
   A. Feet staggered, knees bent (demonstrate this), because it is easier to move quickly from this stance.

3. **GAME 3:** 4 v 4 to target player.

   Conditions: Same as game 1.

   Goal: Apply pressure to opponent.

4. **CLOSURE:** Questions and discussion on where to stand to guard an opposing player.

   Note: Again, the concept of guarding as a means of effective defense is common to all invasion games. Ultimate Frisbee is used only as an example in this case.

LESSON 9

TACTICAL PROBLEM: Defending the goal.

GAME: Hockey, soccer, or team handball.

LESSON FOCUS: Goalkeeper positioning.

OBJECTIVE: Goalkeepers will position to cut down the shooting angle.

1. **GAME 1:** 4 v 4 to a goal with goalkeeper.

   Condition: Rotate goalkeeper frequently so that all get to play goalkeeper in this game.

   Goal: When in goal, make it as difficult as possible for the shooter to score.

   Questions:

   Q. How can the goalkeeper make it hard for the shooter to score?
   A. Stand in the right place.

   Q. Where is the right place?
   A. It depends on where the shooter is shooting from (demonstrate this with shooter from right side and shooter from left side).

2. **PRACTICE TASK:**

   Each player takes a turn in the goal. Three teammates (A, B, C) pass the ball among themselves. Make a minimum of three passes before shooting (figure 4.9).

   Goal: Goalkeeper should cut down the shooting angle by moving toward the player with the ball after each pass (get to positions a, b, c for shots by players A, B, C).

   Cues: Slide the feet across.

   Move toward the ball.

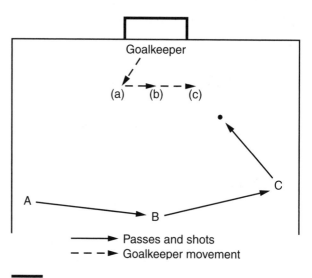

Figure 4.9

3. **GAME 2:** Same as game 1.

4. **CLOSURE:** Question and discussion on goalkeeper's placement.

   Q. What should the goalkeeper do to make it harder for a shooter?
   A. Move to the ball.

LESSON 10

TACTICAL PROBLEM: Starting and restarting play.

GAME: Hockey, soccer, team handball, ultimate Frisbee, or any other invasion game.

LESSON FOCUS: Positioning to get the ball into play.

OBJECTIVE: Players will provide two passing options for the in-bounds pass.

1. **GAME 1:** 4 v 4 to a goal with goalkeeper.

   Conditions: Rotate goalkeepers.

   Restart quickly after ball goes out-of-bounds.

   Goal: Keep possession at each in-bounds pass.

   Questions:

   Q. Where do you take the in-bounds pass or throw-in (soccer) from?
   A. Where the ball went out-of-bounds.

   Q. How should you take it (quickly or slowly)? Why?
   A. Quickly, to take advantage of possession.

   Q. With three players on the court, how many supporting players should the in-bounds passer have?
   A. Two.

2. **PRACTICE TASK:**

Player A must get the ball to player B or C. Player D (the defender) begins by *facing* B and C, and tries to guard them or block the pass. Play 3 v 1 to four passes and then rotate defender (figure 4.10).

Goal: Successful in-bounds pass each time.

Cues: Players B and C:

Each go to a side.

Fake one way and move the other.

Player A:

Pass as soon as a passing lane is open.

Extension: 2 v 2 beginning with in-bounds pass. Four consecutive passes is a score and a turnover. Other team restarts with in-bounds pass.

3. **GAME 2:** Same as game 1.

4. **CLOSURE:** Question and discussion on in-bounds passes.

Q. What is important about the way you take in-bounds passes?

A. Take it as soon as a passing lane opens.

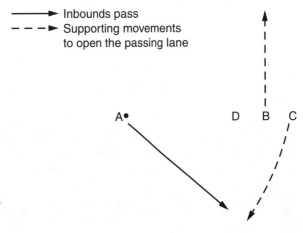

Figure 4.10

Level III

As elementary students develop their abilities to understand and play invasion games, you will be able to increase the complexity of the games they play. The most obvious way to increase complexity is to add to the number of players on each team. This increases the range of options available to players when they have the ball. It also makes it possible for more players to be involved in the game (especially when they don't have the ball) either as supporters to the ball carrier or as defending players. A move to playing 6 v 6 increases the range of offensive possibilities and defensive responsibilities.

Again, progress in game complexity at level III (fourth and fifth grades) is based on the assumption that students have become comfortable in game play of 4 v 4 or fewer. For this reason, it will probably be unnecessary to devote any lessons to teaching students to play the game. They will come to the unit already familiar with playing two or three games at the same time within the same gymnasium or on the same outdoor area. Level III picks up where level II ends. Defensively, students should have learned marking or guarding as a way of defending space; now it is time for players to further address the problems of defending the goal through goalkeeping or rebounding (in basketball). Goalkeeping and rebounding are two of the most important aspects of invasion games, but they often are ignored in games education. On defense, it is also important to learn appropriate ways of winning the ball in games that allow tackling.

The offensive focus of the 6 v 6 game is on penetrating a defense to attack the goal and on transitioning from defensive situations to offense as quickly as possible without losing the ball. Of course, the field of play will be larger to accommodate the increased number of players, making it more difficult for a team to transition from defense to offense. Players will have greater freedom to move with the ball and more opportunities to give longer passes to transition effectively.

The lesson outlines presented in this section encompass a variety of possibilities. Some lessons (4 to 6) are written in a rather generic manner, emphasizing the point that lessons might be used with a variety of games. Others, particularly those relating to defense (1 to 3), are designated for specific games (soccer, floor hockey, basketball). Our goal here, difficult though it might be, is to develop a series of lessons that you can adapt to a single game unit. At this point, you might be concerned that your students have not been sufficiently exposed to any single game, such as basketball, to be able to demonstrate any degree of game-playing proficiency. Do not be too concerned! Remember, they have learned to make appropriate decisions about shooting, passing, and dribbling; and they have learned how to move without the ball offensively to support and defensively to mark or guard. The major feature of basketball not specifically addressed to this point in previous lessons has been shooting (set shots and layups) and dribbling, though this would have been possible with some adaptations to earlier level I and level II lessons. Teams can remain at six-a-side for basketball, allowing for 3 v 3 within team practices and scrimmage games. The use of the Sport Education model (Siedentop, 1994) involving regular competition would provide responsibilities for players not actively playing during basketball game play if games were 5 v 5 or even 4 v 4. Alternatively, if warranted by student ability level, regular season play could remain 3 v 3 with two smaller teams made from the larger team.

Again, it is not necessary to teach specific lessons on restarts. However, it is important at this level to encourage players to take restarts, including throw-ins, corners, and restarts after violations, as quickly as possible to take the most advantage of possession at the restart.

LESSON 1

TACTICAL PROBLEM: Defending the goal.

GAME: Soccer (see note at end of lesson on adaptation to floor hockey).

LESSON FOCUS: Goalkeeping and stopping shots.

OBJECTIVE: Players will get their bodies in line with the ball and hold the ball safely.

1. **START-UP:** Players form or are assigned to teams of six, and they choose or are assigned to home courts. Have students sign team contract.

2. **GAME 1:** 3 v 3 with goalkeepers (2 field players and 1 goalkeeper per team).

   Conditions: Rotate goalkeepers.

   Shorten field to increase number of shots.

   Goals: Goalkeepers stop the shots.

   Field players take lots of shots.

   Questions:

   Q. Where should the goalkeeper be to have the best chance of making a save?
   A. In line with the ball (demonstrate this).

   Q. How should the goalkeeper move into line?
   A. Slide the feet.

   Q. What is the best way for the goalkeeper to hold the ball safely once she has it?
   A. Cradled in her arms and tucked into her chest.

3. **PRACTICE TASK:**

   Do a partner practice by hand-feeding balls to low (feet), medium (waist), high (chest) levels.

   Condition: Use one ball per pair if possible.

   Goals: Get the body in line with the shot.

   Save and hold the ball safely into the chest.

   Cues: Slide the feet to get in line.

   Take the ball into the chest.

Extensions: Vary the direction of the feeds to make the partner move into line as he improves.

Increase the speed of the feeds to give further challenge.

4. **GAME 2:** Same as game 1.

5. **CLOSURE:** Question and discussion on goalkeeper's movements.

Q. How should the goalkeeper move to make saving easier?
A. Slide the feet to get in line with the ball.

Note: Given the amount of time taken for initial organization of teams and home courts, this lesson is quite long and may require a second lesson to cover all the material. The lesson can be applied easily to floor hockey in a following lesson. The same game and practice can apply, though questions and cues would need to address the goalkeeping stance in hockey and the importance of stopping and covering the ball with the hand. Softball gloves to catch or block and cover would be helpful equipment.

LESSON 2

TACTICAL PROBLEM: Defending the basket and winning the ball.

GAME: Basketball.

LESSON FOCUS: Defensive rebounding after shot attempts.

OBJECTIVES: Players will face the basket after a shot attempt to box out the opponent and then players will jump to take the rebound and give an outlet pass.

1. **GAME 1:** 3 v 3 half-court basketball.

    Conditions: (Apply if necessary.) Do not dribble.

    Shoot only from outside the key. (Either of these conditions will increase the likelihood of shots that can be rebounded.)

    Goal: When defending your basket, win the rebounds so that the opposing team does not get the turnover.

    Questions:

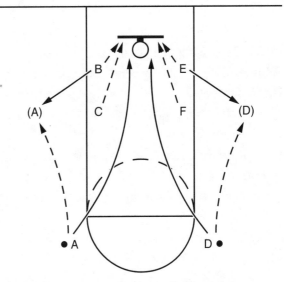

——————► Shot and outlet pass (in task extension)
– – –► Rebounding (B, C, E, F) and moving for outlet pass (A, D)

Figure 4.11

Q. Once you have turned to see the shot, how can you make it harder for your opponent to win the rebound?
A. Block him (box out).

Q. Where should you be when you catch the ball (on the ground or in the air)?
A. In the air. Jump to take the rebound.

2. **PRACTICE TASK:** Three-player rebounding practice.

    Conditions: One feeder (A and D), and two rebounders (B and C, E and F) per group (figure 4.11).

    Two separate groups of three at one basket.

    Players A and D shoot against the backboard.

    Players B, C and E, F go for rebound.

    Rotate positions every three feeds.

Cues: Defenders (B, E) turn to see the ball and box out C, F (demonstrate this).

Jump to take the rebound.

Extension: Rebounder takes the rebound and gives outlet pass to the feeder who has moved to the side.

3. **GAME 2:** Same as game 1.

   Condition: Award an additional point for every rebound taken.

4. **CLOSURE:** Questions and discussion on rebounds.

   Q. What are the two key points to winning a rebound?
   A. Box out and jump to take the ball in the air.

   Q. What do you do after you win a defensive rebound?
   A. Outlet pass.

LESSON 3

TACTICAL PROBLEM: Winning the ball.

GAME: Soccer or floor hockey.

LESSON FOCUS: Winning the ball with a block tackle.

OBJECTIVE: Players will be able to use a strong block tackle to win the ball.

1. **GAME 1:** 3 v 3 without a goal or goalkeeper.

   Condition: Try to dribble around your opponent before you pass.

   Goals: Offense:

   Dribble the ball across the end line under control.

   Defense:

   Tackle the ball carrier to stop her.

   Question:

   Q. Where should you be to make a tackle (close up or back a bit)?
   A. Close up to block.

2. **PRACTICE TASK:** 1 v 1 static block tackle practice; pairs spread in general space.

   Conditions: With a partner, on a count of three both players make a solid block tackle.

   Use the same foot (in soccer) as your partner.

   Goals: "Sandwich" the ball between your foot and your partner's foot (between sticks in hockey).

   Make a firm contact (you will feel and hear a firm contact).

   Cues: Get close to the ball.

   Relax the knee a bit (in soccer).

   Keep firm contact with the ball.

   Push through.

   Extensions: Alternate foot (in soccer).

   Use three-step approach to a tackle.

   Use 1 v 1 game play.

3. **GAME 2:** Same as game 1.

4. **CLOSURE:** Question and discussion on tackling.

   Q. What are the important things in tackling?
   A. Stay on your feet (in soccer), get close to your opponent, make a firm contact, and push through.

LESSON 4

TACTICAL PROBLEM: Transition from defense to offense.

GAME: Soccer, floor hockey, or basketball.

LESSON FOCUS: Quick outlet pass and dribbling at speed.

OBJECTIVE: Players will move effectively from defense to offense by executing a quick outlet pass and dribbling at speed with the ball or puck.

1. **GAME 1:** 6 v 6 including goalkeepers (where appropriate).

   Condition: Use a warm defense.

   Goal: Move the ball forward as quickly as possible to move your team from defense to offense.

   Questions:

   Q. How can you get the ball forward quickly to your own goal?
   A. Pass.

   Q. Where should the first pass go? Why?
   A. Out to the side, because there will be more space outside than in the center.

   Q. After the first pass how can you get the ball forward?
   A. Dribble.

2. **PRACTICE TASK:** Outlet pass and speed dribble.

   Conditions: Use continuous outlet pass and dribble as a team.

   Two feeders (F1 and F2) feed A, B, C, and D in turn.

   Player A takes the feed from F1, speed dribbles to a designated point, and passes to F2, who feeds B.

   Player A then lines up behind D; player B dribbles and passes to F1, who feeds C, and so on.

   Use two balls to give more practice (A and B could be dribbling at the same time) (figure 4.12).

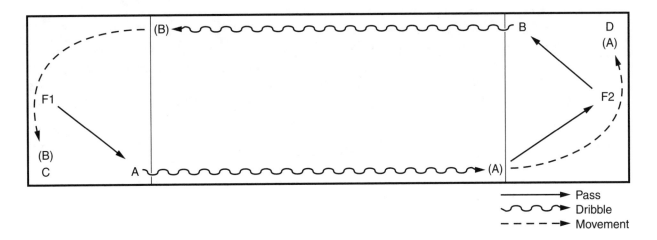

Figure 4.12

Goal: Maximum number of passes or dribbles in 1 minute (team competition).

Cues: Make a quick pass.

Push the ball ahead.

Dribble at speed.

Extension: Go the other way (pass to the left side).

3. **GAME 2:** Same as game 1.

4. **CLOSURE:** Question and discussion on defense and offense positions.

Q. How can you make a good transition from defense to offense?
A. Use a quick outlet pass to the side and dribble the ball forward.

LESSON 5

TACTICAL PROBLEM: Penetrating to attack the goal in a 6 v 6 game.

GAME: Soccer, team handball, hockey, basketball, or ultimate Frisbee.

LESSON FOCUS: Using a target or post player to penetrate and attack.

OBJECTIVE: Students will learn to create depth in attack by using a target or post player.

1. **GAME:** 6 v 6 (includes goalkeepers when game is appropriate).

Goal: Move the ball forward and score.

Extensions: Offense:

Leave a "target" player in the opposing team's half of the field and try to reach this player as quickly as possible with the ball.

Defense:

Guard the target player (use warm or hot defense as abilities allow).

2. **CLOSURE:** Questions and discussion on the role of target players.

Q. How does having a target player help offensively?
A. He helps with transition by being forward.

Q. How can you use the target player most effectively?
A. Give an early pass to the target player.

Note: This is a game play lesson in which it is worthwhile to change the game at least once during the lesson. Include basketball, because the use of a post player does differ a little from that of a target player: A 3-second rule prevents the post player from staying too close to the opponent's basket. Sometimes you will want to freeze game play to reconstruct or rehearse ways of reaching the target early with the ball.

LESSON 6

TACTICAL PROBLEM: Penetrating to attack in a 6 v 6 game.

GAME: Soccer, team handball, hockey, basketball, or ultimate Frisbee.

LESSON FOCUS: Using a target or post player to penetrate and attack.

OBJECTIVE: Students will use a target or post player to create scoring chances.

1. **GAME 1:** 6 v 6 (includes goalkeepers when game is appropriate).

   Conditions: Offense:

   Leave a target player in the opposing team's half of the field and try to reach this player as quickly as possible with the ball.

   Defense:

   Guard the target player (use warm or hot defense as abilities allow).

   Goal: Move the ball forward and score by using the target player.

   Questions:

   Q. How does having a target player help offensively?
   A. It helps spread out your team from end to end (gives depth).

   Q. How can you use the target player to set up shooting chances?
   A. Give a pass to the target player and keep moving for a return pass.

2. **PRACTICE TASK:**

   When shooting from target player feed, each player starts at position S, passes to the target player (Tg), runs to position (S), and shoots the return pass (figure 4.13). Each player collects his own shot and returns to the back of the starting line. Rotate goalkeeper and target player frequently.

   Goal: Use the target player to create shooting opportunities.

   Extension: Shoot from alternate side (weaker hand or foot).

   Cues: Shooter:

   Pass to target.

   Support for the return pass.

   Shoot the return pass.

   Target player:

   Receive and pass ahead of the shooter.

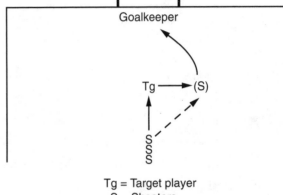

Tg = Target player
S = Shooters

Figure 4.13

3. **GAME 2:** Same as game 1. Play 6 v 6 (including goalkeepers when game is appropriate).

   Condition: Play with target player in attacking half. Goals or points from target player feed count as double.

   Goal: Players will use the target player to create shooting opportunities during game play.

   Cue: Use the target player to set up scoring chances.

4. **CLOSURE:** Questions and discussion on importance of getting ball to target player quickly by early pass and use of target player to create scoring chances.

Teaching Cues for Invasion Game Skills

As previously mentioned, we recommend a thematic approach to teaching games that addresses the tactical problems of game play through several games from the same category.

This approach requires knowledge of many skills and their associated teaching cues, particularly with regard to invasion games where we have advocated that you change the game either between or during lessons. Therefore, for this chapter only we provide the following overview of teaching cues for the skills of passing, receiving, shooting, dribbling, support play, and defensive play. We have deliberately limited cues to those six that are most critical to efficient technical performance. Likewise, we have limited the games used to reflect a balance of throwing, striking, and kicking games. Be aware that some of these teaching cues can be used in other games; for example, many of the basketball and soccer cues could be used for speedball, as could many of the cues used in the team handball lessons. For more detailed and complete teaching cues we recommend Fronske and Wilson (2002).

1. **BASIC PASSING**

   Soccer

   Nonkicking foot beside the ball, pointing to your target.

   Point the toe of the kicking foot out (or in if passing with outside of foot).

   Strike the center of the ball with the inside of the foot.

   Follow through to your target.

   Hockey

   See the target.

   Keep the blade on the ball or puck.

   Push the ball and follow through to target.

   Football (American)

   Grip across the seams.

   Arm back, elbow bent.

   Step with opposite foot.

   Throw and flick the wrist.

   Basketball

   Thumbs behind the ball, elbows in.

   Step and extend.

   Pass the ball flat (i.e., horizontally).

   Finish with palms out.

   Ultimate Frisbee

   Grip with thumb on top, forefinger along outside rim.

   Step with same side (as throwing hand) foot.

   Pass flat and follow through to target.

2. **RECEIVING**

   Soccer

   Move into line with the ball.

   Receive with the inside or outside of the foot.

   Push the ball away to set up the next pass or shot.

   Hockey

   Move into line with the ball or puck.

   Keep blade to the ground.

   Push the ball or puck away to set up the next pass or shot.

   Football (American)

   Move into line with the ball.

   Palms to the ball.

   Thumbs together (high ball) or little fingers together (low ball).

   Cup hands around the ball.

   Bend elbows to cushion the ball ("soft" hands).

   Basketball

   Move into line with the ball.

   Palms to the ball, fingers spread.

   Cup hands around the ball.

   Bend elbows to cushion the ball ("soft" hands).

   Ultimate Frisbee

   Move into line with the Frisbee.

   Fingers point to the Frisbee.

   Thumbs down (high catch) or up (low catch).

   Snap fingers and thumbs together onto the Frisbee.

3. **SHOOTING**

   Soccer

   Take a long step to the ball.

   Get close to the ball (nonkicking foot alongside the ball).

   Strike center of the ball with the laces.

   Keep toe down and follow through to target.

   Hockey

   See the target.

   Keep the blade on the ball or puck.

   Long step.

   Push the ball with a flick of the wrist.

   Follow through to target.

   Basketball (basic set shot)

   See the ball in front of your eyes (for starting position).

   Shooting hand under the ball, supporting hand on side of ball.

   Balance with feet shoulder-width apart.

   Elbow under the ball and pointing to the target.

Extend knees and arm.

Follow through (wrist points down after the shot).

4. **DRIBBLING**

Soccer

Push the ball with inside or outside of foot.

Keep the ball ahead of you, but close.

Hockey

Keep the stick on the ball or puck.

Keep the ball out to the side.

Protect the ball with your body.

Basketball

Keep the ball out to the side.

Protect the ball with your body.

Use the fingertips.

Keep the head up.

Waist-high dribble at speed.

Knee-high dribble to protect the ball.

5. **SUPPORT PLAY (off-the-ball support for all invasion games)**

Move out from behind defenders to open a passing lane.

Move quickly to support the ball carrier.

Signal or call for the ball.

6. **DEFENSIVE PLAY (positioning for all invasion games)**

Mark or guard your immediate opponent; stay between her and the goal.

Get closer to ("pressure") your opponent when he gets closer to his goal.

Pressure your opponent when he receives the ball.

Sideways stance, knees bent.

Position to one side to guide opponent onto her weak side.

Tackle or intercept when you get the chance.

chapter 5

Sport Foundations for Net/Wall Games

Young learners playing the simplest form of a net/wall game need to understand the principles of *ball placement* and *court positioning*. These principles lay the groundwork for solving the tactical problems in net/wall games. Net/wall games provide learners with high levels of activity because they play in a single or small-sided team game (e.g., volleyball) format. These early game-playing experiences are, by necessity, limited by the fundamental skill levels of novice learners. In net/wall games at the elementary level, students progress from simple throw-and-catch games to striking (without and with implements) games in both individual and team situations. Remember, the goal of a tactical games approach is to put the learner into progressively more complex games with clearly outlined tactical problems to be solved.

This chapter has four sections. First, we describe modifications to equipment and playing area for teaching net/wall games. Second, we present game progressions for teaching net/wall games. Third, we present the scope and sequence used to develop the lesson content (i.e., framework and levels of game complexity). Finally, we provide lessons that you can implement across the three levels of game complexity.

Modifications for Net/Wall Games

To teach students to play net/wall games in their simplest form, it is important to consider the range of possible equipment and playing area modifications. Also, as you plan your modifications, keep in mind the primary rule of net/wall games: to propel an object into space so that an opponent is unable to make a return (Griffin, Mitchell, & Oslin, 1997).

Early net/wall games should include a variety of throw-and-catch games because these use the manipulative skills second graders can perform in both practice and game situations. We strongly recommend that you modify the start and restart of the rally or game by eliminating the formal serve. The simplest and most successful way to get the game going is usually a throw. Such a modified serve allows students to begin play and then address tactical problems that are the very essence of net/wall games.

Here are possible modifications of equipment and playing area for net/wall games.

1. *The balls used should be soft and provide an easy bounce.* You should consider offering a variety (i.e., smaller or larger) so that your students can make their own choice based on what works for them. This technique is known as teaching by invitation (Graham, Holt/Hale, & Parker, 2001).

2. *When it is time to switch to using implements in your net/wall games, be sure that your rackets are light and have short handles.* Many teachers we have worked with have used racquetball rackets, badminton rackets, and tennis rackets with shorter handles.

3. *The playing areas are always minicourts.* They can have boundaries that are short and wide, long and narrow, or somewhere in between, depending on your gymnasium or multipurpose room space. The size and shape of your court will depend upon the tactical problem you want your students to work on and solve. You can set up the courts with tape, white shoe polish on a wooden gym floor (easy to remove), cones, or poly spots.

4. *Instead of nets, we recommend using cones initially in early net games lessons.* Cones provide the students with a simple barrier to play over. Once actual nets are used, we recommend badminton or volleyball nets. Both can be easily adjusted to tennis, badminton, or modified volleyball height.

Teach your students how to set up and break down the courts, especially when using cones or equipment that is easy to move. Students are capable and need to be held responsible for all aspects of their learning. As an elementary physical education teacher, you will find your classroom is a revolving door, with one class entering while the other class is departing, so you need to have students help you to maximize their learning time.

Progressions for Teaching Net/Wall Game Play

Progressions begin with simple games that teach the basic concepts of net/wall games. Early game play should involve only a few skills, a few rules, and as few players as possible. As students gain competence in using skills and making decisions, the complexity of the game increases (i.e., increasingly complex skills, more players, and redefined rules).

It is important to understand that you want students to use tactics even in the simplest games. With that in mind, it is important that students learn skills and movements in a game context. In this way, the reasons for using individual or combinations of skills are learned, and students gain an understanding of the relationships among tactical problems across net/wall games. Teaching tactics in a game context leads to increased comfort for students because the game has been the primary learning activity throughout instruction. As in chapter 4, we are concerned with the starting point and progressions for learning the foundations of net/wall game play. The remainder of this chapter answers the following two questions:

1. What type of net/wall game provides the easiest introduction for the elementary school student?

2. What types of net/wall games best enable students to make progress and develop their understanding of game playing to a more advanced level?

The following principles helped guide us in the development of appropriate progressions, represented by three levels of game complexity.

1. *Move students from cooperative situations to competitive situations.* Cooperation (e.g., maintaining a rally) involves working with a partner toward a goal. Competition (e.g., 1 v 1 modified tennis) involves an opponent you work against, and it is important that your students understand that good and appropriate competition needs cooperation, so keeping a rally going is crucial to a competitive net/wall game.

2. *Move from simple to complex.* This idea cuts across skills and movements as well as tactical problems and game conditions.

3. *Move from individual (singles) to small group (2 v 2) to large group (4 v 4) games.* Fewer players will slow down the tempo and flow of the game, which makes it easier to play.

We advocate that at game complexity level I you begin with throw-and-catch games over a net or against the wall because these games are the easiest to introduce. Such simple games allow you to introduce *"about game knowledge"* (what makes a game a game) such as court space, start–restart rules, and fundamental *"in game knowledge"* (how to play throw-and-catch games). In this first step in the progression, we focus on cooperative situations, simple tasks, and singles games.

The second progression, level II, incorporates underarm striking and team throw-and-catch games. The progression principles we follow here relate to moving from cooperative to competitive situations and moving from simple to more complex tactical problems such as creating and defending space, which entail more movements and skills (underhand striking with hand only). The focus of game play in this progression is on individuals and small groups.

Striking with implements in pickleball, badminton, and tennis; striking with the hand; and having more than one contact (i.e., in volleyball) are the foci of the final progression (level III). All aspects of the progression principles are in full use except playing in large groups. We do not advocate 6 v 6 volleyball at the elementary level because the goal is always to maximize involvement for all participants.

Scope and Sequence

In developing the content for this chapter, we asked ourselves the following three questions:

1. What problems or concepts of net/wall games can be realistically addressed at the elementary level?

2. How can these problems be solved in terms of movements that occur without the ball and the skills that are performed with the ball?

3. How can this content be sequenced in levels so that young learners can reasonably be expected to play a developmentally appropriate game at each level?

Remember, in a tactical games approach, rather than teaching discrete skills to be combined into games, the approach places the learner into progressively more complex games with clearly outlined objectives. The basic progression to teaching net/wall games begins with the student throwing and catching over a net and against a wall. Next, the student focuses on underhand striking and team throw and catch. Finally, the student focuses on striking with implements (e.g., pickleball, bad-minton, and tennis) and having more than one contact while striking with her hand(s) (i.e., volleyball).

Table 5.1 presents the tactical framework for net/wall games, whereas table 5.2 sequences the content into three levels of game complexity to allow for instruction that will be developmentally appropriate for the abilities of novice players.

Net/Wall Games Lessons

The following sections provide lesson outlines for net/wall games. As in the previous chapter, our goal is to provide sequenced content suggestions to assist you in developmentally appropriate instruction.

Table 5.1 A Tactical Framework for Net/Wall Games

Tactical goals and problems	Decisions	
	Movements (off-the-ball)	Skills (on-the-ball)
Offense and scoring		
Maintaining a rally	Moving to catch	Underhand throw Underhand strike—forehand and backhand
Setting up an attack	Seeing court spaces—long and short Opening up to teammates	Shots for depth—lob, drive, and clear Approach shot Drop shot Service Passing and setting
Winning a point	Where to attack—attack spaces Power versus accuracy decisions	Downward hitting—volley, smash, and spike
Defense and preventing scoring		
Defending space	Base positioning Covering the court as a team Sliding	
Defending against attacks	Backing up teammates Shifting to cover	Blocking downward hits

Table 5.2 Levels of Game Complexity for Net/Wall Games

Tactical goals and problems	Level of game complexity		
	Level I 1 bounce throw-and-catch games	Level II (1) 1 bounce striking with hand (2) 2 contact/throw-and-catch/no bounce	Level III (1) 0/1 bounce, striking with implement (badminton, pickleball, tennis) (2) 2 contact striking with hands (volleyball)
Offense and scoring			
Maintaining a rally	Moving to catch	Underhand striking—hand only (forehand)	Underhand striking—implement (forehand and backhand)
Setting up an attack	Understanding of court spaces—long and short	Shots for depth—lob, drive, clear Opening up	Clears Drop shots Service Passing and setting
Winning a point		Where to attack	Downward hitting—approach shot, volley, smash, spike, and power versus accuracy
Defense and preventing scoring			
Defending space	Base positioning	Covering the court as a team Sliding	Backing up teammates Shifting to cover
Defending against attacks			Blocking downward hits

Level I

After the initial lesson to establish equipment routines and to teach the basic rules of the game to be played, level I lessons (second and third grades) focus on singles games, beginning with a simple one-bounce throw-and-catch game (e.g., "throw tennis" and one-wall handball). Tactical problems are limited to maintaining a rally, setting up an attack, and defending space. Throughout this level, much time is spent on the fundamental aspects of playing a game, such as court boundaries, etiquette, and start–restart rules. Two basic types of games introduced are the cooperative and the competitive games. These are the essentials so that a beginner can play net/wall games.

For those among you who consider yourselves movement educators, be aware that you might intervene at any point during these level I lessons to teach movement concepts such as force and levels. These concepts are particularly applicable as students learn solutions to the tactical problem of setting up to attack because these solutions will include long and high shots to push an opponent toward the back of a court.

LESSON 1

TACTICAL PROBLEM: Maintaining a rally.

GAME: Throw tennis (singles game with players' choice of ball) using minicourts set up on volleyball court.

LESSON FOCUS: Court spaces, etiquette, and the cooperative game.

OBJECTIVE: Students will learn to recognize court spaces and play a cooperative game while keeping the ball in their own court.

1. **START-UP:** Students select partners and balls. Throw-and-catch warm-up and play with different balls (use one bounce). Explanation of court spaces. Cones (red or yellow) mark the "net" of each court (figure 5.1).

2. **GAME:** Throw and catch over the "net."

   Conditions: All throws *must* be underhand and upward; throw from where you catch (i.e., no moving with the ball).

   Throw over the net; ball *must* bounce only once on the other side of the net.

   Ball cannot bounce on thrower's own side of the net.

   Goal: Rallies of 10 throws while keeping ball in court.

3. **CLOSURE:** Discuss width of court (in line with cones) and depth of court. Set up and take down practice.

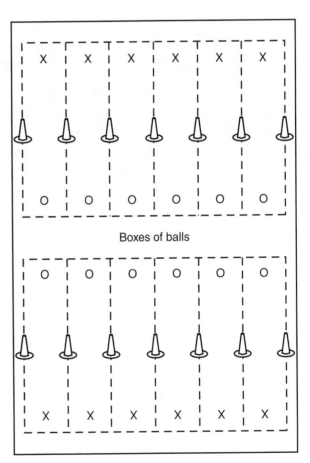

Boxes of balls

Figure 5.1

LESSON 2

TACTICAL PROBLEM: Maintaining a rally.

GAME: Throw tennis (singles).

LESSON FOCUS: Court spaces, etiquette, and the cooperative game.

OBJECTIVE: Students will play a cooperative game while keeping the ball within the defined court.

1. **GAME 1:** Throw and catch over the "net."

   Conditions: All throws must be underhand and upward; throw from where you catch.

   Throw over the net; ball must bounce only once on the other side of the net.

   Ball cannot bounce on thrower's own side of the net.

   Goal: Rallies of 10 throws keeping ball in court.

   Questions:

   Q. What makes it easier to keep the ball in court when you are throwing?
   A. One or two hands (depending on the ball chosen).

   Q. What should your throw look like? (Perhaps present some options here: one-handed or two-handed throw, feet still or stepping, and so on.)
   A. Step as you throw (step with opposite foot).

   Q. What makes it easier to catch the ball? Where should you be?
   A. After it bounces, let it come up and then down so that it is falling when you catch it (this makes it easier to catch and encourages the students to move their feet).

2. **PRACTICE TASK:** Partner throw and catch over the net.

   Goal: Rallies of 10 throws while keeping the ball in court.

   Cues: Throwing:

   Step with the opposite foot (to the throwing hand).

   Swing through to your target.

   Catching:

   Let the ball drop after the bounce.

3. **GAME 2:** Same as game 1.

4. **CLOSURE:** Discuss width of court (in line with cones) and depth of court.

   Q. Where would you throw the ball if you wanted to make it harder for your partner to get it before it bounced twice?
   A. Away from your partner into space.

LESSON 3

TACTICAL PROBLEM: Playing a competitive game and setting up to attack.

GAME: Throw tennis (singles).

LESSON FOCUS: Game rules and use of court spaces.

OBJECTIVE: Students will play a competitive game, with appropriate rules, and try to move their opponent to the back of the court.

1. **GAME:** Throw and catch over the "net."

   Conditions: All throws must be underhand and upward; throw from where you catch.

   Throw over the net; ball must bounce only once on the other side of the net.

   Ball cannot bounce on thrower's own side of the net.

   Goal: Try to make your opponent move around the court.

   Questions (interjected throughout game play):

   Q. What spaces are on the court for you to throw the ball into?
   A. Front and back because the court is long and narrow.

   Q. Is it harder to make a good throw from the front or the back?
   A. Back.

   Q. So where should you try to make your opponent move (front or back)?
   A. Back. Try to get the ball to bounce close to the back line.

2. **QUESTIONS (after continuing game play):**

   Q. When you get your opponent to move back, where is the space now?
   A. In the front.

   Q. So to make it hard for your opponent, where should you throw now?
   A. To the front.

   Q. Should you throw quickly or should you wait to throw? Why?
   A. Quickly, because your opponent will be farther away.

3. **QUESTION (after continuing game play):**

   Q. When should you stop and restart a rally?
   A. Restart a rally if . . .

   the ball bounces twice on opponent's side.

   opponent throws the ball out of court.

   opponent makes the ball bounce on her own side.

   opponent throws overhand.

   opponent catches the ball before it bounces.

   Note: Set up demonstrations of these restarting rules.

4. **CLOSURE:** Review restart rules.

LESSON 4

TACTICAL PROBLEM: Defending space.

GAME: Throw tennis (singles).

LESSON FOCUS: Recovering to a base position.

OBJECTIVE: Students will play a competitive game, with appropriate rules, and try to defend their own space by moving back to the center of the baseline between throws.

1. **GAME 1:** Throw and catch over the "net."

   Conditions: All throws must be underhand and upward; throw from where you catch.

   Throw over the net; ball must bounce only once on the other side of the net.

   Ball cannot bounce on thrower's own side of the net.

   Goal: Try to make your opponent move around the court.

   Cue: Move back to the line between throws.

Questions (interjected during game play):

Q. If your opponent is moving you around your court, where should you move in between your own throws?

A. The middle of your court at the baseline.

Q. Why?

A. So you can move up or back easily to get the next ball.

2. **GAME 2:** Three-minute games against rotating opponents (i.e., rotate the opponent every three minutes).

   Conditions: Alternately, each player serves underhand.

   Follow rules and score the game according to the restart rules.

   A point is scored if . . .

   the ball bounces twice on opponent's side.

   opponent throws the ball out of court.

   opponent makes the ball bounce on his own side.

   opponent throws overhand.

   opponent catches the ball before it bounces.

   Goal: Move your opponent, recover, and score the game.

3. **CLOSURE:** Review court spaces, recovery, and scoring.

   Note: With a competitive game now in full swing, it is worthwhile, at this stage, moving to a wall game to help students understand the tactical similarities between net and wall games. This move is made in lesson 5.

LESSON 5

TACTICAL PROBLEM: Setting up an attack.

GAME: One-wall handball (singles throw and catch).

LESSON FOCUS: Court spaces.

OBJECTIVE: Students will play a cooperative and competitive game of one-wall handball and try to move their opponents around the court.

1. **GAME:** Throw and catch against the wall.

   Conditions: All throws must be underhand and upward; throw from where you catch.

   Ball must bounce once *after* hitting the wall (cannot bounce before hitting the wall).

   Ball must bounce inside the boundaries (cones).

   Goals: 20-throw rally (cooperative game to introduce shift to wall game).

   Try to make your opponent move around the court (competitive game).

   Questions (interjected throughout game play):

   Q. Where should you try to make the ball bounce to make it difficult for your opponent?
   A. Near the back.

   Q. Where on the wall do you need to aim to do this (high or low)?
   A. High up.

2. **QUESTIONS (after continuing game play):**

   Q. When you get your opponent to move back, where is the space now?
   A. In the front.

   Q. So to make it difficult for your opponent, where should you throw now?
   A. The front.

Q. Where on the wall should you aim (high or low)?
A. Low.

3. **QUESTION (after continuing game play):**

   Q. When do you score a point?
   A. You score a point if . . .

   > the ball bounces twice in court.
   >
   > the ball bounces outside the court lines.
   >
   > the ball bounces before it hits the wall.
   >
   > opponent throws overhand.
   >
   > opponent catches the ball before it bounces.

   Note: Set up demonstrations of these scoring rules.

4. **CLOSURE:** Review use of court and restart rules.

LESSON 6

TACTICAL PROBLEM: Defending space.

GAME: One-wall handball (singles throw and catch).

LESSON FOCUS: Recovering to a base position.

OBJECTIVE: Students will play a competitive game, with appropriate rules, and try to defend their own space by moving back to the center of the court between throws.

1. **GAME 1:** One-wall handball.

   Conditions: All throws must be underhand and upward; throw from where you catch.

   > Ball must bounce once after hitting the wall.
   >
   > Ball must bounce inside the boundaries (cones).

   Goal: Try to make your opponent move around the court (competitive game).

   Cue: Move back to the center between throws.

   Questions (interjected during game play):

   Q. If your opponent is moving you around your court, where should you move in between your own throws?
   A. To the middle of your court.

   Q. Why?
   A. So that you can move up or back easily.

2. **GAME 2:** Three-minute games against rotating opponents.

   Conditions: Alternate underhand serve.

   > Follow rules and score the game according to the restart rules.
   >
   > Score a point if . . .
   >
   > > the ball bounces twice in court.
   > >
   > > the ball bounces outside the court lines.
   > >
   > > the ball bounces before it hits the wall.
   > >
   > > the opponent throws overhand.
   > >
   > > the opponent catches the ball before it bounces.

   Note: Set up demonstrations of these scoring rules.

3. **CLOSURE:** Review recovery (to center of the court).

LESSON 7

TACTICAL PROBLEM: Creating space.

GAME: Throw tennis (doubles or team).

LESSON FOCUS: Court spaces (these are wider, with two small courts combined, introducing the possibility of wider spaces).

OBJECTIVE: Students will play a competitive game, with appropriate rules, and try to set up attacks by moving the opposing team from back to front and side to side on the court to create space.

1. **GAME 1:** Throw tennis (2 v 2 or 3 v 3) over tennis-height net.

   Conditions: Alternate throw and catch (each player takes turns to throw and move to back of own line).

   Play a cooperative game.

   Ball must bounce once inside court lines.

   Goal: 20-throw rally.

   Cue: Throw to space.

   Extension: Players can catch the ball without a bounce.

   Questions:

   Q. Now, how can you make it harder for your opponents to catch the ball before the second bounce?
   A. Throw the ball into space.

   Q. Where are the spaces?
   A. Front and back and at the sides.

2. **GAME 2:** Newcome (2 v 2 or 3 v 3; plastic ball or deck ring).

   Conditions: Ball must not bounce.

   Use a badminton-height net.

   Goal: Make the ball bounce in opposing team's court.

   Extension: Two contacts (i.e., can throw the ball or ring to a teammate, who then throws it over).

   Questions: Same as in game 1.

3. **CLOSURE:** Review use of spaces. Question and discussion on moving opponents.

   Q. How can you use the two contacts (throws) to help move your opponents and make space on the other side of the net?
   A. Change the direction with the second throw.

Level II

Level II (third and fourth grades) game progressions move from one-bounce games involving striking with a hand to two-contact games (i.e., two hits or throws per side before the ball crosses the net) using throwing and catching with no bounce. Again, the first lesson establishes the environment and the game. For maintaining a rally, the students will play games that involve underhand striking with their hand only. *It is possible to repeat everything done at level I using striking with the hand as the means of* moving the ball over the net or at the wall. This would present an effective progression to the use of modified rackets. *However, the focus of level II lessons presented here moves to team games, though still using throw-and-catch skills.* Offensively the focus of these lessons is to maintain a rally and to win points. The defensive (score prevention) concepts will focus on covering the court as a team. At this level the students have the opportunity to work with actual nets at varying heights (tennis or badminton heights).

LESSON 1

TACTICAL PROBLEM: Playing a game and maintaining a rally.

GAME: Deck tennis.

LESSON FOCUS: Keeping the projectile (deck ring or quoit) in court.

OBJECTIVE: Enable students to maintain a rally of throw-and-catch deck tennis.

1. **START-UP:** Designation and familiarization (as warm-up) of court spaces (1 through 4). Players form or are assigned to teams of three, and they choose or are assigned to home courts.

2. **PRACTICE TASK:** Triangle passing:

   Goal: 10,15, or 20 consecutive passes.

3. **GAME:** 3 v 3 deck tennis (cooperative).

   Condition: Vary the serving (throws).

   Goal: 10, 15, or 20 consecutive passes.

4. **CLOSURE:** Question and discussion on throwing.

   Q. What are the best ways to throw the ring to keep it in court?
   A. Backhand or forehand.

   Note: Same game to start next lesson.

LESSON 2

TACTICAL PROBLEM: Creating and defending space.

GAME: Deck tennis.

LESSON FOCUS: Throwing quickly to space, judging the lines, covering the court.

OBJECTIVE: Students will be able to play a 3 v 3 competitive game.

1. **GAME 1:** 3 v 3 cooperative game.

   Condition: Vary the throws (backhand and forehand).

   Goal: 10, 15, or 20 consecutive passes.

   Question:

   Q. How would you win a point while playing against the other team?
   A. Land the ring inbounds on the other side of the net. Or if the other team throws the ring out-of-bounds or into the net.

2. **GAME 2:** 3 v 3 competitive game.

   Condition: Alternate serve, with each team serving in turn, by underarm throw from midcourt or back court.

   Goal: Awareness of court spaces and importance of quick catches and throws.

   Questions (interjected during game play):

   Q. To score a point where should you try to throw the ring?
   A. Space.

   Q. What should you do as soon as you catch the ring?
   A. Quickly throw it back into a space.

Q. Why quickly?
A. To catch the other team out of position.

Q. What should you do if the ring comes over the net but is going out-of-bounds?
A. Leave it.

Q. How can you best cover your own court?
A. In a triangle. (One in front, two in back will probably work best.)

Q. Where should the one front player stay?
A. At the net. (This will need to be emphasized because the front player will initially drift back, getting in the way of teammates and taking catches that he shouldn't. This also leaves the front court uncovered.)

3. **CLOSURE:** Questions and discussion on appropriate sport behaviors.

Q. What should you do if you cannot decide on a point?
A. Replay the point.

Q. What should teams do after any game?
A. Find an opponent and shake hands.

LESSON 3

TACTICAL PROBLEM: Maintaining a rally and creating space.

GAME: Deck tennis.

LESSON FOCUS: Backhand and forehand throwing technique.

OBJECTIVE: Use backhand and forehand throw to maintain a rally and create space.

1. **GAME 1:** 3 v 3 competitive game.

   Condition: Alternate serves (backhand and forehand).

   Goal: Score points but keep the ring in court (i.e., don't lose points by throwing out of court).

   Question:

   Q. Which is the easier way to throw accurately (forehand or backhand)?
   A. Backhand. (Some might answer forehand. Practice order doesn't matter.)

2. **PRACTICE TASK 1:** Triangle passing using backhand throw.

   Goal: 10, 15, or 20 consecutive passes with appropriate technique.

   Extension: See how many backhand passes the team can throw in 30 seconds.

   Cues: Step with same foot as hand holding the ring.

   Throw low to high.

   Let go level with your front foot.

   Follow through to your target.

   PRACTICE TASK 2: Triangle passing using forehand throws.

   Goal: 10, 15, or 20 consecutive passes with appropriate technique.

   Extension: See how many forehand passes the team can throw in 30 seconds.

   Cues: Step with opposite foot from hand holding the ring.

   Throw low to high.

   Let go level with your front foot.

   Follow through to your target.

   Note: The cues used here for backhand and forehand resemble those that might be used in teaching tennis backhand and forehand.

Question:

Q. If you are trying to throw quickly, how should you catch the ring?
A. One-handed is quickest, two-handed is safest.

Note: Discuss the trade-off between speed and safety.

3. **GAME 2:** Same as game 1.

4. **CLOSURE:** Review cues and question and discussion of throwing.

   Q. What is the best way to win points in a game?
   A. Throw quickly into space away from opponents.

   Note: Use practice tasks 1 and 2 to start next lesson.

LESSON 4

TACTICAL PROBLEM: Defending space on own side of the net.

GAME: Deck tennis.

LESSON FOCUS: Court coverage and sliding movements.

OBJECTIVE: Students will cover the court using a one forward, two back formation and sliding movements to make catches.

1. **GAME 1:** 3 v 3 competitive game.

   Condition: Alternate serve.

   Goal: Prevent the ring from hitting the floor on your own side of the net.

   Questions:

   Q. What is the best way to position yourselves as a team to keep the ring from hitting the floor on your side? (Ask this during game play.)
   A. One up and two back.

   Q. What type of movement should you use to get to the ring to make a catch? (Ask this after the game.)
   A. Slide.

2. **PRACTICE TASK:** Pressure passing.

   Conditions: Team practice on home court.

   Pressure passing and catching practice in a triangle.

   One passer (A), two feeders (B, C; rotate after 30 seconds).

   Player A passes to B, who passes back to A, who then passes to C, who passes back to A, who passes to B, and so on.

   Note: Feeders (B, C) should pass to the side of a passer (A) to force sliding movements by A (figure 5.2).

   Goal: Zero dropped passes in 30 seconds.

   Extension: See how many passes you can do in 30 seconds.

   Cues: Slide into line.

   Catch and pass quickly.

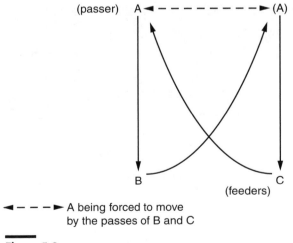

Figure 5.2

3. **GAME 2:** Same as game 1.

   Condition: One up, two back court coverage.

   Goal: Prevent ring from hitting the floor.

4. **CLOSURE:** Question and discussion on defense.

   Q. What is the best formation for defensive coverage?
   A. Two at the back and one at the front.

Level III

Level III (fourth and fifth grades) games progress from one-bounce to no-bounce games, in which players strike with a racket (badminton, pickleball, and tennis), to two-contact games striking with hands (volleyball). All offensive (scoring) concepts are addressed at this level. To maintain a rally, the students will play games that involve underhand striking with a racket. Setting up an attack will encompass introduction of deep, short, and approach (in tennis and pickleball) shots; service; passing; and setting (in volleyball). The tactical problem of winning a point will include downward hitting, which comprises volley, smash, and spike, as well as issues related to power versus accuracy. The defensive (score preventing) concepts of defending space and defending against attacks are also discussed. Defending space includes the decisions and movements associated with backing up teammates and shifting to cover. Defending against attacks includes decisions and movements focused on blocking downward hits.

Note that lessons 1 through 4 are designed for tennis or pickleball; and lessons 5 through 8, though very similar, are designed for badminton. The changes that you see in the specific lessons involve the specific skills and movements taught (such as groundstrokes in tennis versus overhead clears in badminton) and different base positions (recovery) in tennis and pickleball versus badminton. Bear in mind that the skills learned at this level are more difficult, perhaps requiring additional time in practice tasks. Such difficulty may require one lesson being spread over two class periods to allow for this additional practice time.

LESSON 1

TACTICAL PROBLEM: Maintaining a rally.

GAME: Tennis or pickleball (minicourts set up on badminton courts or volleyball courts; use low nets).

LESSON FOCUS: Court spaces, etiquette, and the cooperative game.

OBJECTIVE: Students will learn to recognize court spaces and play a cooperative game while keeping the ball in their own court and striking with a racket.

1. **GAME 1:** No-racket game (toss-bounce-catch game). Students select partners. Throw and catch warm-up; play with different balls and use one bounce. Explain court spaces.

   Conditions: Start rally with an underhand throw over the net.

   Ball cannot bounce on server's own side of the net.

   Ball must bounce only once on the other side of the net.

   Goal: Rallies of 10 throws while attempting to keep ball in court (discuss width of court).

   Question:

   Q. What did you do to keep the rally going?
   A. Throw to each other.

2. **GAME 2:** Tennis or pickleball (singles; short racket and soft-bounce tennis or sponge ball).

    Conditions: Start rally with an underhand throw over the net.

                Ball cannot bounce on server's own side of the net.

                Ball must bounce only once on the other side of the net.

                Use only groundstrokes (forehand and backhand).

    Goal: Rallies of 6 to 10 while attempting to keep ball in court using a racket.

    Cues: Let the ball fall after the bounce.

        Keep racket back and down.

        Step with the foot opposite the hitting arm (forehand).

        Step with the same foot as the hitting arm (backhand).

        Swing low to high.

        Contact the ball level with your front knee.

    Questions:

    Q. What makes it easier to keep the ball in the court when you are using a racket?

    A. Where you point the racket (up, down, or toward the net).

    Q. Where should you make contact?

    A. Level with the front knee.

    Note: This will be a source of difficulty and may also be the source of inconsistent striking accuracy.

3. **CLOSURE:** Review groundstroke technique. Set up and take down practice.

LESSON 2

TACTICAL PROBLEM: Maintaining a rally.

GAME: Tennis or pickleball (minicourts set up on badminton courts or volleyball courts; use low nets).

LESSON FOCUS: Awareness of court.

OBJECTIVE: Students will learn to create space by using underhand striking with a racket (forehand and backhand groundstrokes) in tennis or pickleball.

1. **GAME 1:** Tennis or pickleball (singles; short racket and soft-bounce tennis ball).

    Conditions: Start rally with an underhand throw over the net.

                Ball cannot bounce on server's own side of the net.

                Ball must bounce only once on the other side of the net.

                Groundstrokes only.

    Goal: Rallies of 6 to 10 while attempting to keep ball in court using a racket.

    Cues: "Bounce-hit" (having the hitter say this to herself helps focus attention).

        Racket back and down.

        Step and swing low to high.

    Question:

    Q. What is the best (most reliable) way to hit the ball with your racket?

    A. Forehand or backhand groundstroke.

2. **PRACTICE TASK 1:**

Using an underhand toss, partner A feeds three or four balls to partner B, who focuses on forehand groundstroke. The feeder should begin with three or four balls to create a short, intense trial; then players collect balls and switch roles. Player A calls, "Ball" to prompt player B to be ready for the next groundstroke.

Cues: Let the ball fall after the bounce (move the feet).

Keep racket back and down.

Step with foot opposite (same foot on backhand) to hitting arm.

Swing low to high.

Contact point level with front knee.

Follow through to target.

PRACTICE TASK 2:

Partner backhand groundstroke. Partner A tosses (feeds) three to five balls to partner B, who focuses on backhand groundstrokes. Players switch roles.

Cues: Same as in practice task 1.

3. **GAME 2:** Tennis or pickleball (singles; short racket and soft-bounce tennis ball).

Conditions: Alternate serves; start rally with bounce-hit serve or an underhand throw over the net if needed.

Ball cannot bounce on server's side of the net on the serve.

Ball must bounce only once on the other side of the net.

Use groundstrokes only.

Goal: Rallies of 10 to 15 using forehand or backhand groundstrokes.

4. **CLOSURE:** Review forehand and backhand technique.

LESSON 3

TACTICAL PROBLEM: Setting up to attack in a competitive game.

GAME: Tennis or pickleball (singles).

LESSON FOCUS: Game rules and use of court spaces.

OBJECTIVE: Students will play a competitive game, with appropriate rules, and try to move the opponent to the back of the court.

1. **GAME 1:** Tennis or pickleball (singles; short racket and soft-bounce tennis ball).

Conditions: Alternate serve; with bounce-hit serve or an underhand throw over the net.

Ball cannot bounce on server's side of the net on serve.

Ball must bounce only once on the other side of the net.

Use groundstrokes only.

Goal: Try to make your opponent move around the court.

Extension: Player can come to the net and volley (hit ball before it bounces).

Questions (interjected throughout game play):

Q. When should you stop and restart a rally?
A. Restart a rally if . . .

the ball bounces twice on opponent's side.

opponent hits the ball out of court.

opponent makes the ball bounce on her own side.

Q. What spaces are on the court for you to hit the ball to?
A. Front and back.

Q. Where should you try to make your opponent move (front or back)?
A. Back. Try to get the ball to bounce close to the end line (baseline).

Q. Why?
A. It's harder to return the ball deep from a deep position.

2. **QUESTIONS (after continuing game play):**

   Q. When you get your opponent to move back, where is the space now?
   A. In the front.

   Q. So to make it hard for your opponent, where should you hit the ball?
   A. The front.

   Q. What type of shot can you use?
   A. Drop shot or volley.

3. **CLOSURE:** Review rules.

LESSON 4

TACTICAL PROBLEM: Defending space.

GAME: Tennis or pickleball (singles).

LESSON FOCUS: Recovering to a baseline position.

OBJECTIVE: Students will play a competitive game, with appropriate rules, and try to defend their own space by moving back to the center of the baseline between hits.

1. **GAME 1:** Tennis or pickleball (singles; short racket and soft-bounce tennis ball).

   Conditions: Alternate serve with bounce-hit serve or an underhand throw over the net.

          Ball cannot bounce on your own side of the net on serve.

          Ball must bounce only once on the other side of the net on serve.

          Players can volley.

   Goal: Try to make your opponent move around the court.

   Cue: Move back to the baseline between shots.

   Questions (interjected throughout game play):

   Q. If your opponent is moving you around your court, where should you move to between hits?
   A. The middle of your court at the baseline.

   Q. Why?
   A. It's the best place to be so that you can cover the court by moving forward rather than by moving back.

2. **GAME 2:** 3-minute games against rotating opponents.

   Conditions: Alternate serve with bounce-hit serve or an underhand throw over the net.

          Ball cannot bounce on your own side of the net.

          Ball must bounce only once on the other side of the net.

   Goals: Move your opponent, *recover,* and score the game.

          If you have to come forward to get a short ball, stay at the net and volley.

3. **CLOSURE:** Review court spaces, recovery, and scoring.

LESSON 5

TACTICAL PROBLEM: Maintaining a rally.

GAME: Badminton (minicourts set up on badminton courts or volleyball courts with nets at approximately badminton height).

Note: It would be possible to use a soft ball instead of a shuttle if students find the ball easier to hit. However, the ball must be light enough to fly slowly.

LESSON FOCUS: Court spaces, etiquette, and the cooperative game.

OBJECTIVE: Students will learn to recognize court spaces and play a cooperative game while keeping the shuttle (or soft ball) in their own court and striking with an implement.

1. **GAME 1:** Badminton (singles; short racket and shuttle or soft ball).

   Conditions: Start rally by either striking the shuttle with the racket or using an underhand throw over the net.

   Shuttle cannot land on either side of the net.

   Goal: Rallies of 6 to 10 using either underhand or overhead strokes.

   Cue: Ready position = racket up.

   Questions:

   Q. Which is a stronger shot to use, underhand or overhead stroke?
   A. Overhead.

   Q. What do you have to do to use an overhead stroke?
   A. Move quickly with racket up, get under shuttle, line up to shuttle, hit hard (like a throw), snap the wrist.

2. **GAME 2:** Badminton (singles; short racket and shuttle or soft ball).

   Conditions: Start rally either by striking the shuttle with the racket or by using an underhand throw over the net.

   Shuttle cannot land on either side of the net.

   Goal: Rallies of 6 to 10 using an overhead stroke only.

3. **CLOSURE:** Review need for overhead stroke (i.e., for power). Set up and take down practice.

LESSON 6

TACTICAL PROBLEM: Maintaining a rally.

GAME: Badminton (minicourts set up on badminton courts or volleyball courts with nets at approximately badminton height).

LESSON FOCUS: Awareness of court.

OBJECTIVE: Students will learn to create space by using overhead clear in badminton.

1. **GAME 1:** Badminton (singles; short racket and shuttle or soft ball).

   Conditions: Start rally either by striking the shuttle with the racket or by using an underhand throw over the net.

   Shuttle cannot land on either side of the net.

   Goal: Rallies of 10 while using a racket and attempting to keep shuttle in court.

Cues: Racket up.

Get under shuttle.

Question:

Q. How do you push your partner back?

A. Use an overhead (also known as a clear because you clear the opponent and get the shuttle to the back of the court with this stroke).

2. **PRACTICE TASK:**

Partner A feeds (hits with racket) three or four shuttles to partner B, who focuses on overhead clear. The feeder should begin with three or four shuttles at a time to create a short, intense trial; then players collect shuttles and switch roles. Player A calls "shuttle 1-2-3-4" to prompt player B to be ready for the next shot. Player B scores 2 points for landing the shuttle within 3 feet of the baseline, 1 point for landing it within 6 feet of the baseline.

Cues: Racket up.

Get under shuttle using long strides.

Line up shuttle with nonhitting arm.

Bend elbow.

Throw the racket head at shuttle.

Snap the wrist.

3. **GAME 2:** Badminton (singles; short racket and shuttle).

Conditions: Alternate serve either by striking the shuttle with the racket or by using an overhand throw over the net.

Shuttle cannot land on either side of the net.

Goal: Rallies of 10 to 15 using forehand or backhand clear.

LESSON 7

TACTICAL PROBLEM: Setting up to attack in a competitive game.

GAME: Badminton (singles).

LESSON FOCUS: Game rules and use of court spaces.

OBJECTIVE: Students will play a competitive game, with appropriate rules, and try to move the opponent to the back of the court.

1. **GAME:** Badminton (singles; short racket and shuttle or soft ball).

Conditions: Alternate serve either by striking the shuttle with the racket or by using an overhand throw over the net.

Shuttle cannot land on either side of the net.

Goal: Try to make your opponent move around the court.

Questions (interjected throughout game play):

Q. When should you stop and restart a rally?

A. Restart a rally if . . .

shuttle lands on the court on either side.

opponent hits shuttle out of the court.

If shuttle hits net during rally (if it hits and goes over, it is good).

Q. What spaces are on the court for you to hit the ball to?
A. Front and back.

Q. Where should you try to make your opponent move (front or back)?
A. Back. Try to get the shuttle close to the end line.

Q. Why?
A. It is harder to return.

2. **QUESTIONS (after continuing game play):**

   Q. When you get your opponent to move back, where is the space now?
   A. In the front.

   Q. So to make it hard for your opponent, where should you hit the ball?
   A. The front.

   Q. How do you do that?
   A. Soft shot (drop shot).

3. **CLOSURE:** Review rules.

LESSON 8

TACTICAL PROBLEM: Defending space.

GAME: Badminton (singles).

LESSON FOCUS: Recovering to a base position.

OBJECTIVE: Students will play a competitive game, with appropriate rules, and try to defend their own space by moving to the center of the court.

1. **GAME 1:** Badminton (singles; short racket and shuttle or soft ball).

   Conditions: Alternate serve either by striking the shuttle with the racket or by using an underhand throw over the net.

   Shuttle cannot land on either side of the net.

   Goal: Try to make your opponent move around the court.

   Cue: Recover to center between shots.

   Questions (interjected during game play):

   Q. If your opponent is moving you around your court, where should you move in between hits?
   A. The middle of your court.

   Q. Why?
   A. So that you can move up or back easily for the next shot.

2. **GAME 2:** 3-minute games against rotating opponents.

   Conditions: Alternate serve either by striking the shuttle with the racket or by using an overhand throw over the net.

   Shuttle cannot land on either side of the net.

   Goal: Try to make your opponent move around the court.

3. **CLOSURE:** Review court spaces, recovery, and scoring.

   Note: The recovery position in badminton (center of the court) is different from that in pickleball or tennis (center of the baseline) because the shuttle is not allowed to land in badminton. The bounce of the ball makes the baseline a better recovery position in tennis.

LESSON 9

TACTICAL PROBLEM: Setting up an attack.

GAME: Volleyball.

LESSON FOCUS: Game rules, court space, player rotation, base position.

OBJECTIVE: Students will learn the basic concept of volleyball, focusing on volleying the ball over the net.

> *Note:* As we move to volleyball lesson outlines, it is worth considering the complexity of skill involved. The need for greater practice time may require spreading some of the following lessons over two lessons.

1. **GAME:** Volleyball (3 v 3 using soft, light ball or large trainer volleyball).

   Conditions: Use badminton court or half a volleyball court.

   Place net at badminton height.

   Players start in base position (triad) (figure 5.3).

   Explain the base position (triad) and rotation before play begins. Players start in the base position, and play begins with a free-ball toss (rainbow toss) over the net. Alternate which side makes the initial free-ball toss, and rotate after each rally.

   Serve is free-ball or rainbow toss (two-handed soccer throw-in).

   Back right player tosses from a designated "success" spot.

   Use maximum of three contacts.

   No one player can have consecutive contacts.

   (Add these following conditions later, as game progresses):

   Players practice calling "mine" any time the ball is hit to them.

   Players not playing the ball should turn (pivot) to watch their teammates hit the ball (this is known as opening up).

   Goal: Make the ball bounce in the opposing team's court.

   Note: If you have large classes, we recommend that you play 3 v 3 but rotate players into the game versus adding more players to the game. The games will move quickly because you are rotating after each point and alternating serve.

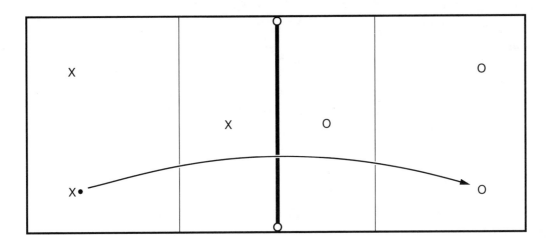

Figure 5.3

Cues: Be in ready position (knees flexed).

Be prepared to go after a ball hit in your direction.

Stand at assigned points (known as base or home position).

Return to those points after playing the ball.

Extension: Minimum of two contacts on a side.

Questions:

Q. How do you win the rally against the other team?
A. Land the ball on the other side of the net. Or, if the other team hits the ball out-of-bounds or into the net.

Q. How do you hit the ball to land it on the other side?
A. Move our feet toward the ball and strike the ball with hands and fingers upward or with a flat surface (off the forearms).

Q. What should you do when the ball is coming over the net but is going out-of-bounds?
A. Leave it.

Q. Is a ball that lands on the line good or out?
A. Good.

2. **QUESTIONS (after continuing game play):**

Q. How do you know who should play the ball?
A. Call "mine" (players who play the ball while moving in the direction of the target have the priority in playing it).

Q. What should players do when they do not play the ball?
A. Turn (pivot) to watch their teammates hit the ball (this is known as opening up).

3. **CLOSURE:** Review base position and rules.

LESSON 10

TACTICAL PROBLEM: Setting up an attack.

GAME: Volleyball.

LESSON FOCUS: Setting up for an attack by using the overhead pass.

OBJECTIVE: Students will play a game using the overhead pass (set).

1. **GAME 1:** Volleyball (3 v 3 using soft, light ball or large trainer volleyball).

Conditions: Use badminton court or volleyball court.

Set net at badminton height.

Players start in base position (triad) (see figure 5.3).

Serve is free-ball or rainbow toss (two-handed soccer throw-in).

Back right player tosses from a designated "success" spot.

Player calls "mine."

Maximum of three contacts.

No one player can have consecutive contacts.

Goal: Team tries to get two contacts on its side of the court before putting the ball over the net.

Question:

Q. What do you have to do to get two contacts on your side?
A. The serve receiver calls "mine," moves his feet toward the ball, strikes the ball with hands upward or with a flat surface. Second player calls for and moves to play the serve receiver's hit.

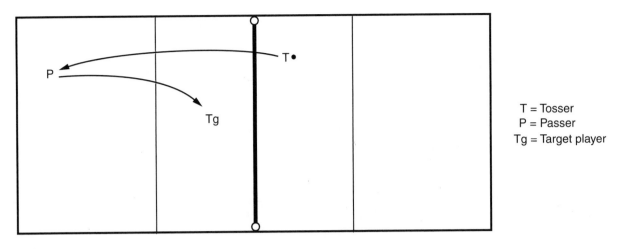

Figure 5.4

2. **PRACTICE TASK:**

Players practice overhead passes in their triad using a toss-pass-catch drill. T (tosser) tosses a free ball (rainbow toss) over the net for P (passer) to overhead pass to Tg (target player), who catches and bounce-passes the ball back to T (tosser). Do three or four trials, then rotate positions (figure 5.4).

Cues: Use your fingerpads.

Bend your legs.

Extend your arms and legs (fly like a superhero).

Give the ball a quick tap, not a catch and throw.

3. **GAME 2:** Volleyball (3 v 3 using soft, light ball or large trainer volleyball).

Conditions: Use badminton court or volleyball court.

Set net at badminton height.

Players start in base position (triad) (see figure 5.3).

First ball is free-ball toss (two-handed soccer throw-in) or rainbow toss.

Back right player tosses from a designated "success" spot.

Players should practice calling "mine" any time the ball is hit to them.

Use a maximum of three contacts.

No one player can have consecutive contacts.

Goal: Team scores a point when they attempt two hits on a side.

4. **CLOSURE:** Questions and discussion on getting two hits on a side.

LESSON 11

TACTICAL PROBLEM: Winning the point.

GAME: Volleyball.

LESSON FOCUS: Attempting to spike to win a point.

OBJECTIVE: Students will set up to spike in a game.

1. **GAME 1:** Volleyball (3 v 3 using soft, light ball or large trainer volleyball).

   Conditions: Use badminton court or volleyball court.

   Set net at badminton height.

   Players start in base position (triad) (see figure 5.3).

   Serve is free-ball or rainbow toss (two-handed soccer throw-in).

   Back right player tosses from a designated "success" spot.

   Player calls "mine."

   Use a minimum of two contacts, maximum of three contacts.

   No one player can have consecutive contacts.

   Goal: Team earns a point for two hits on a side.

   Questions:

   Q. To score a point where should you try to place the ball?
   A. Space.

   Q. What other type of hits are there in volleyball besides the overhead pass?
   A. Spike.

   Q. Which is harder to return, an overhead pass or a spike?
   A. Spike.

   Q. Why?
   A. It's a hard, downward ball.

2. **PRACTICE TASK:**

   In pairs, one player initiates practice of spiking with a high self-toss, then moves to the ball, facing the net, and either swings or jumps and swings, spiking the ball over the net. The other player collects the ball and returns it to the spiker. Have them switch positions after three to five tries.

   Cues: Move the feet to the ball.

   Face the net.

   Swing or jump and swing (depending on the developmental level of the student).

3. **GAME 2:** Volleyball (3 v 3 using soft, light ball or large trainer volleyball).

   Conditions: Use badminton or volleyball court.

   Set net at badminton height.

   Players start in base position (triad) (see figure 5.3).

   First ball is free-ball toss (two-handed soccer throw-in) or rainbow toss.

   Back right player tosses from a designated "success" spot.

   Players should practice calling "mine" any time the ball is hit to them.

   Use a minimum of two contacts, maximum of three contacts.

   No one player can have consecutive contacts.

   Goals: Team scores a point when ball bounces on opponents' side of the net.

   Team members raise their hands when attempting a spike.

4. **CLOSURE:** Questions and discussion on setting up to spike.

   Q. Where should you be facing when you spike?
   A. The net.

   Q. If you jump to spike, in which direction should you jump?
   A. Straight up (so that you don't hit the net on the way back down).

LESSON 12

TACTICAL PROBLEM: Winning the point and defending against the attack.

GAME: Volleyball.

LESSON FOCUS: Attempting to spike to win a point.

OBJECTIVE: Students will set up to spike in a game.

1. **GAME 1:** Volleyball (3 v 3 using soft, light ball or large trainer volleyball).

   Conditions: Use badminton court or volleyball court.

   Set net at badminton height.

   Players start in base position (triad) (see figure 5.3).

   Serve is free-ball or rainbow toss (two-handed soccer throw-in).

   Back right player tosses from a designated "success" spot.

   Players should practice calling "mine" any time the ball is hit to them.

   Use a minimum of two contacts, maximum of three contacts.

   No one player can have consecutive contacts.

   Goals: Team scores a point when ball bounces on opponents' side of the net.

   Team members raise their hands when attempting a spike.

   Questions:

   Q. What does your team have to do so that a teammate has a good chance to spike?
   A. Get the ball high in the air.

   Q. What can the opposing team do to play a spiked ball?
   A. Play low or block it.

   Q. Who would block the ball?
   A. Front-row player.

2. **PRACTICE TASK:**

   Form groups of three to set up to spike and block. Player S (setter) self-tosses to overhead pass (set) the ball to player H (hitter), who attempts to spike the ball over the net. Player B/C (blocker/collector) attempts to block and then collects the ball and returns it to player S. Allow players three to five trials, then have them rotate through positions from setter to hitter to blocker/collector (figure 5.5).

   Cues: Overhead pass (set):

   Use your fingerpads.

   Bend your legs.

   Extend your arms and legs (fly like a superhero).

   Give the ball a quick tap, not a catch and throw.

   Spike:

   Move the feet to the ball.

   Face the net.

   Swing or jump and swing (depending on the developmental level of the student).

   Block:

   Hands high.

   Front the hitter.

   Jump on the arm swing of the hitter.

   Press the ball to the center of the court.

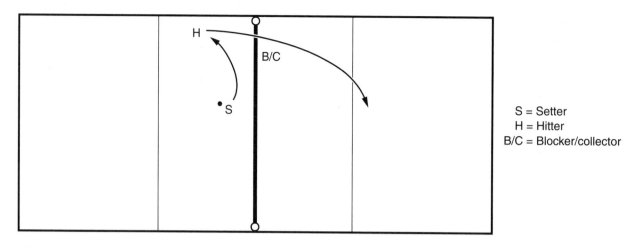

S = Setter
H = Hitter
B/C = Blocker/collector

Figure 5.5

3. **GAME 2:** Volleyball (3 v 3 using soft, light ball or large trainer volleyball).

   Conditions: Use badminton or volleyball court.

   Set net at badminton height.

   Players start in base position (triad) (see figure 5.3).

   Serve is free-ball or rainbow toss (two-handed soccer throw-in).

   Back right player tosses from a designated "success" spot.

   Players should practice calling "mine" any time the ball is hit to them.

   Use a minimum of two contacts, maximum of three contacts.

   No one player can have consecutive contacts.

   Goals: Team scores a point when ball bounces on opponents' side of the net.

   Players jump when attempting a spike.

   Players raise their hands to block the ball.

4. **CLOSURE:** Questions and discussion on spiking and blocking.

   Q. Where do you jump on a spike?
   A. Straight up.

   Q. When do you jump on a block?
   A. On the arm swing of the hitter.

Summary

Decision making is at the heart of all games and makes them challenging and interesting. Our goal is to provide students with many opportunities to learn what to do in various net/wall games. These opportunities will lead to an understanding of these games and will develop improved players. We recommend that you base your instructional units on one level of complexity and individualize instruction as needed with your students and with your facilities and equipment. If your students complete the three levels of game complexity provided in this chapter, they will have gained a fundamental understanding of net/wall games.

chapter 6

Sport Foundations for Striking/Fielding Games

Baseball may be one of America's favorite pastimes, but it can be one of the most boring games to watch and to play. Many modifications, such as softball and T-ball, have been made to the original game to speed up play and create more game-play opportunities. But even with these modifications, it is still a slow game, with most of the action involving 3 or 4 of the 9 or 10 players. This can make it difficult for physical educators and youth sport coaches to provide adequate hitting or fielding opportunities for students and players to improve performance. However, with a bit of reflection on how we learned to play and a few

observations of neighborhood pick-up games, we can learn how to modify the game so that students can learn more during physical education classes.

Many of us learned to play baseball on playgrounds, in vacant lots, on a street in front of the house, or in the driveway. Any number of people could play: 2, 5, 8, or 10, regardless of size, strength, skill, or ability. Space and number of players available would determine the rules, and equipment was varied and optional: a stick or a well-taped bat, a softball, baseball, or wound-up wad of tape, and a base of anything from boxes to shirts. Gloves, of course, were optional; and if there were any, they were shared. We often implemented the following rules: "pitcher's poison"—throws went to the pitcher instead of the first base; no right-field hitting (except when Pedro was up, because he was left-handed, which meant no left-field hitting and the outfielder shifted from left to right); no balls or strikes—three swings, and if you missed on the last swing, you were out; an official pitcher—one pitcher for both teams; you were not allowed to throw Jimmy out at first (he was short for his age and had a hard time running); and if you hit the ball over the fence and onto the tracks, *you* had to go get it.

There were, of course, other games related to baseball, such as running bases, five dollars, and stickball. Each of these games focused on various elements of the "real" game but required far fewer players. Running bases, for example, could be played with three or four people and emphasized baserunning, covering a base, and tagging runners out. Five dollars emphasized fielding, especially outfield play, and hitting the ball long and hard. Stickball was often played in the schoolyard, with a strike zone chalked onto a wall, one batter (usually with a thick stick), and one pitcher. Both pitching and batting were the major emphasis here. There are many variations of stickball—at least one per neighborhood. Many of these same games can be used in physical education or youth sport coaching to help children learn to play baseball and softball. This chapter takes some of these games and other modifications or conditions (see chapter 2) to provide examples of how to teach children the tactics, movements, and skills related to baseball, softball, and other striking/fielding games.

Softball, baseball, and cricket are examples of striking/fielding games. In each, a ball is pitched or bowled to a batter, whose intent is to strike a ball into an area of the field, generally away from fielders, and get on base or to the stumps safely, with the ultimate goal of scoring a run. Tactically, each game involves situations, such as "one out and a runner on first base," which can be isolated for instruction and practice. In the "one out and a runner on first base" example, a number of elements are involved. First, breaking the situation into offense and defense, there are two aspects of each. Offensively, there are the tactics, movements, and skills related to the batter and to the runner. We must remember that sometimes the batter, if successful, becomes the runner; and sometimes there is more than one player running the bases. Defensively, there are tactics, movements, and skills related to the player fielding the ball as well as to the players providing support in the form of backups or base coverage. Support can be verbal as well: Teammates can tell the player which base to throw to.

Remember that games, whether softball, baseball, basketball, or tennis, involve tactics, movements, and skills that are intricately intertwined. *The tactic drives the movement or skill performed.* For example, in a game situation with no outs and a runner on first, the batter should hit behind the runner (to the right side of the diamond) to move the runner into scoring position. This play requires different technique than a normal pull to the left side. Thus, teaching skills in isolation does little to help the child transfer the striking skill to game play. The statement "You can't play the game until you learn the skills" runs contrary to every recreational and pick-up game ever played. The statement also points to our need, as physical educators and coaches, to design games that emphasize the same tactics, movements, and skills required of a full-sized version of the game.

Before you proceed, there are some necessary points of clarification. Throwing, catching, striking, and running are important fundamental skills and precursors to fielding, batting, and baserunning. Fundamental skills should be combined to enhance their transferability among striking/fielding games. Fielding, for example, requires the player to position the body and the ball during the catch so that a quick, accurate throw can be made to get the runner out or to stop the runner from advancing. Batting and running must be combined as a hit and run to first base. Do not forget to teach players to drop the bat; remind them to swing, drop, and run. And if occasionally you cannot get a player to drop the bat, insist that he run with the bat and drop it on the way to first base. Running bases combines quick starts, dodging a tag, changing directions, making the turn (at first, for example), and making sudden stops. Sliding and diving can also be added here, but these are generally taught at the more advanced levels of game play.

Another important point is that sport skills should emerge naturally as a result of the context. In other words, form follows function (Oslin & Mitchell, 1998). For example, with a runner on first and a grounder to the left side of the infield, the shortstop needs only to flip, not throw, the ball to the second-base player to force the out. The skill of "flipping" a ball to the person covering a base has emerged as a result of this force-out situation and is similar to a shovel pass in football. Therefore, it is imperative that skills be taught as part of the game context, as the tactics drive the form of the movement needed to successfully play the game.

Modifications for Striking/Fielding Games

A key characteristic of a tactical games approach is the use of "conditioned" or modified games. Conditioned games are intended to highlight specific situations found in the formal, full-sided version of the game and can be designed as progressions (i.e., a progression of games) from 3 v 3 to 10 v 10. Even advanced players create gamelike conditions during practice to help improve particular aspects of and weaknesses in their game play. In fact, every traditional baseball practice includes the coach calling out situations (e.g., runner on first, no outs) as she hits grounders to the infield.

The following guidelines will assist you in modifying striking/fielding games appropriately.

- *Consider the number of players.* When modifying or designing conditioned games, the first consideration should be given to the number of players. Games can be played 2 v 2, 3 v 3, or even 3 v 1, depending on the situation on which the teacher is focusing. Games for most seven- and eight-year-olds need no more than six players (an infield) because they rarely hit out of the infield, as most Little League spectators can attest. If they do hit to the outfield, give them a home run or let the infield chase the ball down and throw it in to stop the runner from advancing. Either way, each player will get more opportunities to actually catch and throw the ball as well as bat in a game with only six players. It is also important to rotate players so that they get to play all positions.

- *Modify the playing area.* The distances between bases can be shorter than regulation.

Field sizes for players who have difficulty throwing and running can be smaller than fields for more skillful players. Fields can also be made smaller using only first, second, and home base, for example, to emphasize a particular aspect of play. For classes of 20 or more students, position fields in a cloverleaf design, with a large safety zone in the middle (see figure 3.3) and stagger the fields to limit the potential of an errant throw to strike a player on an adjacent field. The safety zone is for members of the batting team as well as for the coach or teacher. Be very strict about safety rules and never tolerate a player who throws the bat.

- *Modify the equipment.* The lessons given in this chapter are prepared with kickball, T-ball, softball, or baseball in mind. In the early stages, it is likely students will find it easier to kick a larger ball than to strike a smaller ball, making more likely understanding and game-play situations will develop because striking and fielding a bigger ball will be easier. As students progress to batting, the use of batting tees, even for the most advanced players, is a must. Tees keep games going quickly and help batters send the ball to the appropriate area depending on the situation. If pitching is provided, limit the number of pitches as well as the number of foul balls and consider a no-walk rule. Soft bats and balls are available at most discount and toy stores. Also consider a variety of lengths, weights, and sizes to accommodate each player. Gloves are optional. Depending on the composition of the ball, gloves can be a deterrent, and they encourage the one-handed rather than two-handed catch. When using gloves, teach how to transfer the ball from the glove to the throwing hand, a skill essential to successful fielding.

- *Modify the rules and, whenever possible, implement rules to speed up play.* The rules should be limited to whatever is necessary to play a particular conditioned game. Additional rules can be added later, when a particular situation requires another rule or modification to existing rules. Rules should be taught as tactics, movements, and skills are introduced. For example, when teaching hit and run to first base, present the rule about not running inside the base path as well as the rationale for the rule. Putting another base outside of the first base line (that is, one inside the line for the base player, one outside for the runner) can protect the player covering first base as well as condition the runner to run outside the base path.

• *Use situations to design or modify conditioned games.* As mentioned previously, all of the tactical problems related to striking/fielding games evolve from situations. One advantage of teaching from game situations relates to the need to individualize games. The whole class can be working on a particular situation, but more advanced players can work on more complex tactics, movements, and skills, while novice players work on more basic ones. For example, players on field A can work on fielding while players on field B can work on base coverage in the same situation.

Progressions for Teaching Striking/Fielding Games

Most elementary specialists recommend focusing on the development of fundamental skills in prekindergarten, first, and second grades, with some introduction of sport skills and sports in third grade. This is not to say that sport skills and movements cannot be learned earlier, because many children do learn these as a result of participating in youth sports and other more advanced-level movement experiences. For the most part, the introduction of a sport skill depends on the complexity of the tactic or skill and the context in which it is used. Whether second grader or adult, we must have some degree of tactical understanding to be successful games players.

Table 6.1 lists tactical decisions and elements of skill execution arising from some game situations common to the offensive tactical problem of scoring. Similarly, table 6.2 lists tactical decisions and movements arising from some game situations common to the defensive tactical problem of preventing scoring. Tables 6.3 and 6.4 identify three levels of game complexity, providing you with a possible progression of game-play development for striking/fielding games. The following lesson out-

Table 6.1   Some Game Situations and Tactical Decisions Common in Scoring in Striking/Fielding Games

Game situation	Tactical decisions	Elements of skill execution
0–1 outs/0 runners	**Batting** Where to hit the ball? Point of contact (power zone)?	Grip and stance Step and swing fast Contact in power zone Follow-through Drop bat
	Batting-to-baserunning (transition) Run through or round first base?	Step and run to first base (outside base path) Running through first base
0–2 outs/runner on first	**Batter and baserunner** Where to hit? Run through or round? Go to second or return to first **Base runner** Ready to run on grounder *or* stay on a line drive or fly ball?	Look for ball Listen for coaches' signal Starting position Timing take-off Watching and listening for coaches' signals Stopping abruptly *or* make turn for third base Stopping at second base Staying in contact with second base

Table 6.2 Some Game Situations and Tactical Decisions Common in Preventing Scoring in Striking/Fielding Games

Game situation	Tactical decisions	Elements of skill execution
0–2 outs/0 runners/infield grounder	**Fielding** Where to throw the ball?	Ready position Feet to the ball Catch and throw Footwork—transition from catch to throw Follow to target (first base)
	Supporting Where to support? Where to back up? Which base to cover (force play)?	Move on contact Positioning to back up play Move to base Right foot on inside edge nearest the play
	Communicating Signal number of outs (prior to pitch) Tell teammates where to throw	Give fielder a target (with glove) Watch ball into glove
0–2 outs/runner on 1st/infield grounder	**Fielding** Throw to first or second? Throw, flip, or tag second?	Catch and shovel pass/flip/toss Flip—underhand throw/toss to second Coverage of second base on force play
	Supporting Who covers second? Back up	Shortstop coverage of second on force play Second-base player coverage of second on force play Positioning to back up play

Table 6.3 Levels of Game Complexity Related to Scoring in Striking/Fielding Games

Game situation	Level of game complexity		
	Level I	Level II	Level III
0–1 outs/0 runners	Batting Hit and run to first base Rounding first base		
0–1 outs/runner on first	Baserunning first to second (take-off and stopping)	Hitting past the infield	Hitting behind the runner
0–2 outs/variable/infield grounder		Baserunning—second to third and third to home Deciding where to hit to advance the runner Hitting to left Hitting to right	
0–1 outs/runner on second/infield grounder		Baserunning on tag situation Feint or fake to draw throw	

(continued)

Table 6.3   (continued)

Game situation	Level of game complexity		
	Level I	Level II	Level III
0–2 outs/runner on first/ outfield hit			Baserunning—tag play Deciding whether to run
0–2 outs/variable			Advancing the runner? Hitting line drives and fly balls to the outfield

Table 6.4   Levels of Game Complexity Related to Preventing Scoring in Striking/Fielding Games

Game situation	Level of game complexity		
	Level I	Level II	Level III
0–2 outs/0 runners/infield grounder	Fielding infield grounders Cutting the lead runner First-base coverage/force play Communication		
0–2 outs/runner on first/infield grounder	Deciding where to throw Second-base coverage/ force play	Positioning to back up Flip/underhand toss	
0–2 outs/variable/infield grounder		Base coverage on force play (third and home plate)	
0–1 outs/runner on second/ infield grounder		Base coverage on tag plays—sweep tag	
1 out/0–1 runners/outfield hit		Fielding—outfield Deciding where to throw Positioning to back up play Communication	
0–1 outs/runner on first/outfield hit (runners attempt to advance)			Cutoffs Relays Tag plays

lines correspond to these levels of game complexity.

Striking/Fielding Game Lessons

In this section, we present lesson outlines for the three levels of game complexity. Bear in mind that in the early stages you may have to devote additional time in the initial lessons to training students to play multiple simultaneous games.

Level I

The game situation of "zero outs/zero runners on base/grounder to infielder" drives the tactical decisions, movements, and skills needed at level I (2nd and 3rd grade). The first several lessons focus on fielding, which extends the skills of catching and throwing to include a transition from receiving the ball to throwing the ball. This transition requires using the proper angle to approach the ball as well as positioning the body and the ball (once it is caught) to throw quickly and accurately. It is

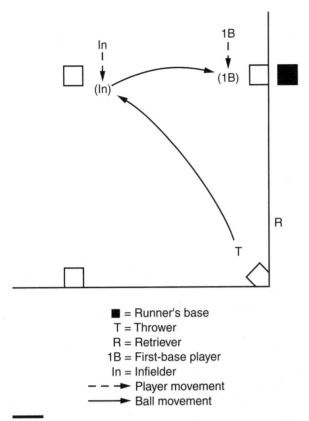

■ = Runner's base
T = Thrower
R = Retriever
1B = First-base player
In = Infielder
− − −▶ Player movement
──────▶ Ball movement

Figure 6.1

recommended that this transition be taught directly.

The first few level I lessons focus on the on-the-ball skill of fielding, then the off-the-ball skill of base coverage. Proper base coverage is important for safety as well as keeping runners off the bases and out of scoring position. An extra base positioned outside the base path (figure 6.1) can help keep the first-base player from colliding with or tripping the runner. It also trains runners to run outside the base path so that they do not interfere with the play, which according to the rules would be an out.

The later level I lessons focus on offensive elements of the game, first on baserunning and then on kicking or batting. Having the offensive team "roll and run" to first during the first few lessons helps maintain the focus on defense while allowing the offense to practice baserunning. Roll and run also eliminates the need to deal with bats, which can be a safety hazard, or (if playing kickball) large balls that can be difficult to throw.

The final few lessons focus on advancing to second base, which extends the role of the base runner both physically (rounding first) and cognitively (decision to stay or run to second). The defense must also decide where to throw. Thus the concept of cutting the lead runner to keep runners out of scoring position is important for students to learn at this level. Allowing the runner to advance will increase the complexity of tactical decisions. Thus, as the complexity of the game situations increases, so too does the complexity of the tactical decisions and the skills required.

Game situations should be used to set up lesson progressions, within and across units of instruction. Each situation involves defensive play, on- and off-the-ball, and offensive play, as a base runner and as a batter. As the teacher, you can decide whether to focus on one or more elements of a particular situation. Then allow that situation to naturally unfold and lead to the next likely situation. For example, when there are zero outs/no runners on base/grounder to the infield, the next situation is likely to involve zero outs/runner on first. The batter must then consider, where is the best place is to hit the ball to advance the runner, and the fielders must consider, where to throw the ball. Thus extending the situation automatically extends the tactical decisions and skills needed to play the game.

LESSON 1

TACTICAL PROBLEM: Throwing out the lead runner.

GAME: Kickball, throwball, T-ball, softball, or baseball.

SITUATION: 0 outs, 0 runners on base, grounder to second-base player.

LESSON FOCUS: Fielding transition from catch to throw.

OBJECTIVE: Students will receive the ball with two hands and immediately bring the ball into throwing position, then step and throw to the player covering the base.

1. **GAME 1:** 2 v 2 half-infield game.

    Conditions: Offense:

   Throw, kick, or bat groundball to second-base player, then run to first base, attempting to beat the throw.

   Defense:

   Field the ball and attempt to get ball to first base ahead of the runner to get the runner out.

   Switch after three runs or three outs, whichever comes first.

    Goal: Defense gets three outs before the offense scores three runs.

    Questions:

   Q. How many of you were able to get three outs before the other pair scored three runs?
   A. No one.

   Q. Why not?
   A. Throw was too late, throw was not caught or was off target, misplay at first.

   Q. What can you do to get the throw to the base more quickly?
   A. Make a good, quick throw to the player at first and a good catch at first.

2. **PRACTICE TASK:**

   Thrower rolls grounders to infielder. As he catches with two hands, he scoops and lifts ball into throwing position, then steps and throws to the target—the first-base player. The first-base player rolls ball back to retriever, who feeds it to the thrower. Defensive players rotate after five trials at second base, then rotate with offensive players who are throwing the ball (see figure 6.1).

    Goal: Demonstrate smooth transition from catch to throw and throw ball accurately to first base.

    Cues: Use two hands.

      Scoop it up.

      Step to the target and throw.

    Extension: After throw, thrower runs to first, and fielder attempts to get ball to first ahead of runner.

3. **GAME 2:** Same as game 1 (2 v 2 half-infield game).

    Condition: Runner must run outside base path to be considered safe at first base.

    Goal: Defense gets three outs before offense gets three runs.

4. **CLOSURE:** Questions and discussion on importance of getting to ball quickly and getting into position to throw runner out at first base. To assess, compare performance in game 1 to performance in game 2.

LESSON 2

TACTICAL PROBLEM: Support and base coverage on force play.

GAME: Kickball, throwball, T-ball, softball, or baseball.

SITUATION: 0 outs, 0 runners on base, grounder to second base.

LESSON FOCUS: Covering first base on a force play.

OBJECTIVE: Students will cover first on a force play using a two-handed target and foot on inside edge of the base.

1. **GAME 1:** 2 v 2 half-infield game.

   Conditions: Offense:

   > Throw, kick, bat groundball to second-base player, then run to first base, attempting to beat the throw.

   > Defense:

   > Field the ball and attempt to get ball to first base ahead of the runner to get the runner out.

   > Switch after three runs or three outs, whichever comes first.

   Goal: Get three outs before the offense scores three runs.

   Questions:

   Q. What is a force-out?
   A. You just have to touch the base for the out when the runner *must* run to a base.

   Q. What should the first-base player do when she is not fielding the ball?
   A. Cover first base (catch the ball and tag the base).

   Q. How can the first-base player help the fielders make an accurate throw?
   A. Give a good target.

2. **PRACTICE TASK:**

   Thrower rolls grounders to infielder, who fields and throws to first base. As soon as the first-base player sees the throw going to second, he moves to first and puts foot on inside edge of base and gives fielder a big two-handed target: big hands, arms extended at chest level. After catching, the first-base player then rolls the ball to the retriever. Rotate after each defensive player has five trials at first base, then rotate with offensive players or throwers (see figure 6.1).

   Goal: Get to base quickly, receive and control the ball.

   Cues: Move quickly to cover first.

   > Keep foot on inside edge of base.

   > Big, two-handed target.

   > Watch ball into the glove (absorb).

   Extension: Use foot opposite throwing hand to tag first base, or add a runner.

3. **GAME 2:** 2 v 2 half-infield game.

   Conditions: Same as in game 1, and spread second and first farther apart as players improve.

   Goal: Get three outs before offense gets three runs.

   Extension: Encourage runners to run it out: run through first, perhaps past a cone placed beyond first.

4. **CLOSURE:** Question and discussion on first-base coverage and support play. Emphasize what to do when not fielding.

LESSON 3

TACTICAL PROBLEM: Defend space and the base.

GAME: Kickball, throwball, T-ball, softball, or baseball.

SITUATION: 0 outs, 0 runners on base, grounder to first base.

LESSON FOCUS: Fielding grounder at first base, then tagging first for the force-out.

OBJECTIVE: The student will move quickly to the ball, field cleanly, then run safely to first and tag the inside edge of the base.

1. **GAME 1:** 2 v 2 half-infield game.

    Conditions: Offense:

    Throws, kicks, or bats groundball to first-base player, then runs to first base, attempting to beat the first-base player to the bag.

    Defense:

    Fields the ball and attempts to get ball to first base ahead of the runner to get the runner out.

    Switch after three runs or three outs, whichever comes first.

    Goal: Get three outs before the offense scores three runs.

    Questions:

    Q. If a player throws or hits a ball toward first base, what should the first-base player do?
    A. Field the ball, then run and tag first base.

    Q. What should the second-base player do?
    A. Back up the first-base player as he fields the ball.

2. **PRACTICE TASK:**

    Thrower rolls grounders between first- and second-base players and runs to first base. The first-base player fields, then runs to first to tag the base ahead of the runner. The fielder (first-base player) should take a curved path (U or C) toward the baseline and then run parallel with the baseline to tag the base. The second-base player should back up, providing support for the first-base player. The first-base player then rolls ball to the retriever. Rotate after each defensive player has five trials at first base, then rotate with offensive players or throwers (figure 6.2).

    Goal: Get to ball quickly, field cleanly, and run to first ahead of the runner.

    Cues: Move quickly to the ball.

    Catch it first, then run to base.

    Touch inside edge of base.

    Stay *inside* the base path.

    Extension: Run a U or C pathway to get runner out.

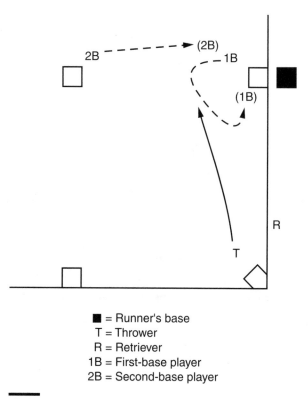

= Runner's base
T = Thrower
R = Retriever
1B = First-base player
2B = Second-base player

Figure 6.2

3. **GAME 2:** 2 v 2 half-infield game.

    Conditions: Throws should be modified to challenge both fielder and runner.

    For example, if the runner is fast, throw closer to the fielders and throw the ball farther from the fielders if the base runner is slower.

    Goal: Get three outs before offense gets three runs.

4. **CLOSURE:** Question and discussion on fielding by first-base player.

LESSON 4

TACTICAL PROBLEM: Score (hit and run to first base).

GAME: Kickball, throwball, T-ball, softball, or baseball.

SITUATION: 0 outs, 0 runners on base, grounder to second base.

LESSON FOCUS: Transition from hit to run.

OBJECTIVE: The student will hit and run (drive right knee and left arm and head and eyes down the line), running as fast as possible through first base.

1. **GAME 1:** 2 v 2 half-infield game.

   Conditions: Offense:

   Hit or kick groundball to second-base player, then run to first base, attempting to beat the throw.

   Defense:

   Field the ball and attempt to get ball to first base ahead of the runner to get the runner out.

   Switch after three runs or three outs, whichever comes first.

   Goal: Get three runs before the defense gets three outs.

   Questions:

   Q. After hitting the ball, what should you do to get to first base as fast as possible?
   A. Run fast.

   Q. What's the first thing you need to do to run fast?
   A. Get a good start.

2. **PRACTICE TASK:**

   All four players start at home plate or three at home and one in coaching box to coach runner to run hard through the base and past the cone; in kickball, work on the transition from kicking to running. From a batting stance, imitate the swing (without bat or ball), then "drive" (knee and opposite arm to first base). After three practice trials, repeat three more times with a bat. Then, if batting, put two players in the field and repeat with bat and ball. Repeat running trials three to five times.

   Goal: Hit and run to first.

   Cues: Drive knee and arm.

   Eyes down the line.

   Run hard through first base.

   Extension: Use stopwatch to time from contact with the ball to contact with the base.

3. **GAME 2:** 2 v 2 half-infield game.

   Condition: Same as in game 1, and extra players can coach first base.

   Goal: Get three outs before offense gets three runs.

4. **CLOSURE:** Question and discussion on hit and run to first base.

LESSON 5

TACTICAL PROBLEM: Score by hitting and running fast through first base.

GAME: Kickball, throwball, T-ball, softball, or baseball.

SITUATION: 0 outs, 0 runners on base, grounder to second base.

LESSON FOCUS: Hit and run through first base.

OBJECTIVE: After hitting, the student will run hard through first base.

1. **GAME 1:** 2 v 2 half-infield game.

   Conditions: Offense:

   > Throw, hit, or kick groundball to second-base player, then run to first base, attempting to beat the throw.

   > Defense:

   > Field the ball and attempt to get ball to first base ahead of the runner to get the runner out.

   > Switch after three runs or three outs, whichever comes first.

   Goal: Get three runs before the defense gets three outs.

   Question:

   Q. Besides getting a good start, what else should you do to get to first base quickly?
   A. Run hard, focus forward, listen to and watch the coach, run through first base.

2. **PRACTICE TASK:**

   Same practice as previous lesson, but emphasize running hard "through" first base. Put a cone about 5 feet beyond first base, and encourage the runner to run as fast as he can past the cone. All four players start at home plate or three at home and one in coaching box to coach runner to run hard through the base and past the cone. From a batting stance, imitate the swing (without bat or ball), then "drive" (knee and opposite arm to first base). After three practice trials, repeat three more times with a bat. Then, if batting, put two players in the field and repeat with bat and ball. Repeat running trials three to five times.

   Note: Adapt this if using throwing or running.

   Goal: Hit and run fast through first base.

   Cues: Hit and run hard.

   > Run "through" the base and past the cone.

   Extension: Use stopwatch to time from contact with the ball to the cone beyond the base.

3. **GAME 2:** 2 v 2 half-infield game.

   Condition: Same as in game 1, and extra players can coach first base.

   Goal: Get three runs before defense gets three outs.

4. **CLOSURE:** Question and discussion on hit and run "through" first base.

LESSON 6

TACTICAL PROBLEM: Advancing runner from first to second.

GAME: Kickball, throwball, T-ball, softball, or baseball.

SITUATION: 0 outs, runner on first, grounder to second base.

LESSON FOCUS: Offense running from first to second base.

OBJECTIVE: The students will be able to start quickly from first base, run hard, and stop suddenly at second base.

1. **GAME 1:** 3 v 3 half-infield game (adding a shortstop).

   Conditions: Start with a runner on first base.

   > Offense:

   > Hit or kick groundball to advance runner to second base; offense scores a run when runner is safe on second.

   > Defense:

   > Field the ball and attempt to get the lead runner out.

   > Switch after three runs or three outs, whichever comes first.

   Goal: Advance the runner to second base.

   Questions:

   Q. What are some things you can do to help you run faster from first to second base?
   A. Get a good take-off, run hard, don't stop too soon or overrun the base.

   Q. According to the rules, when can you leave first base?
   A. When the ball is hit or when it passes the batter.

2. **PRACTICE TASK:**

   For take-off practice, one player is a runner on first in "ready" position. Two players are waiting. One player is at the plate with a bat imitating a swing. Rotate after six to nine swings.

   For stopping practice, about two steps before second base, lean backward and get the heel down ahead of the toe. One step past is allowed, but the runner must keep one foot on the base. During practice, emphasize starting, then stopping, then both. Continue to focus on running hard.

   Goal: Quick start, hard run, sudden stop.

   Cues: Start when batter steps.

   > Run hard.

   > Lean back and heels down to brake.

   Extension: Use stopwatch to time from contact with the ball to the cone beyond the base.

3. **GAME 2:** 3 v 3 half-infield game.

   Conditions: Same as in game 1, and adjust size of field to accommodate level of play.

   Goal: Get three runs before defense gets three outs.

4. **CLOSURE:** Question and discussion on advancing the runner from first to second.

   Q. Where's the best place for the batter to hit in this situation to move the runner to second?
   A. Behind the runner.

LESSON 7

TACTICAL PROBLEM: Cutting the lead runner.

GAME: Kickball, throwball, T-ball, softball, or baseball.

SITUATION: 0 outs, runner on first, grounder to right infield.

LESSON FOCUS: Shortstop coverage of second base on a force play.

OBJECTIVE: Students will demonstrate the proper coverage of second base by the shortstop on a force play from the right side of the infield.

1. **GAME 1:** 3 v 3 half-infield game.

   Conditions: Start with a runner on first base.

   > Offense:
   >
   > Hit or kick ground ball to the right side of the infield to advance the runner to second base.
   >
   > Runs are scored when the runner is safe at second.
   >
   > Defense:
   >
   > Field the ball and attempt to get the runner out at second base.
   >
   > Switch after three runs or three outs, whichever comes first.

   Goal: Get three runs before the defense gets three outs.

   Questions:

   Q. In this situation, which runner should you try to put out first?
   A. The runner going to second.

   Q. Who covers second when the ball is hit to the right side of the infield?
   A. The shortstop.

   Q. If you field the ball close to the base, do you need to throw the ball overhand?
   A. No, you can just "flip" it.

2. **PRACTICE TASK:**

   Use a shortstop and second-base player and a thrower; runners are on first. Thrower throws grounders to second-base player; runners rotate running from first. Focus on second-base player timing "flip" to the base and shortstop placing foot on edge of base closest to the fielder making the play. Rotate after six trials (figure 6.3).

   Goal: Shortstop coverage of second base on force play without interfering with the runner.

   Cues: Second-base player:

   > Watch the ball go into the glove.
   >
   > Flip it to shortstop covering second base.
   >
   > Shortstop:
   >
   > Get to base quickly.
   >
   > Foot on edge closest to play.
   >
   > Give a good target.
   >
   > Watch ball go into hands.

   Extension: Add a base runner.

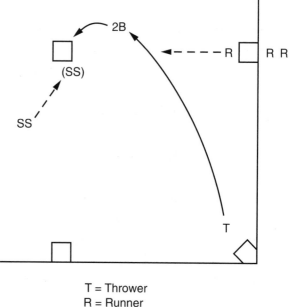

   T = Thrower
   R = Runner
   2B = Second-base player
   SS = Shortstop

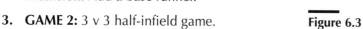

Figure 6.3

3. **GAME 2:** 3 v 3 half-infield game.

   Conditions: Same as in game 1.

   Goal: Get three runs before defense gets three outs.

   Extension: Offense must get the runner on first from home.

   > Then she can advance to second to score.
   >
   > Once on second, the runner does not advance.
   >
   > Offense can hit a groundball anywhere in the infield.

4. **CLOSURE:** Questions and discussion on shortstop coverage of second base on a force play when ball is hit to right side of infield.

LESSON 8

TACTICAL PROBLEM: Cutting the lead runner.

GAME: Kickball, throwball, T-ball, softball, or baseball.

SITUATION: 0 outs, runner on first, grounder to left infield.

LESSON FOCUS: Second-base player's coverage of second base on a force play when ball is hit to left side of infield.

OBJECTIVE: Second-base player will demonstrate proper coverage of second base on a force play from the left side of the infield.

1. **GAME 1:** 3 v 3 half-infield game.

   Conditions: Start with a runner on first base.

   > Offense:

   > Hit or kick groundball to the left side of the infield to advance the runner to second base.

   > Runs are scored when the runner is safe at second.

   > Once on second, the runner does not advance.

   > Defense:

   > Field the ball and attempt to get the runner out at second base.

   > Switch after three runs or three outs, whichever comes first.

   Goal: Get three runs before the defense gets three outs.

   Questions:

   Q. In this situation, which runner should you try to put out first?
   A. The runner going to second.

   Q. Who covers second when the ball is hit to the left side of the infield?
   A. The second-base player.

2. **PRACTICE TASK:**

   Use a shortstop, second-base player, and a thrower. Focus on timing of flip or throw to the base, and place foot on edge of base closest to the play. Rotate after three to five trials.

   Goal: Proper coverage of second base by the second-base player on a force play from the left side of the infield.

   Cues: Get to base quickly.

   > Put foot on edge closest to play.

   > Give a good target.

   > Watch ball go into hands.

   Extension: Add a base runner.

3. **GAME 2:** 3 v 3 half-infield game.

   Condition: Throw, hit, or kick to left side of infield to advance runner.

   Goal: Get three runs before defense gets three outs.

   Extensions: Offense must get the runner on first; then he can advance to second to score.

   > Once on second, the runner does not advance.

   > Offense can hit a groundball anywhere in the infield.

4. **CLOSURE:** Question and discussion on coverage of second base on a force play when ball is hit to left or right side of infield.

LESSON 9

TACTICAL PROBLEM: Cutting the lead runner.

GAME: Kickball, throwball, T-ball, softball, or baseball.

SITUATION: 0 outs, runner on first, grounder to left infield.

LESSON FOCUS: Cutting the lead runner when ball is hit to third-base player.

OBJECTIVE: Students will demonstrate the proper transition from catch to a throw (from third to second base) to cut the lead runner.

1. **GAME 1:** 4 v 4 infield game.

   Conditions: Start with a runner on first base.

   > Offense:
   >
   > Hit or kick groundball toward third base to advance the runner to second base.
   >
   > Runs are scored when the runner is safe at second.
   >
   > Defense:
   >
   > Field the ball and attempt to get the runner out at second base.
   >
   > Switch after three runs or three outs, whichever comes first.

   Goal: Get three outs before offense scores three runs.

   Questions:

   Q. In this situation, which runner should you try to put out first?
   A. The runner going to second.

   Q. Who covers second when the ball is hit to the third-base player?
   A. The second-base player.

   Q. Where does the shortstop go?
   A. Backs up play, then covers third base.

   Q. Why is it more difficult to get a runner out at second from third than shortstop?
   A. Farther away.

   Q. What can you do to improve the speed of the throw?
   A. Charge the ball, watch ball go into hands, catch first, *then* throw.

2. **PRACTICE TASK:**

   Three players are at third, one on the field and two waiting; three players are at second, one playing second base and two waiting. Two players are throwing and retrieving. Throw ball to third-base position; player charges ball, scoops, steps to second, and throws *to* the base. Extra players rotate in after each trial, and all players rotate after nine throws. Or, after fielding the ball at third, that player should go play second base and second-base player can go to third baseline.

   Goal: Make the force play at second from third base.

   Cues: Charge the ball.

   > Scoop it up with two hands.
   >
   > Step to target and throw.

   Extension: Add a base runner.

3. **GAME 2:** 4 v 4 infield game.

   Condition: Same as in game 1.

   Goal: Get three runs before defense gets three outs.

Extensions: Offense must get the runner on first, then she can advance to second to score.

Once on second, the runner does not advance.

Offense can hit a grounder anywhere in the infield.

4. **CLOSURE:** Questions and discussion on cutting the lead runner, fielding grounders from third base.

LESSON 10

TACTICAL PROBLEM: Cutting the lead runner.

GAME: Kickball, throwball, T-ball, softball, or baseball.

SITUATION: 0 outs, runners on first and second, grounder to the infield.

LESSON FOCUS: Cutting the lead runner when ball is hit to third-base player.

OBJECTIVE: Students will demonstrate the proper transition from catch to a throw (from third to second base) to cut the lead runner.

1. **GAME 1:** 4 v 4 infield game.

Conditions: Start with a runner on first and second base.

Offense:

Throw, hit, and kick groundball anywhere in the infield to advance the runner to third base.

Runs are scored when the runner is safe at third.

Defense:

Field the ball and attempt to get the runner out at third base.

Switch after three runs or three outs, whichever comes first.

Goal: Get three runs before the defense gets three outs.

Questions:

Q. In this situation, which runner should you try to put out first?
A. The runner going to third.

Q. Who covers third?
A. The third-base player.

Q. What if the third-base player fields the ball?
A. The shortstop covers third.

Q. Why should you cut the lead runner, whenever possible?
A. To keep the other team from scoring.

Q. In this situation, what should the third-base player do to help the player fielding the ball?
A. Get to the base quickly, give a good target, catch and control the ball.

2. **PRACTICE TASK:**

Thrower alternates grounders to shortstop and second-base players, who field and throw to third base. The third-base player moves quickly to the base; uses foot to touch inside edge of base closest to play; and gives a big, two-handed target. Emphasize watching ball go into the hands and positioning away from incoming runner. After three to five trials at third, rotate infield, throwing, and retrieving duties.

Goal: Make the force play at third base to cut the lead runner.

Cues: Move quickly to the base.

Foot on inside edge closest to play (but out of runner's path and so that runner cannot block throw).

Big, two-handed target.

Watch it go in.

Extension: Add a base runner.

3. **GAME 2:** 4 v 4 infield game.

Conditions: Same as in game 1.

Goal: Get three runs before defense gets three outs.

Extensions: Offense must get the runner on first and second, then she can advance to third to score.

Once on third, the runner can advance to home plate and score an additional run.

Offense can hit a grounder anywhere in the infield.

4. **CLOSURE:** Question and discussion on cutting the lead runner and covering bases on force plays.

Level II

Level II lessons (third and fourth grades), beginning where level I left off (with zero outs, runner on first or second, infield grounder) allow a review of the tactics, movements, and skills needed for throwing out the lead runner. This series of lessons highlights offensive play during the early lessons, because most students should be ready to demonstrate some degree of bat control and hit and run and be able to decide to run through *or* round first base.

Most level II lessons focus on tag plays (i.e., tagging a runner who is not forced to run). These lessons include coverage of second base, particularly when it is appropriate for the shortstop as well as when it is appropriate for the second-base player to cover second. The situations expand to include tag plays at third and home plate and expand the number of players needed to play the modified games as well as the practice situations.

The number of players for each situation can be easily adjusted with the addition of a player from the offensive team (offensive players can rotate or take turns playing for the defensive team). Remember that conditions can be adjusted to accommodate any and all situations, and students can also be quite helpful if asked for suggestions on modifying game conditions.

Finally, level II lessons also focus on outfield play. It is important here to emphasize getting the ball into the infield quickly. Off-the-ball communication is important here as well as backing up the player fielding the ball, which is another off-the-ball skill and should be taught as such. Good teams communicate, provide plenty of backup, and always know where to throw the ball *before* the batter hits the ball. These are tactics and skills that anyone can successfully master.

LESSON 1

TACTICAL PROBLEMS: Defending space and bases; throwing out the lead runner.

GAME: T-ball, softball, or baseball.

SITUATION: 0 outs, runner on first, infield grounder.

LESSON FOCUS: Fielding grounders and base coverage on force play.

OBJECTIVE: When fielding a grounder hit to the infield, the students will move to the ball, field it cleanly, and throw it accurately, making the correct play for the situation.

1. **GAME 1:** 4 v 4 infield game.

   Conditions: Start with runner on first.

   Offense:

   Hit groundball to the infield, then run to first base, attempting to beat the throw.

   If a runner advances to second and batter is out at first, the offensive team must fill empty base to create a force situation.

   Defense:

   To get the runner out, field the ball and attempt to get the ball to base ahead of the runner.

   Switch after three runs or three outs, whichever comes first.

   Goal: Defense gets lead runner out.

   Questions:

   Q. How many of you were able to get three outs before the other pair scored three runs?
   A. No one.

   Q. Why not?
   A. Throw was too late, throw was not caught or off target, misplay at first.

   Q. What can the fielder do to get the ball to the base more quickly?
   A. Get to the ball as quickly as possible, make a clean catch and a good throw.

   Q. What can the player covering the base do to support the fielder?
   A. Get to base quickly, give a good target, stop and catch the ball.

2. **PRACTICE TASK:**

   Divide infield in half; one thrower throws to left side (shortstop; second-base player covers second), and one thrower throws to the right side (first and second base) (figure 6.4). Extra player can be a retriever or coach. Players on left side make plays at second base, and players on right side make plays at first base. The throwers roll grounders to infielder; as she catches with two hands, she scoops and lifts ball into throwing position, then steps and throws to the target (second-base player or first-base player). The first-base player rolls ball back to retriever, who feeds it to the thrower. Defensive players rotate after five trials at second base, then rotate with offensive players who are throwing the ball. Review fielding grounders: transition from catch to throw and cover bases on force play.

   Goal: Demonstrate smooth transition from catch to throw, and throw ball accurately to first base.

   Cues: Thrower:

   Two hands.

   Scoop it up.

   Step to the target and throw.

   Base player:

   Move quickly to cover base.

   Keep foot on inside edge of base (edge closest to the play).

   Use big, two-handed target.

   Watch ball into the glove (absorb).

   Extension: Have players hit off a tee instead of using a throw.

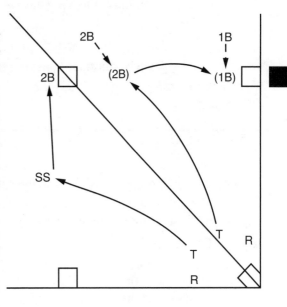

■ = Runner's base
T = Thrower
R = Retriever
1B = First-base player
2B = Second-base player
SS = Shortstop

Figure 6.4

3. **GAME 2:** Same as game 1 (4 v 4 infield game).

   Conditions: Same as in game 1.

   Goal: Defense gets lead runner out.

4. **CLOSURE:** Questions and discussion on importance of getting to ball quickly and into position to throw runner out, as well as the support of players covering bases. Also review proper base coverage.

LESSON 2

TACTICAL PROBLEM: Score by hitting to get on base and advance the runner.

GAME: T-ball, softball, or baseball.

SITUATION: 0 outs, runner on first, infield grounder.

LESSON FOCUS: Hitting to get on base and advance the runner.

OBJECTIVE: Students will hit the ball where it is most likely to advance the runner and get on base.

1. **GAME 1:** 4 v 4 infield game.

   Conditions: Start with a runner on first.

   > Offense:

   > Throw, kick, or bat groundball to the infield, then run to first base, attempting to beat the throw. If a runner advances to second and batter is thrown out at first, the offensive team must fill empty base to create a force situation.

   > Defense:

   > Field the ball and attempt to get ball to base ahead of the runner to get the runner out.

   > Switch after three runs or three outs, whichever comes first.

   Goal: Offense gets on base *and,* when possible, advances the runner to the next base.

   Questions:

   Q. If there are zero outs and no runner at first, where is the best place to hit the ball? Why?
   A. To the left side of the infield, because the play is farther from first.

   Q. What if there is a runner on first? Where is the best place to hit the ball? Why?
   A. Right side of the infield, behind the runner. Allows the runner to get to second base.

   Q. Why is it important to get the runner to second base?
   A. To give the runner a better chance of scoring on the next hit.

2. **PRACTICE TASK:**

   Batting practice from a tee, with a fence 8 to 10 feet (2.5 to 3 meters) in front of tee. Mark three areas indicating left, center, and right fields. Hit three left, three center, and three right, then rotate. It is best to work in pairs, but you can work in fours with batter on deck and two players on safety patrol or coach.

   Goal: Hit the ball at least two out of three times to left, center, and right.

   Cues: Align stance with tee (to position ball in appropriate area of the contact zone).

   > Spot ball (focus on the place where you want to hit the ball).

   > Hit, step, and follow through to infield target.

   Extension: Hit off tee to infield.

3. **GAME 2:** Same as in game 1 (4 v 4 infield game).

   Conditions: Same as in game 1.

   Goal: Score by getting on base and advancing the runners.

4. **CLOSURE:** Questions and discussion on importance of getting runners into scoring position. Review batting technique.

LESSON 3

TACTICAL PROBLEM: Score by base running and advancing past first base.

GAME: T-ball, softball, or baseball.

SITUATION: 0 outs, runners variable, infield grounder.

LESSON FOCUS: Baserunning.

OBJECTIVE: The student will run through and make the turn to run to second base, according to the situation.

1. **GAME 1:** 4 v 4 infield game.

   Conditions: Offense:

   > Throw, kick, or bat groundball to the infield, then run to first base, attempting to advance to second if possible.

   > Runs are scored when offensive team gets a runner to second base safely. Once at second, base runners can continue running and score again if they reach home plate.

   > A coach must be on first at all times.

   > Defense:

   > Field the ball and attempt to get ball to base ahead of the runner to get the lead runner out.

   > Switch after three runs or three outs, whichever comes first.

   Goal: Offense gets runners to second base.

   Questions:

   Q. As a base runner, how do you know when to run through first base and when to make the turn?
   A. Watch and listen to the coach; when ball gets through infield or on an overthrow.

   Q. How should you run to first when you need to make the turn or go to second base?
   A. Curve out before getting to the base.

2. **PRACTICE TASK:**

   Players line up behind home plate; one at a time they step up to the tee, imitate a swing, and run to first base. They listen for the coach and follow his instructions and hand signals ("run it out," "make the turn," "go two"). The runners continue around the base path and get back in line. First player around replaces the coach.

   Goal: Act immediately on the coach's signals and commands, and adjust running path to make the turn toward second base.

   Cues: Look and listen for the coach.

   Start C-turn three steps before first base.

   Extension: Hit ball off the tee.

3. **GAME 2:** Same as game 1 (4 v 4 infield game).

    Conditions: Same as in game 1.

    Goal: Offense gets to second base to score.

4. **CLOSURE:** Question and discussion on running technique and watching the coach.

LESSON 4

TACTICAL PROBLEM: Defend space or base in a tag situation.

GAME: T-ball, softball, or baseball.

SITUATION: 0 outs, runners variable, infield grounder.

LESSON FOCUS: Tag plays.

OBJECTIVE: The student will demonstrate proper position to receive throw and make a tag on an incoming runner.

1. **GAME 1:** 4 v 4 infield game.

    Conditions: Offense:

    > Throw, kick, or bat groundball to the infield, then run to first base, attempting to advance to second if possible.

    > Runs are scored when offensive team gets a runner to second base safely. Once at second, base runners can continue running and score again if they reach home plate.

    > A coach must be on first at all times.

    > Defense:

    > Field the ball and attempt to get ball to base ahead of the runner to get the lead runner out.

    > Switch after three runs or three outs, whichever comes first.

    Goal: Defense keeps runner from advancing to second base.

    Questions:

    Q. How can you keep the runner from advancing to second base?
    A. Get runner out at first by getting ball to base ahead of the runner.

    Q. If the batter hits and chooses to run to second base, what does the infielder have to do to get the runner out?
    A. Tag the runner.

2. **PRACTICE TASK:**

    For offense, on the signal, the runner takes off, and then the thrower sends grounders to players on left side of the infield (third and shortstop), who then throw to second-base player moving to cover second base for the tag play. Runners start halfway down first baseline. Thrower times throw to a make tag play close at second base.

    Rotate after three to five trials by second-base player. Focus on safe positioning to avoid interference from the runner.

    The sweep tag (catch and sweep the ball back and down to tag the runner) is recommended.

    Goal: Catch and tag the runner before he reaches the base.

    Cues: Quickly move into position (so runner cannot come between you and the fielder).

    > Catch first, then tag.

    > Sweep low (at edge of base closest to the runner).

    Extension: Hit ball off tee.

3. **GAME 2:** Same as in game 1 (4 v 4 infield game).

   Conditions: Same as game 1.

   Goal: Defense tags runner out at second base.

4. **CLOSURE:** Question and discussion on tag situations and proper, safe technique.

LESSON 5

TACTICAL PROBLEM: Defend space or base in a tag situation.

GAME: T-ball, softball, or baseball.

SITUATION: 0 outs, runners variable, infield grounder.

LESSON FOCUS: Tag plays.

OBJECTIVE: The student will demonstrate proper position to receive a throw and make a tag on an incoming runner.

1. **GAME 1:** 4 v 4 infield game.

   Conditions: Offense:

   > Throw, kick, or bat groundball to the infield, then run to first base, attempting to advance to second if possible.

   > Runs are scored when offensive team gets a runner to second base safely.

   > Once at second, base runners can continue running and score again if they reach home plate.

   > A coach must be on first at all times.

   > Defense:

   > Field the ball and attempt to get ball to base ahead of the runner to get the lead runner out.

   > Switch after three runs or three outs, whichever comes first.

   Goal: Defense keeps runner from advancing to second base.

   Questions:

   Q. How can you keep the runner from advancing to second base?
   A. Get runner out at first by getting ball to base ahead of the runner.

   Q. If the batter hits and chooses to run to second base, what does the infielder have to do to get the runner out?
   A. Tag the runner.

2. **PRACTICE TASK:**

   For offense, on the signal, the runner takes off, and then the thrower sends grounders to players on right side of the infield (first and second; can also add pitcher, who then throws to shortstop moving to cover second base for the tag play). Runners start halfway down first baseline. Thrower times throw to make tag play close at second base. Rotate after three to five trials by second-base player. Focus on safe positioning to avoid interference from the runner. The sweep tag is recommended.

   Goal: Catch and tag the runner before she reaches the base.

   Cues: Quickly move into position (so that runner cannot come between you and the fielder).

   > Catch first, then tag.

   > Sweep low (at edge of base closest to the runner).

   Extension: Hit ball off tee.

3. **GAME 2:** Same as game 1 (4 v 4 infield game).

   Conditions: Same as in game 1.

   Goal: Defense tags runner out at second base.

4. **CLOSURE:** Questions and discussion on tag situations and proper, safe technique.

LESSONS 6 AND 7

TACTICAL PROBLEM: Defend space or base in a tag situation.

GAME: T-ball, softball, or baseball.

SITUATION: 0 outs, runner on second, infield grounder.

LESSON FOCUS: Tag plays.

OBJECTIVE: The student will make the appropriate decision, depending on the situation and position of the ball.

> *Note:* Two lessons are given to this situation because of the complexity of possible solutions. There are three possibilities for fielders to defend space or the base here:
> - Look the runner back and throw to first or hold the ball.
> - Field and throw to third.
> - Field and throw to first, then throw to third or home.

1. **GAME 1:** 4 v 4 infield game.

   Conditions: Offense:

   > Start with a runner at second base.

   > Throw, kick, or bat groundball to the infield and attempt to advance the runner *and* get on first.

   > Runs are scored when offensive team gets a runner to third base safely.

   > Once at third base, runners can continue running and score again if they reach home plate.

   > Defense:

   > Field the ball and attempt to get the lead runner out.

   > Switch after three runs or three outs, whichever comes first.

   Goal: Defense keeps the runner from advancing to third base.

   Questions:

   Q. How can you keep the runner from advancing to third base?
   A. Catch the ball and look runner back before throwing to first; throw ball to third base as soon as you catch it.

   Q. What does the third-base player need to do to get the runner out?
   A. Tag the runner.

2. **PRACTICE TASK:**

   Offense starts with a runner on second. The thrower sends grounders to players on the left side of the infield (third base and shortstop), then runs to first base. The fielder catches the ball and looks the runner back, then makes the throw or holds the ball depending on the situation. When the runner attempts to advance to third, the ball is thrown to third and the third-base player attempts to position and tag the runner out. Focus on safe positioning to avoid interference from the runner. The sweep tag is recommended.

Goal: Defense keeps runner from reaching third base safely.

Cues: Fielding by shortstop or third-base player:

Get to ball quickly.

Look at runner as you bring the ball back.

If in doubt, hold the ball (to keep runner from advancing to third).

Third-base coverage:

Quickly move into position (so that runner cannot come between you and the fielder).

Catch first, then tag.

Sweep low (at edge of base closest to the runner).

Extension: Hit ball off tee.

3. **GAME 2:** Same as game 1 (4 v 4 infield game).

Conditions: Same as in game 1.

Goal: Defense keeps runner from advancing to third base.

4. **CLOSURE:** Questions and discussion on tag situations; looking back the runner; and proper, safe technique.

LESSON 8

TACTICAL PROBLEMS: Defend space or base in a tag situation; advance runners into scoring position.

GAME: T-ball, softball, or baseball.

SITUATION: 0 outs, runner on second, infield grounder.

LESSON FOCUS: Tag plays; fakes and feints to draw the throw.

OBJECTIVE: The student will make the appropriate defensive decision, depending on the situation and position of the ball. The student will make the appropriate offensive decision, depending on the situation.

1. **GAME 1:** 4 v 4 infield game.

Conditions: Offense:

Start with a runner at second base.

Throw, kick, or bat groundball to the infield and attempt to advance the runner and get on first.

Runs are scored when offensive team gets a runner to third base safely.

Once at third base, runners can continue running and score again if they reach home plate.

Defense:

Field the ball and attempt to get the lead runner out.

Switch after three runs or three outs, whichever comes first.

Goals: Defense keeps the runner from advancing to third base.

Offense gets to third base to score.

Questions:

Q. How can you keep the runner from advancing to third base?
A. Catch the ball and look runner back before throwing to first; throw ball to third base as soon as you catch it.

Q. What does the third-base player need to do to get the runner out?
A. Tag the runner.

Q. As a runner on second base, what can you do to distract the fielder so that you can run to third or your teammate can get on first safely?
A. Fake like you're running to third; wait for throw then run to third.

2. **PRACTICE TASK:**

Offense starts with a runner on second; the thrower sends grounders to players anywhere in the infield, then runs to first base. The fielder catches the ball and looks the runner back, then makes the throw or holds the ball depending on the situation. When the runner attempts to advance to third, the ball is thrown to third and the third-base player attempts to position and tag the runner out. Focus on safe positioning to avoid interference from the runner. The runner fakes the run and attempts to draw or delay the throw to first.

Goal: Keep runner from reaching third base safely. Base runner draws or delays the throw.

Cues: Fielder:

> Get to ball quickly.
>
> Look at runner as you bring the ball back.
>
> If in doubt, hold the ball (to keep runner from advancing to third).
>
> Base coverage:
>
> Quickly move into position at the base.
>
> Catch first, then tag.
>
> Sweep low (at edge of base closest to the runner).
>
> Runner:
>
> Use one-step fake.
>
> Stay balanced.
>
> Watch the ball.

Extension: Hit ball off tee.

3. **GAME 2:** Same as game 1 (4 v 4 infield game).

Conditions: Same as in game 1.

Goal: Keep runner from advancing to third base. Runner draws or delays the throw.

4. **CLOSURE:** Questions and discussion on tag situations, looking back the runner, and drawing or delaying the throw.

LESSON 9

TACTICAL PROBLEM: Defend space.

GAME: T-ball, softball, or baseball.

SITUATION: 0 outs, runner on first, right side of field.

LESSON FOCUS: Outfield play.

OBJECTIVE: The student will move to the ball or position as quickly as possible to catch the ball and *immediately* throw the ball to second base.

1. **GAME 1:** 4 v 4 half-field game (right center, right field, shortstop, second base).

   Conditions: Offense:

   Start with a runner at first base.

   Throw, kick, or bat groundball to the right side of the field and attempt to advance the runner *and* get on first.

   Runs are scored when offensive team gets a runner to second base safely.

   Once at second base, runners can continue running and score again if they reach home plate. (Third-base player and catcher can be added from the batting team.)

   Defense:

   Field the ball and attempt to get the lead runner out.

   Switch after three runs or three outs, whichever comes first.

   Goal: Defense gets runner out at second.

   Questions:

   Q. As an outfielder, what is your objective?
   A. Catch the ball and get it in the infield as soon as possible.

   Q. What are some things you can do to get to the ball quickly?
   A. Watch it off the bat; know the situation.

   Q. What are some things you can do to throw the ball quickly?
   A. Catch it over the throwing shoulder; position body to transition ball quickly to throwing hand.

2. **PRACTICE TASK:**

   One partner throws high flyballs to a partner. The partner should move under and catch the ball in position to throw quickly, then throw quickly and accurately (within one step) back to the partner. Rotate after five trials.

   Cues: Move quickly to the ball.

   Time the catch.

   Catch over the throwing shoulder.

   Throw immediately to base or cut off player.

   Extension: Add a base runner.

3. **GAME 2:** Same as game 1 (4 v 4 infield game).

   Conditions: Same as in game 1.

   Goal: Defense keeps runner from advancing to second base.

4. **CLOSURE:** Questions and discussion on fielding flyballs and advantage of getting ball into infield quickly.

LESSON 10

TACTICAL PROBLEM: Defend space.

GAME: T-ball, softball, or baseball.

SITUATION: 0 outs, runner on first, left side of field.

LESSON FOCUS: Outfield play.

OBJECTIVE: The student will move to the ball or position as quickly as possible to catch the ball and *immediately* throw the ball to second base.

1. **GAME 1:** 4 v 4 half-field game (left center, left field, shortstop, second base).

   Conditions: Offense:

   Start with a runner at first base.

   Offense throws, kicks, or bats groundball to the left side of the field and attempts to advance the runner *and* get on first.

   Runs are scored when offensive team gets a runner to second base safely.

   Once at second base, runners can continue running and score again if they reach home plate. (Third-base player and catcher can be added from the batting team.)

   Defense:

   Field the ball and attempt to get the lead runner out.

   Switch after three runs or three outs, whichever comes first.

   Goal: Defense gets runner out at second.

   Questions:

   Q. As an outfielder, what is your objective?
   A. Catch the ball and get it in the infield as soon as possible.

   Q. What are some things you can do to get to the ball quickly?
   A. Watch it off the bat; know the situation.

   Q. What are some things you can do to throw the ball quickly?
   A. Catch it over the throwing shoulder; position body to transfer ball quickly to throwing hand.

2. **PRACTICE TASK:**

   In outfield practice, three people are in left field. Three people are in left center (one ready to field and two waiting). Other players should be playing second and third and a runner should be at first. The designated thrower stands at about the shortstop position and throws flys, line drives, and grounders between the left and left-center fielders. On the throw, the runner takes off from first and attempts to advance to second and third if possible. One player calls the ball and fields it, and the other backs up and communicates where to throw the ball. These two fielders switch positions and wait until the other two players take their turn before having another trial. After 15 balls are thrown, players should switch roles until all players have had five opportunities to field or back up in the outfield.

   Cues: Call ball and move quickly to ball.

   Time the catch.

   Catch over the throwing shoulder and throw immediately to base or cut off player.

3. **GAME 2:** Same as game 1 (4 v 4 infield game).

   Conditions: Same as in game 1.

   Goal: Defense keeps runner from advancing to second base.

4. **CLOSURE:** Questions and discussion on fielding flyballs, advantage of getting ball into infield quickly, and off-the-ball responsibilities of backing up and communicating where to throw the ball.

Level III

Level III (fourth and fifth grades) play focuses primarily on outfield play. Activities also entail support, or off-the-ball, play, such as backing up, base coverage, cutoffs, and relays. Although it takes time to develop the strength and accuracy to consistently perform these skills, it takes very little time to develop the movements needed for support play. Yet, support play is essential to successful team play and often is not addressed with novices. If a player moves on every play, he will feel more involved in the game, and this will also serve to keep his attention focused on the game.

Organizing teams of 5 v 5 allows for an easy shift to 10 v 10 play. When additional defensive players are needed, members of the offensive team can step in. But remember to rotate these players so that everyone gets an opportunity to play key defensive positions and so that the same player doesn't always get sent to the other team. Students who have played organized T-ball, baseball, or softball will be more likely to request the "real" game (to which you might reply, "What's not real about this game?"); you might want to occasionally provide an opportunity for full-sided game play. However, the decrease in opportunities to respond severely limits the degree to which a 10 v 10 game is useful in an instructional and practice setting, where the emphasis is on learning how to play the game. If all small-sided games, drills, and practices reflect specific aspects of the "real" game, shifting from small-sided games to the full game

should not pose a problem for novice or experienced players.

The form of the game, such as kickball, T-ball, or baseball, is dependent on the students, teacher, and context. Some forms, such as kickball and Wiffle ball, are more conducive for indoor play than for outdoor play and can be used when outdoor play is prohibitive. When forced to play indoors, also consider setting up specific situations. However, you do not have to wait for inclement weather to chase you indoors so that you can set up small areas or stations for students to practice situations. Regardless of the game form or context, the tactics, movements, and skills needed for successful play are very similar and there is no need to take a day off when inclement weather keeps you indoors.

LESSON 1

TACTICAL PROBLEM: Defend space.

GAME: T-ball, softball, or baseball.

SITUATION: 0 outs, runner on first, ball hit to left side of the field.

LESSON FOCUS: Outfield play (extend and review content from previous lessons).

OBJECTIVE: The student will move to the ball or position as quickly as possible to catch the ball and *immediately* throw the ball to second base. When not fielding the ball, the student will provide support by backing up the play or covering a base and communicating where to throw the ball.

1. **GAME 1:** 5 v 5 half-field game (left center, left field, pitcher, second, shortstop).

   Conditions: Offense:

   Start with a runner at first base.

   Hit groundball to the left side of the field and attempt to advance the runner *and* get on first.

   Runs are scored when offensive team gets a runner to second base safely.

   Once at second base, runners can continue running and score again if they reach home plate. (A third-base player can be added from the batting team.)

   Defense:

   Field the ball and attempt to get the lead runner out.

   Switch after three runs or three outs, whichever comes first.

   Goal: Defense gets runner out at second.

   Questions:

   Q. As an outfielder, what is your objective?
   A. Catch the ball and get it in the infield as soon as possible.

   Q. What are some things you can do to get to the ball quickly?
   A. Watch it off the bat; know the situation.

   Q. What are some things you can do to throw the ball quickly?
   A. Catch it over the throwing shoulder; position the body to transfer ball quickly to throwing hand.

2. **PRACTICE TASK:**

In outfield practice, three people are in left field. Three people are in left center; one is ready to field and two are waiting. Other players should be playing second and third, and a runner should be at first. The designated thrower stands at about the shortstop position and throws flyballs, line drives and grounders between the fielders. On the throw, the runner takes off from first and attempts to advance to second and third if possible. One player calls the ball and fields it, and the other backs up and communicates where to throw the ball. These two fielders switch positions and wait until the other two players take their turn before having another trial. After 15 balls are thrown, players should switch roles until all players have had three to five opportunities to field or back up in the outfield.

Cues: Call ball and move quickly to ball.

Time the catch.

Catch over the throwing shoulder and throw immediately to base or cut off player.

3. **GAME 2:** Same as game 1 (4 v 4 infield game).

Conditions: Same as in game 1.

Goal: Defense keeps runner from advancing to second base.

4. **CLOSURE:** Questions and discussion on fielding flyballs, advantage of getting ball into infield quickly, and off-the-ball responsibilities of backing up and communicating where to throw the ball.

LESSON 2

TACTICAL PROBLEM: Advance the base runner.

GAME: T-ball, softball, or baseball.

SITUATION: 0 outs, runner on first, ball hit to the left side of the field.

LESSON FOCUS: Hit to outfield.

OBJECTIVE: The student will be able to hit the ball through or over the infield, hitting a line drive or flyball.

1. **GAME 1:** 5 v 5 half-field game (second, third, shortstop, left field, left center).

Conditions: Offense:

Start with a runner at first base.

Hit ball to the left side of the field and attempt to advance the runner *and* get on first.

Runs are scored when offensive team gets a runner to second base safely.

Once at second base, runners can continue running and score again if they reach home plate. (A first-base player can be added from the batting team.)

Defense:

Field the ball and attempt to get the lead runner out at second base.

Switch after three runs or three outs, whichever comes first.

Goal: Offense advances the base runner from first to second base.

Questions:

Q. In a 0 out, runner on first situation, what is the batter's responsibility?
A. Move the runner to second base.

Q. What do you have to do to do this?
A. Hit ball past the infield into the outfield.

2. **PRACTICE TASK:**

Work in threes (a hitter, a coach, a safety patrol). Hit a ball suspended from a rope or pole. Hit the ball so that it swings around the pole as many times as possible. This requires a fast bat and solid contact. A second station can include a batting tee, from which the batters hit Wiffle balls as far as possible. In either drill, the coach observes the point of contact to ensure the ball is being struck in the power zone and the safety patrol is watching to be sure no one else is in the area and is ready to yell, "Freeze!" if anyone comes near the batter.

Cues: Watch the center of the ball.

Swing fast.

Contact in the power zone.

3. **GAME 2:** Same as game 1 (5 v 5 half-field game).

Conditions: Same as in game 1.

Goal: Defense keeps runner from advancing to second base.

4. **CLOSURE:** Questions and discussion on hitting line drives and flyballs through or past the infield.

LESSON 3

TACTICAL PROBLEM: Advance the base runner; defend space (outfield).

GAME: T-ball, softball, or baseball.

SITUATION: 0 outs, runner on first, ball hit to left side of field.

LESSON FOCUS: Hit to outfield; field ball in the outfield.

OBJECTIVE: The student will be able to hit the ball through or over the infield, hitting a line drive or flyball. The student will move to the ball or position as quickly as possible to catch the ball and *immediately* throw the ball to second base. When not fielding the ball, the student will provide support by backing up the play or covering a base and communicating where to throw the ball.

1. **GAME 1:** 5 v 5 half-field game (second, third, shortstop, left center, left field).

Conditions: Offense:

Start with a runner at first base.

Throw, kick, or bat ball to the left side of the field and attempt to advance the runner *and* get on first.

Runs are scored when offensive team gets a runner to second base safely.

Once at second base, runners can continue running and score again if they reach home plate. (A first-base player can be added from the batting team.)

Defense:

Field the ball and attempt to get the lead runner out at second base.

Switch after three runs or three outs, whichever comes first.

Goals: Offense advances the base runner from first to second base.

Defense keeps runners from advancing to second base.

Questions:

Q. What does the batter do in this situation, and how?
A. Move the runner to second base with a hit through or over infield.

Q. What does the fielder do in this situation, and how?
A. Field ball to catch and throw immediately.

2. **PRACTICE TASK:**

Two stations (one batting station and one fielding station).

Station 1: Work in threes (a hitter, a coach, a safety patrol). Hit a ball suspended from a rope or pole. Hit the ball so that it swings around the pole as many times as possible. This requires a fast bat and solid contact. A second station can include a batting tee, from which the batters hit Wiffle balls as far as possible. In either drill, the coach observes the point of contact to ensure the ball is being struck in the power zone and the safety patrol is watching to be sure no one else is in the area and is ready to yell, "Freeze!" if any one comes near the batter.

Station 2: In outfield practice, three people are in left center (one is ready to field and two are waiting). Other players should be playing second and third and a runner is at first. The designated thrower stands at about the shortstop position and throws flyballs, line drives, and grounders between the fielders. On the throw, the runner takes off from first and attempts to advance to second and third if possible. One player calls the ball and fields it, and the other backs up and communicates where to throw the ball. These two fielders switch positions and wait until the other two players take their turn before having another trial. After 15 balls are thrown, players should switch roles until all players have had three to five opportunities to field or back up in the outfield.

Cues: Station 1:

    Watch the center of the ball.

    Swing fast.

    Contact in the power zone.

    Station 2:

    Call ball and move quickly to the ball.

    Time the catch.

    Catch over the throwing shoulder.

    Throw immediately to base or cut off player.

3. **GAME 3:** Same as game 1 (5 v 5 half-field game).

    Conditions: Same as in game 1.

    Goal: Defense keeps runner from advancing to second base.

        Offense gets runner to second base and into scoring position.

4. **CLOSURE:** Questions and discussion on hitting and defending and fielding in the outfield.

LESSON 4

TACTICAL PROBLEM: Tag up on a flyball to advance to the next base.

GAME: T-ball, softball, or baseball.

SITUATION: 0 outs, runner on first, ball hit to left side of field.

LESSON FOCUS: Tag up on flyball.

OBJECTIVE: The student will be able to tag up on a flyball, then advance to the next base.

1. **GAME 1:** 5 v 5 half-field game (second, third, shortstop, left field, left center).

    Conditions: Offense:

        Start with a runner at first base.

        Hit ball to the left side of the field and attempt to advance the runner *and* get on first.

        Runs are scored when offensive team gets a runner to second base safely.

Two runs are scored if runner tags and advances to second base on a flyball.

Once at second base, runners can continue running and score again if they reach home plate. (A first-base player can be added from the batting team.)

Defense:

Field the ball and attempt to get the lead runner out at second base.

Switch after three runs or three outs, whichever comes first.

Goal: Offense attempts to advance on a flyball.

Questions:

Q. What does the runner on first do when the batter hits a flyball?
A. Waits in starting position until the ball is touched by a fielder, then runs to the next base.

Q. What if the base runner doesn't think she will beat the throw to the base?
A. She can stay on base and does not have to run.

2. **PRACTICE TASK:**

   Player stands at the shortstop position and throws flyballs to the left fielder and then to the left-center fielder. A runner tags up and attempts to run to second ahead of the throw. A player can also be at second base to make the play on the runner. Extra runners should stand in the coach's box and step in as soon as the previous runner takes off.

   Cues: Ready position.

   Go on contact.

3. **GAME 2:** Same as game 1 (5 v 5 half-field game).

   Conditions: Same as in game 1.

   Goal: Offense gets runner to second base on tag-up.

4. **CLOSURE:** Questions and discussion on advancing to next base on flyball.

LESSON 5

TACTICAL PROBLEM: Defending second on hit up the middle.

GAME: T-ball, softball, or baseball.

SITUATION: 0 outs, runner on first, ball hit to center field.

LESSON FOCUS: Coverage of second base on force play when ball is hit up the middle of the field. Review of outfield hitting and fielding skills.

OBJECTIVE: The student will demonstrate proper coverage of second base from the second base and shortstop positions when a ball is hit to the center of the field.

1. **GAME 1:** 5 v 5 half-field game (first, second, shortstop, left center, right center).

   Conditions: Offense:

   Start with a runner at first base.

   Hit ball to center field and attempt to advance the runner *and* get on first. Runs are scored when offensive team gets a runner to second base safely.

   Runners can continue running and score again if they reach home plate (third and catcher positions can be added from batting team).

   Defense:

   Field the ball and attempt to get the lead runner out at second base.

   Switch after three runs or three outs, whichever comes first.

Goal: Defense gets runner out at second.

Questions:

Q. When a ball is hit to right-center field, who covers second?
A. Shortstop.

Q. When a ball is hit to left-center field, who covers second?
A. Second-base player.

Q. Where and how should second base be played in these situations?
A. Position outside second base, on edge closest to the play. Give a good target and call for the ball. Put foot opposite glove hand on outside edge of base to make the force play.

2. **PRACTICE TASK:**

    Five players practice defense and five players serve as throwers, runners, and retrievers and run the drill or practice. Defensive positions include left-center fielder, right-center fielder, shortstop, and second-base player. Extra players can step in at any position and alternate with that player. Thrower throws flyballs, line drives, or groundballs from pitcher's mound alternately to left- and right-center field. Runner at first takes off with the throw. Fielder who calls ball catches it and throws to second to get runner out. Adjacent fielder backs up play and communicates where to throw ball. Shortstop and second-base players make the play at second base, and when off the ball, they should back up the throws into second base. Rotate after 8 to 10 throws to the outfield. Emphasize backup on every play and communication.

    Cues: (Force play at second base):

    Position quickly outside base path (between fielder and base).

    Show a target (signal with the glove) and call for the ball.

    Right foot on edge of base (left foot if left-handed).

    Watch ball into glove.

3. **GAME 2:** Return to 5 v 5 three-quarter-field game.

4. **CLOSURE:** Questions and discussion on force plays at second when there are 0 outs, runner on first, hit to center field.

LESSON 6

TACTICAL PROBLEM: Advancing runner to second (scoring position).

GAME: T-ball, softball, or baseball.

SITUATION: 0 outs, runner on first, ball hit to right field.

LESSON FOCUS: Offense hits behind the runner to right side of the field.

OBJECTIVE: The student will advance the runner to second base by hitting behind the runner.

1. **GAME 1:** 5 v 5 three-quarter-field game (first, second, shortstop, right center, right field).

    Conditions: Offense:

    Start with a runner at first base.

    Hit ball to center field and attempt to advance the runner *and* get on first.

    Runs are scored when offensive team gets a runner to second base safely.

    Runners can continue running and score again if they reach home plate. (Third and catcher positions can be added from batting team.)

Defense:

Field the ball and attempt to get the lead runner out at second base.

Switch after three runs or three outs, whichever comes first.

Goal: Offense advances the runner to second base.

Questions:

Q. In a 0 out, runner on first situation, where is the best place to hit the ball to advance the runner to second base?
A. To the right side of the field behind the runner.

Q. As a batter, what do you need to do to hit to right field?
A. Adjust stance; look for outside pitch to hit; contact ball on right side of plate.

2. **PRACTICE TASK:**

Station 1: Use batting tees, position so that batter contacts ball in front and to the right of home plate.

Station 2: Suspend ball on horizontal pole or rope. Players practice adjusting stance and contact point to hit ball to right side of field. Batter tries to hit ball to right.

Station 3: Once the batter is ready, move to a station where she can hit a pitched ball.

Use multiple stations; for example, have three to five batting tees and three to five balls suspended from ropes and two to three pitching stations. Extra players can serve as coaches or safety patrol.

Cues: Determine contact point and adjust stance.

Contact ball in power zone at right or front of plate.

Step and swing.

Fast bat.

3. **GAME 2:** Return to 5 v 5 half-field game.

4. **CLOSURE:** Questions and discussion on hitting behind the runner and critical elements for hitting to right field.

LESSON 7

TACTICAL PROBLEM: Defending bases on tag play.

GAME: T-ball, softball, or baseball.

SITUATION: 0 outs, no runner on first, ball hit to left field.

LESSON FOCUS: Defense—tag plays at second, third, and home.

OBJECTIVE: The student will cover the base (second, third, or home) to efficiently and safely tag out the advancing runner.

1. **GAME 1:** 5 v 5 half-field game (second, third, shortstop, left, left center).

Conditions: Offense:

Start with no runner at first base.

Hit ball to left or left-center field and attempt to advance to as many bases as possible.

Runs are scored when offensive team gets a runner to second base safely, and additional runs are scored for advancing to third and again to home plate. (Catcher, right-center, and first base positions can be added from batting team.)

Defense:

Field the ball and attempt to get the runner out.

Switch after three runs or three outs, whichever comes first.

Goal: Defense gets runner out at second.

Questions:

Q. In a 0 out, no runners on, hit to left-field situation, where should the ball be thrown?
A. Second base.

Q. Since the runner is not forced to run in this situation, what does the second-base player need to do to get the out?
A. Tag the runner.

2. **PRACTICE TASK:**

Players in left and left center, two players at second base to alternate (after each play), and one player at third. The designated thrower stands at about the shortstop position and throws flyballs, line drives, and grounders between the fielders. On the throw, the runner takes off from first and attempts to advance to second and third if possible. One player calls the ball and fields it, and the other backs up and communicates where to throw the ball. The second-base player positions himself between the ball and the bag, retrieves the throw, and attempts to tag the runner. After each attempt, the second-base player should serve as a coach as the other players take their turn. Rotate after each second-base player has had three to five practice opportunities.

Cues: Position quickly between base and ball.

Target and talk.

Catch and sweep low (to edge of base closest to incoming runner).

3. **GAME 2:** Return to 5 v 5 half-field game.

4. **CLOSURE:** Questions and discussion on tag plays.

LESSON 8

TACTICAL PROBLEM: Defending bases with cutoff.

GAME: T-ball, softball, or baseball.

SITUATION: 0 outs, no runner on first, ball hit to left field.

LESSON FOCUS: Defense uses cut off play to keep runners from advancing.

OBJECTIVE: The student will throw to cut off when runner is or will be safe at second.

1. **GAME 1:** 5 v 5 half-field game (second, third, shortstop, left, left center).

Conditions: Offense:

Start with no runner at first base.

Hit ball to left or left-center field and attempt to advance to as many bases as possible.

Runs are scored when offensive team gets a runner to second base safely, and additional runs are scored for advancing to third and again to home plate. (Catcher, right-center, and first-base positions can be added from batting team.)

Defense:

Field the ball and attempt to get the runner out.

Switch after three runs or three outs, whichever comes first.

Goal: Defense gets runner out at second.

Questions:

Q. In a 0 out, no runners on, hit to left-field situation, where should the ball be thrown?
A. Second base.

Q. If it is obvious that the runner is or will be safe at second, where should the ball be thrown to keep the runner from advancing?
A. Second base, third base, shortstop.

Q. What are the advantages of throwing to shortstop?
A. It keeps runner from advancing and shortstop can redirect throw if necessary.

2. **PRACTICE TASK:**

Players in left, left center, second base, and third should rotate in after each play. The designated thrower stands to the left-field side of pitcher's mound and throws flyballs, line drives, and grounders between the fielders. On the throw, the runner takes off from first and attempts to advance to second and third if possible. One player calls the ball and fields it, and the other backs up and communicates where to throw the ball. The second-base player positions herself between the ball and the bag, retrieves the throw, and attempts to tag the runner. The shortstop moves toward left field and prepares to receive "cutoff" if the pitcher or thrower calls for the cutoff. After each attempt, the second-base player should serve as a coach as the other players take their turn. Rotate after each player has had two to three practice opportunities at shortstop.

Cues: Position quickly between the play and second base.

Target and call for ball.

Catch and turn (left or glove side) toward target.

Run ball in quickly (if no throw).

3. **GAME 2:** Return to 5 v 5 half-field game.

4. **CLOSURE:** Questions and discussion on cutoffs.

LESSON 9

TACTICAL PROBLEM: Defending bases with cutoff and relay.

GAME: T-ball, softball, or baseball.

SITUATION: 0 outs, no runner on first, ball hit to right field.

LESSON FOCUS: Defense uses cut off play to keep runners from advancing; uses relay to put out advancing runner.

OBJECTIVE: The student will throw to cut off when runner is or will be safe at second. The student will relay the ball to third when the runner attempts to advance.

1. **GAME 1:** 5 v 5 half-field game (second, third, shortstop, right field, right center).

Conditions: Offense:

Start with a runner at first base.

Hit ball to right field or right center and attempt to advance to as many bases as possible.

Runs are scored when offensive team gets a runner to second base safely, and additional runs are scored for advancing to third and again to home plate. (Catcher, right-center, and first-base positions can be added from batting team.)

Defense:

Field the ball and attempt to get the runner out.

Switch after three runs or three outs, whichever comes first.

Goal: Defense gets runner out at second.

Questions:

Q. In a 0 out, no runners on, hit to left-field situation, where should the ball be thrown?
A. Second base.

Q. Who covers second base?
A. Shortstop.

Q. If it is obvious that the runner is or will be safe at second, where should the ball be thrown to keep the runner from advancing?
A. Second base, third base, shortstop.

Q. What are the advantages of throwing to second-base player if there is no play at second?
A. It keeps runner from advancing and second-base player can redirect throw if necessary.

Q. What if the runner continues to run to third?
A. Second-base player can relay throw to third.

2. **PRACTICE TASK:**

Players in right field and right center, second base, and third. The designated thrower stands to the right-field side of pitcher's mound and throws flyballs, line drives, and grounders between the fielders. On the throw, the runner takes off from first and attempts to advance to second and third if possible. One player calls the ball and fields it, and the other backs up and communicates where to throw the ball. The shortstop positions himself between the ball and the base, retrieves the throw, and attempts to tag the runner. The second-base player moves toward right field and prepares to receive "cutoff" or "relay" if the pitcher or thrower calls for the cutoff or a relay to third base. After each attempt, the second-base player should serve as a coach as the other players take their turn. Rotate after each player has had two to three practice opportunities at shortstop.

Cues: Position quickly between the play and second base.

Target and call for ball.

Catch, turn (left or glove side), and step toward target.

Use throw motion (don't release if no play).

Run ball in quickly if no throw.

3. **GAME 2:** Return to 5 v 5 half-field game.

4. **CLOSURE:** Questions and discussion on cutoffs and relays.

LESSON 10

TACTICAL PROBLEM: Defending space.

GAME: T-ball, softball, or baseball.

SITUATION: 0 outs, no runner on first, hit with situation.

LESSON FOCUS: Defense uses off-the-ball play as a team.

OBJECTIVE: In a full field game, defense will provide appropriate backup for players fielding the ball and cover for base players in all fielding situations.

1. **GAME 1:** 10 v 10 full-field game.

   Conditions: Offense:

   > Start with no runners on base.
   >
   > Throw or bat ball depending on the situation and attempt to advance to as many bases as possible.
   >
   > Runs are scored when offensive team gets a runner to any base safely, but score one run for first, two runs for second, three runs for third, and four runs for home.
   >
   > Defense:
   >
   > Field the ball, attempt to get the runners out, and keep runners from advancing.
   >
   > Switch after five runs or three outs, whichever comes first.

   Goal: Defense gets three outs before offense gets five runs.

   Questions:

   Q. Who moves when the ball is hit?
   A. Everyone should move.

   Q. Where should they move?
   A. Depends on situation, but off-the-ball players should back up, cover bases, set up for cutoff, or relay plays and communicate.

2. **PRACTICE TASK:**

   Situation practice of 10 players on the field; 1, 2, or 3 players set up and run situations. The defensive team scores runs for performing proper backups and coverage in each situation, but all 10 players must perform properly to score. One run is scored each time all 10 defensive players provide proper support for the player fielding the ball. Players rotate positions after five situations, with the 1 to 3 players setting up situations rotating in as well.

   Cues: Know the situation and where to throw.

   > Watch the ball and move on contact.
   >
   > On first, make the play or back up the play.
   >
   > If not fielding, move to or toward nearest base to back up or cover (except for second-base player and shortstop).
   >
   > Communicate.

3. **GAME 2:** Return to 10 v 10 game.

4. **CLOSURE:** Questions and discussion on off-the-ball play.

chapter 7

Sport Foundations for Target Games

This chapter is intended to provide a rationale for including target games as part of the elementary physical education curriculum and also to provide a scope and sequence of target game activities specifically designed to promote understanding of the tactical problems common to most target games. Just as in invasion, net/wall, and striking/fielding games, tactical similarities across target games can help the transfer of learning not only from one target game to another but across games categories as well.

There are two subcategories of target games (Almond, 1986). In one subcategory, the player performs independently of the opponent (*unopposed,* such as in golf, bowling, archery, and darts). A second subcategory, *opposed,* includes games such as billiards, horseshoe throwing, bocce, croquet, and shuffleboard, which allow the performer to counterattack. This means they can choose to challenge a shot by blocking, knocking away a disk, or sending a croquet ball out of a playing area. Ring toss, beanbag toss, and rolling or bowling at a pin or target are examples of some of the less complex target game activities that are frequently found in elementary physical education.

Target games are frequently included in elementary curricula to develop and refine manipulative skills with little if any consideration given to concepts or tactical problems common to most target games. However, these types of games provide a perfect context for developing the decision-making skills needed for game play. Compared with other games, such as invasion and net/wall games, in which decision making is more spontaneous, decision making in target games is done before performing the skill. Consequently, target games provide an excellent context for young learners to develop manipulative skills as well as basic decision-making skills, which can serve as a basis for more complex skills and tactics.

Similar to invasion, net/wall, and striking/fielding games, target games involve tactical problems or concepts and skills. Target games provide more time to make decisions before executing the skill. As shown in table 7.1, several preshot decisions are needed to solve the tactical problems. The primary tactical problem in target games is accuracy, which involves determining the proper direction and distance. The more proficient the learner becomes at making preshot decisions, the more likely she is to put herself into position to successfully execute the skill.

Modifications for Target Games

All that is needed for a target game is a target and an object to roll, toss, or slide. Targets can range from a single bowling pin to a box, hoop, or target drawn on the floor, and several inexpensive games can be found at toy or discount stores that include objects and targets (for example, Tic Tac Throw, 10-pin bowling sets, dart games, and plastic golf sets). Many of these games have been designed specifically for young children, and others have been designed as leisure activities that families can play outdoors.

When setting up multiple target games in a gymnasium, remember that objects can roll or slide into other playing areas; therefore, it is useful to have some long objects, such as 2 × 4s or Funnoodle™ pool floats, to serve as a barricade and to define and divide the playing areas. Figure 7.1 shows how a gym might be set up during a target games lesson. Notice that the stations are set up so that the objects are sent outward, toward the wall, allowing the teacher to easily monitor from the center of the activity area. Two to four students can be assigned to a station, and at least one student is responsible for returning the object safely to his partner(s).

The courts should be arranged so that they can be lengthened as skill and accuracy improve. Again, this is a good reason to have students send objects from the center toward the wall. Target sizes should also vary to accommodate the skill level of each student; for example, different size boxes can be used, or a target with various-sized concentric rings (such as an archery target) on the floor or wall. The type, size, and weight of the objects can also vary, or the students can have a variety of objects (e.g., different-sized balls, beanbags, or rings) to select from.

Several targeting aids should also be available; these include footprints drawn on the floor (or mat) to mark the starting position, arrows taped to the floor to identify the target line, or

Table 7.1 A Tactical Framework for Target Games (Bowling)

Tactical concepts for accuracy	Preshot decisions	Skill execution
Direction	Determine—starting point, target line, intermediate target, and release point	Setup Stance Grip Ball position (from start to release)
Distance	Determine—length of step and speed of approach, and length of backswing	Approach Backswing Follow-through

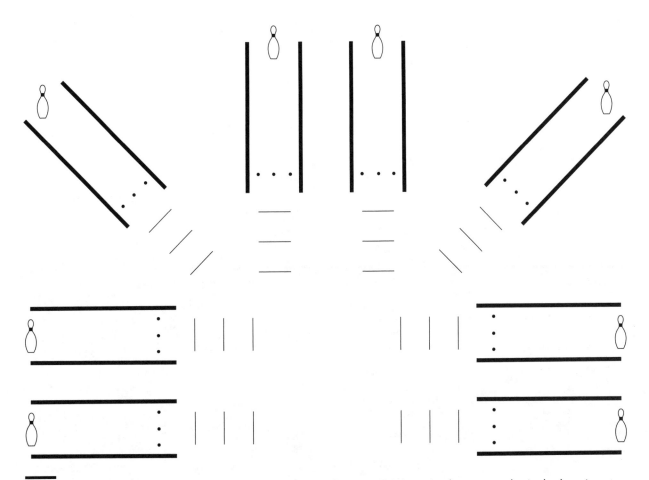

Figure 7.1 Organization of space and equipment for teaching target games in elementary physical education.

stickers that can be used to mark an intermediate target. Use colored floor tape to designate various distances from the target (see figure 7.1). This allows students to move back after a certain number of successful rolls or tosses.

Progressions for Teaching Target Games

Target games are appropriate for very young learners (ages four and up) because they involve basic sending skills, such as rolling a ball, sliding a puck, or throwing or tossing underhanded. These are essentially the same skills needed to play even the most advanced forms of target games, although the objects may be heavier and the distances longer. It is easiest to begin with rolling a ball at a target or pin. Initially, the target should be close and large, and the ball should be small enough to grip with one hand. Wiffle balls, tennis balls, and soft foam balls are excellent because they are easy to manipulate.

A developmental task analysis (Siedentop, Herkowitz, & Rink, 1984) can be used to determine how to increase and decrease complexity of a target game activity (table 7.2). Significant elements of the task are listed across the top, and criteria are listed from simple to complex. Other criteria, such as ball weight and color, could also be added here. An initial task might require the student to roll a 5-inch (12.7-centimeter) Wiffle ball at a small target from 10 feet (3 meters), with the tactical focus on the starting point. To increase or decrease task complexity, change *one* element at a time. Thus, task complexity can be modified to accommodate each learner as she improves in skill and accuracy.

Students should learn skills and tactics together within a game context. If students do this consistently, they will come to understand the relationship between tactics and skills as well as the similarities between games. Table 7.3

Table 7.2   Developmental Task Analysis for Increasing and Decreasing the Complexity of a Target

Task complexity	Task elements				
	Ball size	Ball composite	Distance from target	Target size	Tactic
Simple	3" (7.5 cm) 5" (12.5 cm) 7" (18 cm)	Foam ball Wiffle ball Team handball	5' (1.5 m) 10' (3 m) 15' (4.5 m)	Large Medium-large Medium	Starting point Target line Intermediate target
Complex	9" (23 cm)	Playground ball	20' (6 m)	Small	Release point

Modified from Siedentop, Herkowitz, & Rink, 1984.

Table 7.3   Levels of Tactical Complexity

Tactical problems and concepts for accuracy	Level of game complexity		
	Level I 1 player unopposed	Level II 1 v 1 unopposed	Level III 1 v 1 opposed
Direction	Roll, slide, setup Where to start Where to roll (target line and intermediate target)	Toss, setup Where to release	Strike, setup Where to contact
Distance	Determine length of backswing Determine length of step	Determine speed of approach	2- to 3-step approach—adjust backswing, step, and approach relative to shot

illustrates a possible progression for tactics and skills, from level I to level III. Children, even as young as four years of age, are able to understand tactics related to a consistent starting point, a target line, and an intermediate target. Initially, instructional aids should be used to give them the idea and then gradually withdrawn. For example, footprints can be used to mark the starting point, and an arrow or line taped on the floor can serve as a target line.

As with invasion, net/wall, and striking/fielding games, principles guide the development of appropriate progressions.

First, *move from cooperative to competitive situations*. Competition should begin with the individual learner, where he is challenged to improve his own score. As the students improve, then include competition against other students.

Second, *move from simple to complex*. This principle applies to both skills and tactics (see tables 7.2 and 7.3).

Third, *move from unopposed to opposed target games*. The game form should be the primary basis for increasing complexity. Begin with very basic target games, such as rolling a ball at a pin or sliding a beanbag at a target on the floor. Then, introduce variations of more advanced target games, such as five-pin bowling or lawn darts (with weight ends in place of pointed darts). Games that are opposed (e.g., horseshoe throwing or ring toss as a variation, shuffleboard, and bocce ball) should then be introduced. As shown in table 7.4, some target games are naturally more complex than others mostly because of the type of game and age appropriateness of the equipment, yet all target games share many tactical similarities. Manufacturers have produced smaller versions of these games, for example golf bags and plastic, large-faced clubs and miniature pool tables, to encourage children to play target games that are similar to those played by their parents.

Table 7.4   Target Games From Simple to Complex and the Related Preshot Decisions

Target game	Skill	Preshot decision					
		Setup	Target line	Intermediate target	Release point	Point of contact	Length of backswing and step or speed of approach
Bocce, bowling, skittles, ten pin	Rolling a ball	Y	Y	Y	Y	N	Y
Horseshoe throwing, ring toss, lawn darts	Tossing underhand	Y	Y	N	Y	N	Y
Shuffleboard	Pushing a cue	Y	Y	Y	Y	N	Y
Curling	Sliding a stone	Y	Y	Y	Y	N	Y
Golf	Putting	Y	Y	Y	N	Y	Y
Croquet	Hitting with a mallet	Y	Y	Y	N	Y	Y
Billiards, pool, snooker	Shooting with a cue	Y	Y	Y	N	Y	Y
Golf	Swinging a club	Y	Y	Y	N	Y	Y

Bowling As an Exemplar for Teaching Target Games

Bowling is the quintessential target game and serves as an excellent example of the relationship between preshot decisions and skill execution. In bowling, spots on the approach lane help the bowler position his feet when shooting strikes and spares, and arrows serve as intermediate targets. In addition, a row of spots just beyond the foul line serves as a marker for the release point. Rolling the ball over an arrow, rather than shooting at the pins, increases accuracy. This combination of spots and arrows allows the bowler to consistently shoot for strikes and the various spares. Of course, this assumes that the delivery is consistent not only in the grip or hand position but also in the point of release. Thus, the greater the alignments among the starting point, point of release, and intermediate target, the greater the accuracy.

We can take this concept of spots (as starting points) and arrows (as intermediate targets) and apply it to all target games. When putting, for instance, the golfer locates a spot (i.e., a mark on the green or a few blades of grass) just in front of the ball along the path he wants the ball to travel, and he uses this as an intermediate target. The golfer's stance or starting position is determined once the ball path has been determined, as the stance must be parallel to the ball path. Once the starting position and intermediate target are determined, the performer needs only to execute the putt or, as in the case of other target games, execute the shot, throw, push a cue, or roll the object to hit the target.

Target games that involve throwing, such as horseshoes and darts, do not have an intermediate target per se, but they do require a specific release point. Identifying a specific, consistent spot or area in the background during the release of the object may aid in improving the consistency of the release and may well serve as an intermediate target. Most often the release point is dependent on the kinesthetic sense of the performer.

While some target games involve a release point, others such as golf, billiards, and croquet, involve a contact point. The contact point is the point on the ball that must be struck in order to send the object in the desired direction with the appropriate spin. During a pitch shot, for example, the performer must strike below the midpoint of the ball and with a downward motion in order to send the ball up and land it on the green with sufficient backspin so that the ball stays on the green and does not roll off.

Target games that include counterattacks by an opponent also require the selection of a starting point, intermediate target, and release point. To counterattack, the performer must make a number of tactical adjustments and precisely execute the shot. For example, in shuffleboard a player may want to knock the opponent out of scoring position, which requires that they adjust their stance and intermediate target and judge the distance and speed (power) needed to not only reach the opponent's disk but also to send their disk and their opponent's disk to the desired locations.

We must reiterate that even the most novice players can play target games quite successfully. The tactical problems are basic, easy-to-understand concepts that can easily be extended to challenge more advanced players. The following samples of lesson activities illustrate how you might introduce tactical concepts to primary- and elementary-aged children. By substituting different objects, such as deck rings, beanbags, or horseshoes, the same lesson can be taught several times and in several different contexts to provide the repetition that young children need to develop motor skills and to realize the tactical similarities among games.

Keep one thing in mind: Many of the same concepts that apply to target games also apply to other game categories. For example, striking

a ball with a paddle or bat, a forearm pass in volleyball, or a throw in baseball, although all representing more "open" skills (Gentile, 1972), incorporate the tactical concepts related to accuracy, direction, and distance. If we are to promote ". . . competency in many and proficiency in a few motor skills" (NASPE, 1995), it is essential that skill development *and* tactical understanding be taught intentionally as well as integrated in kindergarten through 12th-grade physical education curriculum.

Target Games Lessons

Target games differ from other games categories in that skill execution is similar across games. For example, rolling or bowling a ball is very similar to tossing a bocce ball, throwing a horseshoe, or striking a ball with a club. The only difference is the concept of "intermediate target," which does not apply to most tossing and throwing games, such as horseshoe throwing and darts. With most target games that involve tossing or throwing, the concept of release point can be applied. Similarly, in target games that involve striking, the concept of the contact point applies as well as the intermediate target.

Another difference between target games and other categories of games is that they involve basically *one* tactical problem—accuracy—and therefore target games tend to be far less complex than other games, particularly at the elementary level. Because of the simplicity of target games, we have presented five level I lessons focusing on accuracy (distance and direction) as the main tactical problem, and many of these lessons can be combined depending on the age or grade level at which they are introduced. The same sequence of lessons can be used to teach the underhand toss, ring toss, and numerous other activities related to target games, which could perhaps be considered level II lessons. In fact, the same sequence of lessons can be used to teach horseshoe throwing, except the nature of the equipment would not make this game appropriate until level III.

Level I Lessons

LESSON 1

TACTICAL PROBLEM: Rolling for accuracy and direction.

GAME: Rolling a ball at a pin.

LESSON FOCUS: Setting up and determining starting position.

OBJECTIVE: Demonstrate a consistent starting position (same spot, balanced stance, same grip and hand position on the ball, eyes focused on the target) before executing the roll.

1. **GAME 1:** Knockdown (roll a ball to knock down a pin).

    Conditions: Pin and partner at on one end and roller at the other end, approximately 10 to 15 feet (3 to 4.5 meters) apart.

    Partners switch after every five trials.

    Goal: Knock down pin three times in a row.

    Questions:

    Q. How many of you were able to knock down the pin three times in a row?
    A. No one or only a few of them.

    Q. If you want to knock down the pin every time, what should you do before you roll the ball? (Have children stand and pretend they are getting ready to roll.) *What are you doing?*
    A. Aiming, holding the ball, standing still.

    Q. How are you standing, holding the ball?
    A. Standing still, holding ball with both hands in front of body.

    Q. Where are you standing? Where are you aiming?
    A. Standing in line with the pin, aiming at the pin.

    Q. When do you decide where and how to stand?
    A. Before you roll the ball.

2. **PRACTICE TASK:**

    Partner stands 10 to 15 feet (3 to 4.5 meters) away and forms a V with his feet (heels together and toes pointing out). Think about where and how to stand before you roll the ball. Start in the same place every time; stand the same way, hold the ball the same way, and aim the same way on every roll.

    Goal: Roll the ball so that it goes exactly to the V formed by the partner's feet, five times in a row. (The partner forming the V must stand perfectly still until the ball hits his feet.)

    Cue: *Same* start, *same* stance, *same* hold.

3. **GAME 2:** Knockdown (roll a ball to knock down a pin).

    Conditions: Same as in game 1.

    Goal: Same as in game 1.

4. **CLOSURE:** Review what to do to roll the ball the *same* way every time. Think about where and how to stand before doing the roll.

LESSON 2

TACTICAL PROBLEM: Rolling for accuracy and direction.

GAME: Rolling a ball at a pin.

LESSON FOCUS: Step and arm swing.

OBJECTIVE: Demonstrate smooth and consistent form and rhythm on the step and arm swing (swing back, step forward, swing forward, follow through toward the target, and release the ball low).

1. **GAME 1:** Knockdown (roll a ball to knock down a pin).

   Conditions: Pin and partner are at one end and roller at the other, approximately 10 to 15 feet (3 to 4.5 meters) apart. Partners switch after every 10 trials.

   Goal: Knock down pin three times in a row.

   Questions:

   Q. How did you roll the ball to knock down the pin?
   A. Stepped, rolled the ball at the pin.

   Q. Did you start with your feet together or apart?
   A. Feet together.

   Q. What foot did you step with?
   A. Foot opposite the throwing hand.

   Q. Stand and show me your start position, now your backswing. When do you do your backswing, before or after your step?
   A. Before.

   Q. What do you do when your arm swings forward?
   A. Step and release the ball.

2. **PRACTICE TASK:**

   As you roll the ball, sing, "Swing back," then step long and low (bend to get low) and swing forward and release. Release the ball low and smooth so that it rolls *all* the way to your partner without bouncing. Then the partner returns the ball back to you in the same manner.

   Goal: Roll ball low and smooth with no bounces.

   Cues: Low and smooth.

   Swing back and step.

3. **GAME 2:** Knockdown (roll a ball to knock down a pin).

   Conditions: Same as in game 1.

   Goal: Same as in game 1.

4. **CLOSURE:** Review the backswing and step and forward swing, as well as a low, smooth, no-bounce release.

LESSON 3

TACTICAL PROBLEM: Rolling for accuracy and direction.

GAME: Rolling a ball at a pin.

LESSON FOCUS: Step and follow through toward the target.

OBJECTIVE: Identify the target line, and then send the ball in the direction of the pin by stepping and following through along the target line.

1. **GAME 1:** Knockdown (roll a ball to knock down a pin).

   Conditions: Pin and partner are at one end and roller at the other, approximately 10 to 15 feet (3 to 4.5 meters) apart. Partners switch after every 10 trials. Tape or draw a line from the foul line to the pin to serve as a target line.

Goal: Knock down pin three times in a row.

Questions:

Q. How did you roll the ball to knock down the pin?
A. Start position, aimed, stepped, rolled the ball at the pin.

Q. In which direction did you step?
A. Straight, toward the pin.

Q. What other body parts went straight toward the pin?
A. The hand on the forward swing and follow-through.

Q. When is the best time to think about the direction of your step and follow-through?
A. Before you roll the ball.

2. **PRACTICE TASK 1:**

Perform five rolls; freeze at the end of the roll and have partner check to see if step and release hand are pointing directly toward the pin. If the pin is knocked down, take one step back. If you miss the pin, take one step forward. After five rolls, switch with your partner. Think about and pick a good starting position before you roll the ball. See how far back you can go and still knock down the pin.

Cues: Step *to* the target.

Follow through *to* the target.

Think before you roll.

Question:

Q. Besides stepping and following through to the target, was there anything else that you used to get the ball to roll straight to the target?
A. Target line.

PRACTICE TASK 2:

Repeat the practice; use the target line as you step and follow through *to* the target. Freeze at the end of the roll and have partner check to see if step and release hand are pointing directly toward the pin. If you knock down the pin, take one step back. If you miss the pin, take one step forward. After five rolls, switch with your partner. See if you can get farther back than you did before.

Cues: Step *to* the target.

Follow through *to* the target.

Think before you roll.

3. **GAME 2:** Knockdown (roll a ball to knock down a pin).

Conditions: If the player knocks down the pin three times in a row, he should step back one step and roll again. Once the player misses, switch places with partner.

Goal: Knock down pin three times on three rolls from three increasingly longer distances.

4. **CLOSURE:** Review the key elements of the roll (step and follow through *to* the target) and target line that influence the direction the ball travels. Emphasize looking where to throw (use the target line) before throwing.

LESSON 4

TACTICAL PROBLEM: Rolling for accuracy and direction.

GAME: Rolling a ball at a pin.

LESSON FOCUS: Selecting an intermediate target.

OBJECTIVE: Select the intermediate target that will result in consistently knocking down the pin.

1. **GAME 1:** Knockdown (roll a ball to knock down a pin).

   Conditions: Students work in pairs; one rolls the ball and the other retrieves the ball, rolls it back, and sets up the pin.

   The pin is approximately 15 to 20 feet (4.5 to 6 meters) away.

   Students switch after three turns.

   Class is set up with pairs parallel to each other, all rolling the same direction (figure 7.2).

   Place three stickers on the floor to designate a starting position behind the foul line; place three stickers slightly ahead of the foul line, 6 to 18 inches (15 to 45 centimeters), to serve as intermediate targets.

   Use one plastic bowling pin per pair and an assortment of balls so that the children can choose the one that works best for them (Graham, Holt/Hale, & Parker, 2001).

   Goal: Roll the ball and knock down the pin three times in a row.

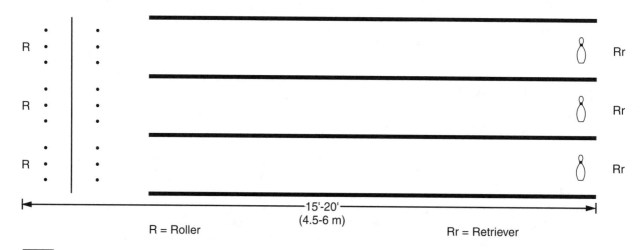

R = Roller   Rr = Retriever

Figure 7.2

   Questions:

   Q. How many of you were able to knock down the pin three times in a row?
   A. No one or very few.

   Q. Why is it so hard to hit the pin three times in a row?
   A. Pin is too far away.

   Q. Instead of aiming for the pin, way down there, where else could you aim?
   A. At the stickers in front of the line.

   Q. Which sticker would work best?
   A. Don't know.

2. **PRACTICE TASK:**

   Select one of the stickers behind the line so that you have the same starting place every time. Roll two balls over the first sticker, two over the second sticker, and two over the third sticker. Determine which sticker will work the best to help you knock down the pin. Be sure to roll the ball right over the intermediate target sticker.

   Cues: Start the *same.*

   Roll ball *over* the sticker.

   Questions:

   Q. Which sticker worked the best for you?
   A. Left, right, middle.

Q. Why does aiming at the sticker work better than aiming at the pin?
A. Because it is closer.

Q. Does anyone know what you call a target that is closer?
A. An intermediate target.

Q. Why do you want to always start the same and use an intermediate target?
A. So that you can knock down the pin on every roll.

3. **GAME 2:** Knockdown (roll a ball to knock down a pin).

    Conditions: Same as in game 1.

    Goal: Same as in game 1.

4. **CLOSURE:** Review the key points related to starting in the *same* spot and using an intermediate target.

LESSON 5

TACTICAL PROBLEM: Rolling for accuracy and distance.

GAME: Rolling a ball at a pin.

LESSON FOCUS: The relationship of the length of the backswing and step to the generation of force necessary to roll the ball a greater distance.

OBJECTIVE: The students will demonstrate understanding of the concept that the longer the backswing, the greater the force and the farther the ball will roll; they will be able to adjust the backswing relative to the distance needed to consistently knock down the pin.

1. **GAME 1:** Knockdown (roll a ball to knock down a pin).

    Conditions: Students work in pairs; one rolls the ball and the other retrieves the ball and rolls it back and sets up the pin.

    Students switch after two turns at each of the three distances.

    The pin is set at the closest spot for the first two trials, middle spot for the next two trials, and the farthest spot for the last two trials (figure 7.3).

    Remind students to start the same and use an intermediate target to send the ball in the right direction.

    Goal: Roll the ball and knock the pin down two times at each distance.

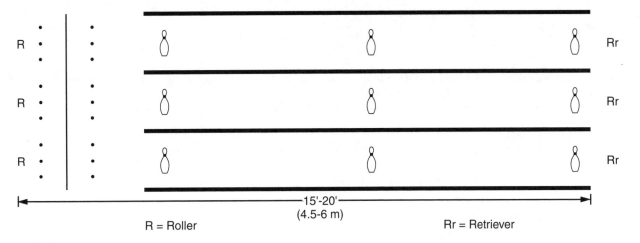

R = Roller   Rr = Retriever

Figure 7.3

Questions:

Q. How did you swing your arm when you rolled the ball at the spot nearest you, compared to when you rolled the ball at the spot farthest from you? (Stand up and show me how you moved your arm when the spot was near. Now, show me how you moved your arm when the spot was far away.)
A. More arm swing when the pin is far away, and less when it is near.

Q. Why does the ball go farther or a longer distance when your arm goes back farther?
A. It gives us more power and speed.

Q. When would you want more force?
A. When the pin is far away.

Q. And how do you swing your arm back when you want more force?
A. Way back.

Q. When would you want less force?
A. When the pin is near us.

Q. And, how do you swing your arm back when you want less force?
A. Just a little bit.

2. **PRACTICE TASK:**

Return to game 1. Practice using a shorter backswing when the pin is near and a longer backswing when the pin is far away. If you reach the goal, ask your partner to set the pin even farther back, one step. Determine the farthest distance you can roll the ball and still hit the pin.

Cues: Big swing *far.*

Little swing *near.*

Goal: Knock down pin two times in a row at each distance.

Questions:

Q. Besides swinging your arm back farther, what can you do to roll the ball a farther distance?
A. Use a longer step; use a longer forward swing and follow-through.

Q. Besides helping you create more force and roll the ball a farther distance, how does the step and follow-through help you knock down the pin?
A. It helps us to roll the ball in the right direction toward the pin.

3. **GAME 2:** Knockdown (roll a ball to knock down a pin).

Conditions: Return to game 1, except have partner set up the pin one step farther every time you knock it down.

Switch after two misses in a row.

Use a longer step when the pin is far away and (no step) a shorter step when the pin is near.

4. **CLOSURE:** Review the key points related to the concept of the longer the step and arm swing, the greater the force and the farther the roll.

Level II Lessons

Level II lessons emphasize the need to adjust the starting point, target line, and intermediate target. Although three pins may seem to be a bigger target, more accuracy is required to knock down all three pins because of the need to hit the "pocket." You may choose to use terms similar to those used in bowling, such as headpin and pocket. We do recommend referring to the pins by number: number one (1) for the headpin, number two (2) for the 2-pin, and number three (3) for the 3-pin. Level II lessons can be expanded to include more pins, with 5-pin being the most logical extension. This will involve more adjustments in preshot decisions and will be a good lead-in to 10-pin bowling. Scoring can also be added when students are ready, and it is often good content to integrate into the classroom setting.

LESSON 1

TACTICAL PROBLEM: Rolling for accuracy and direction.

GAME: 3-pin.

LESSON FOCUS: Adjusting start position, target line, and intermediate target.

OBJECTIVE: The students will adjust their start position, target line, and intermediate target to consistently hit the pocket.

1. **GAME 1:** 3-pin.

   Conditions: Three pins (1, 2, and 3) and partner are at one end and roller at the other end approximately 15 to 20 feet (4.5 to 6 meters) apart.

   Partners switch after every three trials.

   Goal: Knock down all three pins three times in a row.

   Questions:

   Q. (Pointing to the three-pin setup) *Will someone show me the best place to hit the pins so that they all fall down?*
   A. Between the 1 and 2 (2 and 3 for left-handed rollers).

   Q. *When you had just one pin, you rolled the ball right down the middle. Where do you want to roll the ball to hit between the 1- and 2-pins?*
   A. From the right side of the lane.

   Q. *If you want to roll the ball down the right side, where should you stand?*
   A. On the right side of the lane.

2. **PRACTICE TASK 1:**

   Use footprints to find a good starting point. When you go back to your lane, put the footprints in what you think will be a good spot and try them out by taking two rolls. If after two turns you do not hit between the 1- and 2-pin, adjust the footprints again and take another two rolls. Once you get your footprints in a good starting point, let your partner set up her footprints.

   Goal: Adjust the footprints to obtain a good start position.

   Cue: Adjust the footprints and take two rolls.

   Questions:

   Q. *How many of you were able to find a good starting point?*
   A. All.

   Q. *Besides a starting point, what should you think about before you roll?*
   A. Target line and intermediate target.

   Q. *Where is the target line?*
   A. Between the ball (where the ball is released) and the 1- and 2-pins.

   Q. *Where is the intermediate target?*
   A. The dot (marked on the lane) that goes along that line.

   Q. *Why do you want to use an intermediate target?*
   A. It is closer to aim at than the pins way down the lane.

   PRACTICE TASK 2:

   Go back to your lanes and look for your target line and the dot (intermediate target) that you will use to aim. Try out your intermediate target two times to see if it works. If not, pick another intermediate target and try it two times. After you find your intermediate target, mark it (with a sticker) so that you will know where it is when you roll the ball. After you find your intermediate target, give your partner a turn while you go to the other end to set pins and roll the ball back.

Cues: Pick an intermediate target.

Take two rolls.

3. **GAME 2:** 3-pin.

Conditions: Same as game 1.

Goal: Same as game 1.

4. **CLOSURE:** Review how to make adjustments to starting point, target line, and intermediate target when shooting at three pins instead of one pin. Emphasize thinking about where and how to stand before rolling the ball.

LESSON 2

TACTICAL PROBLEM: Rolling for accuracy and direction.

GAME: 3-pin.

LESSON FOCUS: Adjust start position, target line, and intermediate target.

OBJECTIVE: The students will adjust their start position, target line, and intermediate target on the second roll to consistently hit the remaining pin(s).

1. **GAME 1:** 3-pin.

Conditions: Three pins (1, 2, and 3) and partner are at one end and roller is at the other end approximately 15 to 20 feet (4.5 to 6 meters) apart.

Attempt to knock down all three pins with first ball and remaining pins on the second ball.

Partners switch after every six trials.

Goal: If you do not knock down all three pins with the first ball, knock down the remaining pins with the second ball.

Questions:

Q. Is knocking down three pins the same as knocking down one pin? (Point to a 3-pin setup and a setup with one pin remaining.)
A. No.

Q. If you do not knock down all the pins with the first ball, what should you do to be sure you knock down the remaining pins?
A. Change the starting point and intermediate target.

Q. What if you have the 1-pin (headpin) and another pin remaining? Do you need to change your starting point and intermediate target?
A. No.

2. **PRACTICE TASK 1:**

Use the footprints to find a starting point and dots to find an intermediate target when aiming for the 3-pin. Put the footprints in what you think will be a good spot and try them out by taking two rolls. If after two rolls you do not hit between the 3-pin, adjust the footprints again and take another two rolls. Once you get your footprints in a good starting point, let your partner set up her footprints.

Cue: Line up your footprints with your intermediate target.

Questions:

Q. How many of you were able to find a good starting point and intermediate target to knock down the 3-pin?
A. All.

Q. If you left the 2-pin, would your start position and intermediate target be the same?
A. No.

Q. Where would they be?

A. Not sure.

PRACTICE TASK 2:

Use the footprints to find a starting point and dots to find an intermediate target when aiming for the 2-pin. Put the footprints in what you think will be a good spot and try them out by taking two rolls. If after two rolls you do not hit between the 2-pin, adjust the footprints again and take another two rolls. Once you get your footprints in a good starting point, let your partner set up her footprints.

Cue: Line up your footprints with your intermediate target.

3. **GAME 2:** 3-pin.

    Conditions: Same as in game 1.

    Goal: Same as in game 1.

4. **CLOSURE:** Review how to make adjustments to starting point, target line, and intermediate target when shooting at three pins instead of one pin. Emphasize thinking about where and how to stand before rolling the ball.

LESSON 3

TACTICAL PROBLEM: Rolling for accuracy and direction.

GAME: 3-pin.

LESSON FOCUS: Adjust start position, target line, and intermediate target.

OBJECTIVE: The students will adjust start position, target line, and intermediate target on the second roll to consistently hit the remaining pin(s).

1. **GAME 1:** 3-pin.

    Conditions: Three pins (1, 2, and 3) and partner are at one end and roller at the other end approximately 15 to 20 feet (4.5 to 6 meters) apart.

    Attempt to knock down all three pins with first ball and remaining pins on the second ball. Keep score to see how many pins you knock down after four rolls.

    If you do not knock down all three pins after the second roll, set up three pins for third roll.

    Partners switch after every four rolls.

    Goal: If you do not knock down all three pins with the first ball, knock down the remaining pins with the second ball.

    Questions:

    Q. How many of you were able to knock down 12 pins on four rolls?

    A. No one.

    Q. How many of you are hitting between the 1- and 2-pin when three pins are standing?

    A. Some.

    Q. What should you do before you roll to knock down the pins?

    A. Find a starting point, target line, and intermediate target.

    Q. What happens to your starting point, target line, and intermediate target when you're aiming at the 2-pin or the 3-pin?

    A. They are different.

2. **PRACTICE TASK:**

    Use the footprints to find a starting point and dots to find an intermediate target when aiming for the three setups (all three pins, 2-pin, and 3-pin). First, figure out where your footprints and intermediate target are when all three pins are standing. Take two turns to be sure it's right. Then, let your partner have a turn to figure out where her footprints and intermediate targets are. Repeat for the 2-pin and 3-pin. (Different-colored dry-erase markers can be used to mark starting positions and intermediate targets.)

    Cue: Line up your footprints with your intermediate target.

3. **GAME 2:** 3-pin.

    Conditions: Same as in game 1.

    Goal: Same as in game 1. Compare score of game 1 and game 2.

4. **CLOSURE:** Review how to make adjustments to starting point, target line, and intermediate target when shooting at three pins instead of one pin. Emphasize thinking about where and how to stand before rolling the ball.

Level III Lessons

Level III lessons involve a different game, bocce ball. However, bocce skills and tactics transfer easily from bowling. The emphasis here should be on adjusting the starting point, target line, and intermediate target as the target changes, and on adjusting the speed of the arm swing and length of the backswing as the target gets closer or farther away. Although this sounds simple enough, accuracy requires control and consistency, which takes considerable practice and time to develop. Initially, some students may have to be prompted to take their time and intentionally think through the preshot decisions.

LESSON 1

TACTICAL PROBLEM: Rolling for accuracy and direction.

GAME: Bocce ball.

LESSON FOCUS: Adjust start position, target line, and intermediate target.

OBJECTIVE: The students will determine their start position, target line, and intermediate target to get the ball close to the jack on each roll.

1. **GAME 1:** Bocce ball.

    Conditions: Play on grass or carpet.

    Foam balls can be used on fast surface.

    Place jack in permanent position; players, who each have two balls, try to get their balls closest to the jack.

    Players alternate until their two balls have been rolled.

    The ball closest to the jack scores 2 points.

    If one player has two balls closer than the other player, she scores 4 points—2 points for each ball that is closest to the jack.

    Goal: Score 2 points on every roll.

    Questions:

    Q. How many of you were able to score 2 points on every roll?
    A. No one.

    Q. If you were rolling a ball at some pins, what would you do before you rolled to knock down the pins?
    A. Pick a starting point, target line, and intermediate target.

Q. Since this too is a target game, do you think that tactic will work here?
A. Yes.

2. **PRACTICE TASK:**

Use the footprints to find a starting point and dots to find an intermediate target when aiming for the jack. First, figure out where your footprints and intermediate target are and then let your partner figure out where to place his footprints and intermediate target. Take two or three turns to be sure it's right. (You can use stickers to mark starting positions and intermediate targets.)

Cue: Line up your footprints with your intermediate target.

3. **GAME 2:** Bocce ball.

Conditions: Same as in game 1.

Goal: Same as in game 1. Compare scores of game 1 to game 2.

4. **CLOSURE:** Review how to make adjustments to starting point, target line, and intermediate target when shooting at the jack. Emphasize the similarities among target games.

LESSON 2

TACTICAL PROBLEM: Rolling for accuracy and direction.

GAME: Bocce ball.

LESSON FOCUS: Adjust start position, target line, and intermediate target.

OBJECTIVE: The students will determine the start position, target line, and intermediate target to get the ball close to the jack on each roll.

1. **GAME 1:** Bocce ball.

Conditions: Play on grass or carpet. Foam balls can be used on fast surface.

Player who will go second rolls the jack out about 15 to 20 feet (4.5 to 6 meters).

Players, who each have two balls, try to get their balls closest to the jack.

Players alternate until they have rolled their two balls.

The ball closest to the jack scores 2 points. If one player has 2 balls closer than the other player, he scores 4 points—2 points for each ball that is closest to the jack.

Goal: Score 2 points on every roll.

Questions:

Q. How many of you were able to score 2 points on every roll?
A. No one.

Q. What happens to your starting point, target line, and intermediate target when the jack is in a different place?
A. They change.

Q. What should you do before you roll?
A. Figure out the new starting point, target line, and intermediate target.

2. **PRACTICE TASK:**

Play three rounds using footprints and dots to mark your intermediate target. Every time the jack is in a new position, figure out where your footprints and intermediate target are and then let your partner figure out where to place her footprints and intermediate target. Then play the round. Repeat on each new roll of the jack.

Cue: Line up your footprints with your intermediate target.

3. **GAME 2:** Bocce ball (without footprints, but intermediate target can still be used).

    Goal: Compare scores of game 1 and game 2.

4. **CLOSURE:** Review how to make adjustments to starting point, target line, and intermediate target when shooting at the jack. Emphasize the similarities among target games.

LESSON 3

TACTICAL PROBLEM: Rolling for accuracy and distance.

GAME: Bocce ball.

LESSON FOCUS: Adjust the speed of the arm swing and length of backswing.

OBJECTIVE: The students will adjust the speed and length of the backswing depending on the distance from the jack.

1. **GAME 1:** Bocce ball.

    Conditions: Play on grass or carpet.

    Foam balls can be used on fast surface.

    Place jack in permanent position; players, who each have two balls, try to get their balls closest to the jack.

    Players alternate until they have rolled their two balls.

    The ball closest to the jack scores 2 points.

    If one player has two balls closer than the other player, he scores 4 points—2 points for each ball that is closest to the jack.

    Goal: Score 2 points on every roll.

    Questions:

    Q. How many of you were able to score 2 points on every roll?
    A. No one.

    Q. Why aren't you getting your ball close to the jack?
    A. Rolling too long or too short or not consistently.

    Q. Last lesson we worked on adjusting starting point and intermediate target. What do you need to adjust when the roll is too long or too short?
    A. The arm swing.

    Q. Watch my arm as I roll the ball at the jack 20 feet (6 meters) away, then 10 feet (3 meters) away. How is it different?
    A. Faster at 20 feet (6 meters) and longer backswing.

2. **PRACTICE TASK:**

    Place a jack at 10, 15, and 20 feet (3, 4.5, and 6 meters). Players throw six balls (two balls at each jack). Combine two teams and take turns rolling and retrieving. Adjust speed of the arm swing and length of the backswing according to distance from the jack.

    Cue: The farther, the faster, and the longer the backswing.

3. **GAME 2:** Bocce ball.

    Conditions: Same as in game 1.

    Goal: Same as in game 1. Compare scores of game 1 and game 2.

4. **CLOSURE:** Review how to make adjustments to the varying distances of the jack by changing the speed of the arm and length of the backswing. Emphasize the use of feedback from the previous throw to adjust the next throw.

Transfer of Target Game Concepts to Other Games Categories

In closing, we emphasize the fact that the tactical problems related to target games transfer across games categories to invasion, net/wall, and striking/fielding games. For example, the concept of contact point is applicable in batting, volleyball, tennis, soccer, and many other games. The concept of release point relates to throwing a baseball and shooting a basketball, just to name a few. This provides further justification for including target games in the elementary physical education curriculum.

PART III

Assessment and the Curriculum

chapter 8

Assessing Learning Outcomes

This chapter addresses the role of assessment in the teaching and learning of games. We will examine what to assess and what your students should know and do (i.e., learning outcomes) and also align assessment with the National Association for Sport and Physical Education (NASPE) Standards (NASPE, 1995). Assessment of learning outcomes is important, but it is not something that has been done effectively in physical education. In addition to the assessment ideas in this chapter, we hope that the management structures and lesson outlines provided in other chapters will

make assessment easier for you as teachers. For example, the use of sport education seasons in which students are assigned to permanent teams enables you to assess one team per lesson with a focus on the tactical problem addressed during that lesson. If you are assessing game performance, an important focus in this chapter, this observation and assessment can take place during the lesson's closing game. Furthermore, the regular use of question and answer segments during lessons provides you with an informal means of assessment. In this chapter we will first share our beliefs about assessment, then outline practical considerations for assessing students.

Beliefs About Assessment

We have four major beliefs about assessment:

1. Assessment should be ongoing and routine.

2. Assessment should be authentic.

3. Planning what to teach is the same as planning what to assess.

4. Assessment serves as a means of holding teachers and students accountable for teaching and learning.

1. *We believe that assessment should be an ongoing and routine part of sport-related games teaching* (Griffin, Mitchell, & Oslin, 1997). That is, assessment must occur throughout the school year, as well as during each sport-related games unit and every games lesson. Both summative and formative assessment must be ongoing and routine. Formative assessment (checking on student progress, providing feedback for diagnosing strengths and weaknesses) provides feedback for the teacher and the individual students about strengths and weaknesses and checks on students' progress. In fact, every tactical games lesson includes a question and answer segment that is a formative assessment measure. A variety of summative and formative assessments used throughout a unit not only provides a picture of student learning but also provides students with in-depth knowledge about what is important to learn in the unit (Zessoules & Gardner, 1991). Summative assessment, usually in the form of evaluation and assigning grades, involves systematically determining the extent to which objectives have been met (Veal, 1993); such assessment can be based on several formative assessments taken over the course of a unit.

Another valuable aspect of ongoing and routine assessment is that it provides teachers with many opportunities to find out what their students might already know about games. The role of prior knowledge in games teaching and learning is important for two reasons. First, students generally know something about games because they have played them in their neigh-

borhoods or community leagues or watched them as spectators. Because of all of these possible experiences, the knowledge students have about games may differ from the knowledge we, as teachers, want them to have about games (Clement, 1993; Griffin & Placek, 2001; Wandersee, Mintzes, & Novak, 1994). Second, students may have *alternative conceptions* about various aspects of game play (e.g., their roles in particular positions in a game or how best to "get open" in an invasion game to support teammates). *Alternative conceptions* are defined as reasonably different ideas about an aspect of game play based on a learner's experience that would be brought into a formal instruction setting (Dodds, Griffin, & Placek, 2001; Wandersee, Mintzes, & Novak, 1994). Teachers need to acknowledge that their students usually know something about game playing; thus, it is important to have a sense of their prior knowledge to better build more developmentally appropriate instruction.

2. *Assessment should be authentic.* When implementing a tactical games approach, the teacher's goals for students focus on successful game play, so assessment should also focus on game play (Veal, 1993). That is, if the goal of games teaching is to improve student game performance, then it is essential that assessment measures take into consideration two critical components. First, assessment measures should encompass all aspects of performance, including concepts related to tactical awareness or understanding as well as skill performance. Second, assessment measures need to measure game playing in context, whether in full-sided games or, in the case of elementary students, in modified or conditioned games.

Typically, physical educators rely on skill testing to assess student game performance, and there are many examples of common skill tests in any measurement textbook. Using skill tests to assess game performance is problematic for four reasons: (1) Skills tests do not predict playing performance. (2) Skills test do not take into account the social dimensions of games. (3) Skills tests measure skills out of context, in situations not related to game play. (4) Skills tests do not reflect a broader view of game performance (Griffin, Mitchell, & Oslin, 1997; Oslin, Mitchell, & Griffin, 1998).

3. *Planning what to teach is the same as planning what to assess.* The notion of integrating instructional goals with instructional processes and assessment is known as instructional alignment (Cohen, 1987). Instructional alignment helps the teacher establish a relationship of assessment to the goals and learning activities of a lesson or unit, thus informing students of expected learning outcomes. Each tactical lesson in the earlier chapters begins with the tactical problem to be solved, a lesson focus, and specific lesson objectives. Considering these aspects of instructional alignment in your planning will help you limit your scope of content (to do a few things well), allow time for assessment, and enhance your ability to sequence the games content appropriately. Relating assessment criteria to what has been taught is critical for performance in game situations (Mitchell & Oslin, 1999a).

For example, in a tactical games lesson and unit teachers are asking students to (1) *confront* a situation or problem to solve, (2) engage in an *action* situation (i.e., practice or game) to solve the problem, and (3) *reflect* on their actions (i.e., critical thinking). This instructional process will help you and your students stay focused during each learning activity by asking yourself, *What aspects of the lesson do I want my students to reflect upon?* Answering this question will help decide on what type of assessment measures (e.g., assessing game play, asking questions) to use.

4. *Assessment serves as an accountability measure for teachers and students.* From our work with teachers, we have learned that assessment holds teachers accountable for teaching and students responsible for learning (James, Griffin, & France, 2000). Assessment helps teachers improve their instruction and clarifies expected learning outcomes to students. As noted by Oslin, Collier, and Mitchell (2001), assessment is necessary not only to evaluate the extent to which students have learned lesson content but also to ensure that they stay focused.

Assessment helps teachers and students (1) to establish ongoing and regular feedback about solving a particular tactical problem and (2) to demonstrate whether students have achieved particular goals or standards relative to game performance. In summary, student assessment does not simply measure student performance but improves it.

Practical Considerations for Implementing Assessment

Here we address some practical issues associated with assessing learning. Whether it is the teacher or students who are the assessors, but particularly if it is students, you should be aware of these practical considerations.

Assessments by Teachers

Although we have shared why we believe assessment is vital to the teaching–learning process, we also recognize that teachers need to take into account practical considerations to make assessment effective in their classrooms. We acknowledge that many teachers believe that there is too much paperwork and not enough time to make assessment part of classroom life, but these factors should not keep teachers from providing students with a complete learning experience that includes assessment and accountability. In this section, we identify the decisions the teacher needs to make about assessment and the various assessment strategies the teacher can use.

As the teacher, you know that you will need to keep track of student learning. The first assessment decision has to do with matching the assessment to the focus of the lesson (i.e., lesson objective). Second, the teacher must decide whether assessment will be formative or summative. Finally, the teacher's choice of assessment strategy will take into account (1) *who* will do the assessment and (2) the *type* of assessment tool to be used.

It is important to balance the *type* of assessment with *who* assesses because this balance provides you and your students with a broader overall picture of progress toward becoming better games players. Who will assess is one of the keys to addressing the issues of paperwork and time. Both teacher and students can assess in a classroom. The teacher can and should assess but *not do all* the assessment all the time. Teachers can assess for both formative and summative purposes. Students can assess and should do so in various formative situations.

The type of assessment you choose might range from the use of an observation instrument,

Table 8.1   Recommended Use of Assessment Types for Teachers and Students

Assessment type	Recommended for use by	
	Teacher	Students
Written test	Yes	No
Question and answer session	Yes	No
Game Performance Assessment Instrument (GPAI)	Yes	Yes
Monitoring and observation	Yes	No
Rubric	Yes	Yes
Checklist	Yes	Yes
Self-report or journal		Yes

which will be explained in greater detail later in the chapter, to the use of student self-report. Table 8.1 shows the various types of assessment and who, teacher or student, is a better fit when using them.

Involving Students in Assessment

Involving students in assessment can be time effective for the teacher. Students have shared with us how much they enjoy and benefit from the opportunity of being involved in assessment; they can assess each other (peer assessment), they can assess as a group (group problem solving), and they can assess themselves (self-assessment or reporting).

When involving students in assessment, you should take into consideration the following guidelines.

1. *Teach students how to assess, what it means, and how to use the information.* We believe that these three important considerations will lead to success in involving students with assessment. Take the time to teach all three of these considerations. In fact each one serves as a lesson in itself. For example, after the first two lessons of a badminton unit with a combined fifth- and sixth-grade class, the teacher introduced partner assessment to her students. The students were going to keep track of overhead clears. The teacher set up a demonstration game for the students to practice. The students were organized to observe in pairs so that they could check for understanding; then she had students share their results as a class. The activity was repeated a second time to be sure that students

understood their roles and expectations. The time spent was short, but the teacher was able to be clear about her expectations through practice. This example also was used to teach the students what the information means (i.e., the importance of pushing the opponent back in the court to create space on the front) as well as setting up students to give specific feedback to each other.

2. *Establish an assessment routine.* For assessment to be a routine part of your class, you need to create a consistent system for organizing students, equipment, and space. First, students need to know whom they are assessing. There are endless ways to organize; the following are just two examples:

- Partner assessment, in which Student A assesses Student B, then switches roles, and this continues throughout the unit.
- Team assessment, in which teams take turns observing game play with each player assessing a member of another team.

3. *You will need to organize equipment for assessment.* On what and with what will the students write? Also, how will the assessment forms be collected? You can consider several options, such as pencils attached to clip boards or student or team portfolios. Finally, you need to consider space in the assessment process. How will observers use the space? Where will they sit to assess each other? Also, where will the equipment be prior to assessing and at the end of class?

4. *Hold students accountable for assessment by monitoring the process and checking the results of student assessments.* Simply put, you need to follow up on all aspects of assessment. In other words, if you do not value follow-up and don't take care in implementing aspects of assessment in the teaching–learning process, then neither will your students. Take time to briefly discuss results and their meaning because this indicates the importance you attach to the process of assessment.

5. *Consider "do-ability" in assessment.* Do-ability involves the need to consider *how much to do* and *who will do* the assessment. We believe that you should *limit* how much to observe and measure in a particular lesson or across a whole unit, regardless of whether the teacher or student is involved in the assessment. Limiting assessment will ensure that you set assessment tasks that can be accomplished within constraints of available time, equipment, facilities, and people.

Assessing Four Domains of Learning Outcomes

The concept of four domains of learning outcomes—psychomotor, cognitive, behavioral and social, and affective—is a way to help identify the range of learning outcomes that reflects a broad view of game performance. Figure 8.1 presents our proposed learning outcomes in diagrammatic form and indicates the relationships among these outcomes. We believe that improvement in game performance, the primary goal of a tactical games approach, will lead to increased enjoyment, interest, and perceived competence. These motivational outcomes increase the likelihood that students will play games later in life, hence increasing the likelihood of students maintaining a physically active lifestyle after school and into adulthood, as specified by NASPE Content

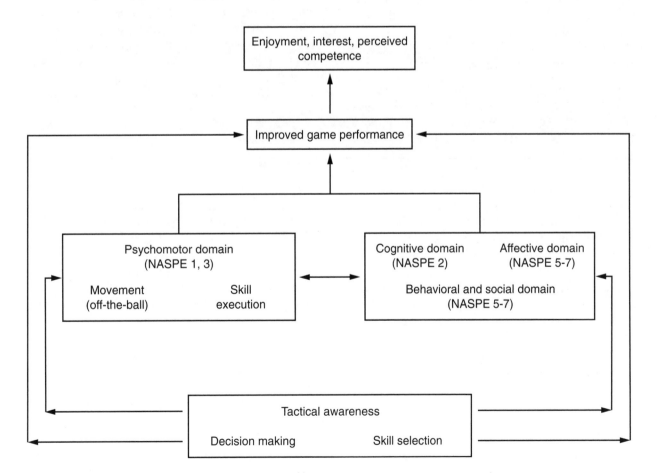

Figure 8.1 Anticipated learning outcomes.

Adapted, by permission, from L.L. Griffin, S.A. Mitchell, and J.L. Oslin, 1997, *Teaching sport concepts and skills* (Champaign, IL: Human Kinetics), 218.

Standard 3 (NASPE, 1995). Figure 8.1 matches other tactical games outcomes with the NASPE Standards. Improved game performance stems from increased tactical awareness. Tactical awareness is the ability of students to identify problems and their solutions in game situations and thus become better decision makers. The link between tactical awareness and game performance occurs through the integration and interaction of the psychomotor, cognitive, and affective domains.

The *psychomotor domain* encompasses game performance; the *cognitive domain* reflects the understanding or knowing of game-related knowledge; the *behavioral and social domain* addresses students' socialization into sport; and the *affective domain* considers dimensions of sport and games, such as good sport behaviors, teamwork, and cooperation. In the end, one domain influences the other, and this combination reflects the multiple dimensions and complex nature of game play. The following sections discuss assessment as related to each domain.

Psychomotor Domain

In teaching and learning tactical games, the psychomotor domain encompasses off-the-ball movements (e.g., support, guard, and mark) and on-the-ball skills, which include skill selection and skill execution (see figure 8.1). This domain parallels the NASPE Content Standard 1 (NASPE, 1995), which states, "A physically educated person demonstrates competency in many movement forms and proficiency in a few movement forms" (p. 1). A tactical games approach primarily focuses on improved game performance (i.e., competent and proficient games players). The assessment of game-playing ability should include decisions players make about what to do with the ball and movements players make when they do not have the ball because both on-the-ball skills and off-the-ball movements are vital components to becoming competent or proficient games players. For example, in a small-sided (3 v 3) basketball game, we can assess what players are doing with the ball. But it is also just as important to assess how a player moves in positive ways to get the ball.

Recent efforts to measure performance more completely in game play have included assessing aspects of decision making, skill execution,

and individual player performance (French, Werner, Rink, Taylor, & Hussey, 1996; Gréhaigne, Godbout, & Bouthier, 1997; Mitchell, Oslin, & Griffin, 1995; Nevett, Rovengo, & Babiarz, 2001; Oslin, Mitchell, & Griffin, 1998; Turner & Martinek, 1992). These types of measurements are valuable for three reasons:

1. They assess students in game play.
2. They can provide information about a player's thinking process. For example, in an invasion game a player may receive credit for attempting to pass to an open player even if the pass is not well executed.
3. They can be a valuable source of information from which a teacher can plan the next lesson.

As we have been maintaining, game play should be measured authentically, that is, within the context of actual game-playing situations. In the next section, we will introduce the Game Performance Assessment Instrument (GPAI) and teach you how to use the GPAI to assess elements of the psychomotor domain in your teaching. The GPAI is a flexible, authentic assessment tool that is easy to use and adapt to what has been taught and learned (Mitchell & Oslin, 1999a).

The Game Performance Assessment Instrument

The Game Performance Assessment Instrument (GPAI) was developed as a comprehensive assessment tool for teachers to use and adapt for a variety of games. This flexibility means that teachers can adapt the GPAI for different games across the classification system (e.g., invasion, net/wall) or within a particular classification (e.g., basketball, soccer), eliminating the need to become familiar with many different assessment instruments.

Seven components of game performance are defined in the GPAI (table 8.2). It is important to note that not all components apply to all games. For example, in tennis the component "base" is critical to court coverage, but players do not have to guard or mark opponents. The seven components in table 8.2 constitute a broad definition of game performance that entails much more than skill execution (Mitchell & Oslin, 1999a).

Following are brief descriptions and examples of each game performance component.

1. *Base* is a position to which players should return between skill attempts. For example, in net games, players should return to a specific place on the court that provides them with optimal opportunity for court cover-age. Table 8.3 provides some examples of how base applies to various games.

2. Decision making is choosing a movement or skill to execute in response to a tactical problem. Table 8.4 provides some decision-making examples across the games classification system.

Table 8.2 Components of Game Performance

Game performance component	Decision, skill, or movement
Base	Appropriate return of performer to a recovery (base) position between skill attempts
Decision making	Making appropriate decisions about what to do with the ball (or projectile) during a game
Skill execution	Efficient execution of selected skills
Support	Provides appropriate support for a teammate with the ball (or projectile) by being in position to receive a pass
Guard or mark	Appropriate guarding or marking of an opponent who may or may not have the ball (or projectile)
Cover	Provides appropriate defensive cover, help, or backup for a player making a challenge for the ball (or projectile)
Adjust	Movement of performer, either offensively or defensively, as necessitated by the flow of the game

Adapted, by permission, from L.L. Griffin, S.A. Mitchell, and J.L. Oslin, 1997, *Teaching sport concepts and skills* (Champaign, IL: Human Kinetics), 220.

Table 8.3 Examples of Base in Various Games

Game	Base movement
Invasion games	
Basketball	Player sets up in position in a zone defense
Net/wall games	
Badminton	Players return to about the "T" at center court between shots
Tennis	Players return to the center of the baseline between shots
Volleyball	Players return to a designated playing area when ball is returned over the net during a rally
Striking/fielding games	
Softball	Player starts in base (fielding position) prior to each pitch
Target games	
Golf	Player starts in a setup or stance position

Table 8.4 Examples of Decision Making in the Four Game Categories

Game category	Skill choice
Invasion games	Decide whether to shoot, pass, or dribble
Net/wall games	Decide shot selection and placement

(continued)

Table 8.4 (continued)

Game category	Skill choice
Striking/fielding games	**Batters** Decide pitch and placement of shot **Fielders** Decide where to throw the ball **Pitchers** Decide how to deliver the ball
Target games	**Golf** Decide what club to use **Croquet** Decide shot selection

Table 8.5 Examples of Skill Execution in the Four Game Categories

Game category	Skill
Invasion games	Player shoots when open Player passes to open player Player controls the ball from a pass
Net/wall games	**Badminton** Player executes a high clear deep in opponent's court **Tennis, pickleball, badminton** Player executes drop shot close to net in front of service line **Volleyball** Player passes ball to set up an attack
Striking/fielding games	Player fields cleanly Player throws accurately to target Player hits effectively (maximize scoring; minimize outs)
Target games	Player executes a chip Player shoots an arrow Player delivers the ball Player throws a horseshoe

3. After a player decides what she is going to perform, *skill execution* must be efficient to achieve the desired outcome. Table 8.5 lists some skill execution examples in various games.

4. *Support* is important primarily to invasion games, where keeping possession is vital to scoring. To keep possession as a team, players with the ball must be able to pass to teammates who are ready and available to receive a pass. Hence, being available to support teammates (an off-the-ball move-

ment) is critical to keeping possession of the ball and scoring in an invasion game and thus to solid overall game performance.

5. Off-the-ball movements are critical aspects of defensive game play. All invasion games require players to *guard* or *mark* their opponents in order to deny them the ball and prevent them from scoring.

6. *Covering,* another defensive aspect of a game, usually involves providing backup to teammates who make challenges for the ball. In invasion games, a defender makes a

Table 8.6 Examples of Adjustments in Game Categories

Game category	Adjustment
Invasion games	Ball at the opposite end of the field—the defender will adjust position by moving at least to the halfway line in a position to support the attack if needed and to deny space should opponents counterattack.
Net/wall games	Badminton doubles pairs should adjust offensive front-back formation to a defensive side-side formation when necessary.
	Volleyball players in the front row should adjust (open up) when the ball goes to the back row (face the ball).
Striking/fielding games	Softball or cricket fielders should adjust their position according to strengths and weaknesses of batters or whether the batter is left- or right-handed.

challenge for the ball and a teammate covers the space behind him. In basketball, this is called "help" defense, and in soccer it is simply known as cover. In striking/fielding games such as softball, the fielder making a play on a ball should have a teammate covering (backup) in case of a fielding error. In net games such as volleyball, players provide cover for teammates who are attempting to spike, in case the spike is blocked.

7. *Adjust* refers to a player's ability to make adjustments to positioning as needed in the game. In other words, don't stand rooted during a game. Table 8.6 provides examples of adjustments that players may make in invasion, striking/fielding, and net/wall games.

Using the Game Performance Assessment Instrument

The appeal of the GPAI is that you as the teacher can adapt and use the instrument according to the type and focus of the game being played in your lesson, according to your students, and according to your gymnasium or playing area. The GPAI uses two basic scoring methods: (1) the 1 to 5 system (figure 8.2) and (2) a tally system (figures 8.3, 8.4, and 8.5).

Mitchell and Oslin (1999a) pointed out that the 1 to 5 scoring system is efficient for two reasons. First, observers (who are primarily you, the teachers) do not have to record each time a player is involved in the game. In invasion games and some net/wall games, this is impossible to do effectively because of the tempo, flow, and unpredictability of those games when

players have a wide range of skill levels. Second, the 1 to 5 scoring system provides for a wide range of scoring but not so broad as to make consistency of scoring difficult to achieve. As the teacher, you need to create criteria for the five indicators (that is, from very effective performance to very weak performance). These indicators will be based on your objectives, student abilities, and time available for physical education.

The tally system can be used with striking/fielding and some net/wall games because they are played at a slower pace, which gives the observer an opportunity to score or tally every event. The tally system also provides a more precise game performance measure. As you can see in the net/wall and striking/fielding game GPAI forms (see figures 8.4 and 8.5), components are scored as either "appropriate" or "inappropriate," or "efficient" or "inefficient." You can then develop percentage scores for assessed GPAI components (Mitchell & Oslin, 1999a). For example, an appropriate decision-making percentage would be calculated by dividing the number of appropriate decisions made by the total (appropriate and inappropriate) decisions made. Likewise, you could calculate a skill execution percentage by dividing efficient skill execution attempts by total skill execution attempts.

You can also give your students the bigger picture of their game play by calculating game involvement and overall game performance scores. Game involvement can be measured by adding together all responses that indicate involvement in the game, including inappropriate decisions made and inefficient skill execution (see Griffin, Mitchell, & Oslin, 1997). Do not include inappropriate guard and mark, support,

Game Performance Assessment Instrument
Invasion Games

Class: _____   Evaluator: _____   Team: _____   Game: _____

Observation dates: (a) _____   (b) _____   (c) _____   (d) _____

Scoring key: 5 = Very effective performance
4 = Effective performance
3 = Moderately effective performance
2 = Weak performance
1 = Very weak performance

Components/Criteria

1. **Skill execution**—Students pass the ball accurately, reaching the intended receiver

2. **Decision making**—Students make appropriate choices when passing (i.e., passing to unguarded teammates to set up a scoring opportunity)

3. **Support**—Students attempt to move into position to receive a pass from teammate (i.e., forward toward the goal)

Name	Skill execution	Decision making	Support

Figure 8.2   GPAI for an invasion games unit.

From *Sport Foundations for Elementary Physical Education* by Stephen Mitchell, Judith Oslin, and Linda Griffin, 2003, Champaign, IL: Human Kinetics.

adjust, and cover responses because an inappropriate response in these components indicates that the player was not involved in the game. Game performance is a more precise measure of performance quality and is calculated by adding scores from all components assessed and dividing by the number of components assessed (e.g., the percentage of decisions plus the percentage of skills executed divided by two).

In fact, each sport foundation chapter has been designed to assist you in creating GPAIs that align to each lesson and across the unit. Let's take a closer look at the chapters and suggest GPAI adaptations appropriate for those chapters. For example, each sport foundation chapter has levels of game complexity. In chapter 4, Sport Foundations for Invasion Games, there are three levels of game complexity, which

Game Performance Assessment Instrument
Support in Invasion Games

Scorer: _____ Player: _____ Game: _____

What you are looking for: Support—Students should attempt to move into position to receive a pass from a teammate.

Examples of appropriate (good) support:

- Moving forward to space after pass is made
- Positioning self in a "passing lane"
- Moving quickly and calling for the ball

Recording directions: Read the three points listed previously that tell you about good support. Referring to these points, use a tally to mark each player's attempt to support during the game.

Date	Appropriate (good supporting)	Inappropriate (not supporting)

Figure 8.3 GPAI for peer assessment of support.

From *Sport Foundations for Elementary Physical Education* by Stephen Mitchell, Judith Oslin, and Linda Griffin, 2003, Champaign, IL: Human Kinetics.

provide a scope and sequence to your instructional unit. Table 8.7 shows only game complexity level I. As you can see, it limits your instructional focus to three offensive tactical problems (keeping possession, penetrating and attacking, and overall tactics related to starting and restarting play). The levels also limit the size of the games to be played (level I uses three-a-side

Game Performance Assessment Instrument
Net/Wall Games

Class: _____ Evaluator: _____ Team: _____ Game: _____

Observation dates: (a) _____ (b) _____ (c) _____ (d) _____

Components and Criteria:

- **Skill execution**—Students perform underhand groundstrokes into opponent's court
- **Decision making**—Students make appropriate choices when to place a long (deep) or short shot
- **Base**—Students return to recovery position between skill attempts

Recording procedures: Use a tally to mark the observed category. Mark each player's responses during the game. If the student you are evaluating strikes the ball long or short, be sure to mark whether an appropriate (A) or inappropriate (IA) decision was made and whether the underhand groundstrokes were executed efficiently (E) or inefficiently (IE).

Name	Skill execution		Decision making		Base	
	E	IE	A	IA	A	IA

Figure 8.4 GPAI for a net/wall games unit.

Adapted, by permission, from L.L. Griffin, S.A. Mitchell, and J.L. Oslin, 1997, *Teaching sport concepts and skills* (Champaign, IL: Human Kinetics), 225.

From *Sport Foundations for Elementary Physical Education* by Stephen Mitchell, Judith Oslin, and Linda Griffin, 2003, Champaign, IL: Human Kinetics.

Game Performance Assessment Instrument
Striking/Fielding Games

Class: _____ **Evaluator:** _____ **Team:** _____ **Game:** _____

Observation dates: (a) _____ (b) _____ (c) _____ (d) _____

Components and Criteria:

- **Skill execution**—Students field ball cleanly
- **Decision making**—Students make appropriate play, considering the situation
- **Base**—Students are in appropriate starting position

Recording procedures: Use a tally to mark the observed category. Mark each player's responses during the game. If the student you are evaluating fields the ball, be sure to mark whether he made an appropriate (A) or inappropriate (IA) decision and whether the fielding was executed efficiently (E) or inefficiently (IE).

Name	Skill execution		Decision making		Base	
	E	IE	A	IA	A	IA

Figure 8.5 GPAI for a striking/fielding games unit.

From *Sport Foundations for Elementary Physical Education* by Stephen Mitchell, Judith Oslin, and Linda Griffin, 2003, Champaign, IL: Human Kinetics.

Table 8.7   Sport Foundations for Invasion Games, Complexity Level I, Three-a-Side Maximum

Tactical goals and problems	Skill
Offense and scoring	
Keeping possession	Pass, receive, footwork
	When to pass
Penetrating/attacking	Shooting, moving with the ball (dribbling)
	When to dribble
Starting and restarting play	
Beginning the game	Initiating play
Restarting from sideline and end line	Putting ball in play
Restarting from violations	Putting ball in play

maximum) as well as the skills and movements that you will teach.

You can limit the focus of your GPAI instrument to the objectives of your overall unit. Figure 8.2 is a possible GPAI for an invasion games unit. This GPAI focuses on the components of skill execution, decision making, and support. Spaces are provided for six players because level I calls for three-a-side games. Now you have an idea of how the levels of game complexity can help you link assessment with instruction.

Next, we'll examine how the lessons are designed by looking at a specific lesson (Level I, lesson 6 in chapter 4, Sport Foundations for Invasion Games). All lessons begin with the same format by stating (1) the tactical problem to be solved, (2) the game to be played, (3) the general lesson focus, and (4) the specific objective for the lesson.

TACTICAL PROBLEM: Keeping the ball and attacking.

GAME: Team handball (sponge ball).

LESSON FOCUS: Moving forward to support the passer.

OBJECTIVE: In a 3 v 3 game students will keep the ball and attack goal by moving forward to support the player with the ball.

In this lesson, the focus is on "moving forward to support the passer with the ball," which means that you should limit your GPAI use to support only. Games are complex, and with that in mind we recommend that teachers limit the observation focus for themselves as well as their students (Mitchell & Oslin, 1999a).

Now let's consider what you might arrange in the way of assessment measures. First, you can use the GPAI in figure 8.3 that focuses only on support and limit the number of students (e.g., perhaps by observing just one team) or use this form as a peer assessment tool. The goal is always to align your instruction by linking objectives, instructional activities, and assessment.

At this point, you are probably asking yourself, *Can I really do this and be accurate?* The answer is yes! Both teachers and students (peer assessment) who used a version of the GPAI in live settings to assess game performance have been considered reliable. That is, in their assessment of performance, they have been consistent with a fellow observer approximately 80% of the time. (Griffin, Dodds, & James, 1999; Oslin, Mitchell, & Griffin, 1998). You can make your GPAI measures more objective and less subjective by having two observers independently collect GPAI data and then compare scores to establish interobserver agreement. The key to establishing reliability is in the quality of the criteria stated for observation: The criteria should be specific and observable (Mitchell & Oslin, 1999a).

The GPAI examples provided are primarily *product* measures. Product measures make it easy for the observer to identify the effectiveness of the performance. For example, if supporting your teammates and passing were scored low during game play, then both teacher and student will see that there is a need to work on the techniques of those particular skills.

Process measures, which focus on the execution of movements or skills, are particularly important at the elementary level. We envision that movements and skills can be assessed during practice situations using rubrics and checklists focused on specific critical elements of specific movements or skills. As teachers, you probably use a number of these forms in your teaching on a regular basis. Both measures, product and process, can be used and combined to develop a summative evaluation.

This section has familiarized you with the GPAI as an authentic and comprehensive means for assessing game performance in the psychomotor domain that can be used successfully by both teachers and students. Because it provides all players credit for simple game involvement and for decisions and performance with and without the ball, all students—regardless of skill level—will value game improvement.

The Cognitive Domain

In teaching and learning tactical games, the cognitive domain encompasses the students' ability to know and articulate solutions to solve tactical problems (i.e., What to do?) and explains how they are going to execute particular skills and movements (i.e., How to do it?).

The cognitive domain parallels the NASPE Content Standard 2 (NASPE, 1995), which states, "A physically educated person applies movement concepts and principles to the learning and development of motor skills" (p. 1). Assessment in the cognitive domain would consist of testing students' ability to articulate aspects of game understanding.

As teachers, you know that there are many ways to assess students' knowledge and understanding about sport-related games. We know you will be familiar with many types of assessment tools mentioned in school reform literature such as written tests, reflective journals, checklists, portfolios, role-playing, student logs, and demonstrations, to name a few. We encourage you to use other resources such as *Moving Into the Future: National Physical Education Standards* (NASPE, 1995), *Teaching Middle School Physical Education* (Mohnsen, 2003), and *Teaching for Outcomes in Elementary Physical Education* (Hopple, 1995) for additional assessment tools. The following are some of the ways you can get started assessing cognitive aspects of game performance that emphasize a tactical approach.

1. *Question and answer* sessions, such as those provided in our books, provide two opportunities for formative question-and-answer-type assessment. The first time is right after the initial game (game 1), when the teacher can ask the questions regarding (1) What to do? (i.e., tactical awareness) and (2) How to do it? (i.e., skill execution). A question and answer session that targets the focus and specific objective of the lesson serves three functions. First, it shifts the students to the center of the learning environment and you to the role of facilitator. Second, students share what they already know (i.e., prior knowledge) and begin to think critically about the tactical problem that you have presented in your small-sided conditioned game. Third, as students develop game understanding, they will begin to connect the tactical similarities among games, and this tactical understanding can transfer to other games (Mitchell & Oslin, 1999b). The second opportunity in our lesson outlines for a question and answer session is at the end of the lesson, during closure. You should see this as an opportunity to debrief your students by asking three questions: (1) What happened? (2) What does it mean? (3) Now what?

2. A *"one-minute quiz"* is a written or verbal test used at the end of a lesson as a check for understanding (Griffin & Oslin, 1990). Quiz questions are simple and hold students accountable for learning lesson content. "Think tactically" when you design questions. For example, have your students (1) solve a tactical problem, (2) make connections among games from the same category, and (3) describe different skills and movements practiced in class. The following questions show a tactical focus:

> *Q. What are the ways we tried to maintain possession of the ball?* (The focus of this question is on the different skills or movements used to solve the tactical problem of maintaining possession of the ball in an invasion game, for example, in basketball, soccer, or hockey.)

> A. Pass, dribble, or support, depending on the lesson focus.

> *Q. How are volleyball, tennis, badminton, and handball similar?* (The focus of this question is on understanding the similarities that these games have because they

are in the same classification, such as net/wall games).

A. All are net or wall games, in which the primary rule is to propel an object over the net or against the wall in such as way that it cannot be returned by an opponent.

Q. What are the learning cues for support that we used today?

A. Quick straight movement, call for a pass.

3. In *scenario activities,* students would be asked to solve tactical problems that you design as an activity. Figures 8.6 and 8.7 are examples of possible invasion game scenarios, whereas figures 8.8 and 8.9 are net/wall game examples. Scenarios could be completed by the student as a worksheet on which they could draw and write or by a class as a verbal discussion. Sometimes students know what to do in a game but cannot always execute it, so scenarios provide students with opportunity to show their game play knowledge. We encourage you to use the scenarios provided as a beginning but to develop your own based on the content taught.

4. Use of *self-report journals* allows the teacher and students a simple way to keep track of written assignments. Students can self-report or use their journals for the "one-minute quizzes" or to reflect on their game performance assessment measures (GPAI; e.g., how they might improve their performance). Self-report journals provide a medium for students to give

---

Invasion Games Scenario 1

Solving the tactical problem: Attack and penetration

Situation: This is a 2 v 2 situation in an invasion game such as soccer, team handball, or basketball. Team O is on offense and team D is on defense. You are player O1; you have the ball. How can you and your teammate (O2) work together to beat the defenders on team D and attack the goal? Try to think of two different ways. Explain below what you would do and draw lines on the figure to illustrate.

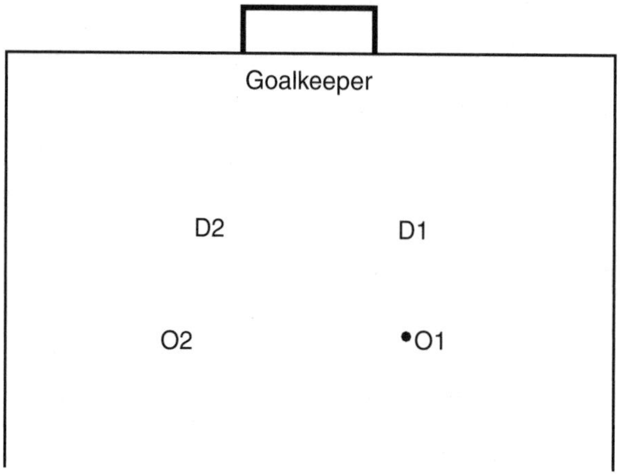

1. I could . . .

2. I could . . .

Figure 8.6 Invasion games scenario 1.

From *Sport Foundations for Elementary Physical Education* by Stephen Mitchell, Judith Oslin, and Linda Griffin, 2003, Champaign, IL: Human Kinetics.

Invasion Games Scenario 2

Solving the tactical problem: Defending space

Situation: This is a 3 v 3 basketball game situation, with team O on offense. You are on team D, and player O1 on team O has the ball. Team D is not defending very well! Draw arrows on the court to show where you and your teammates can position yourselves to make it harder for team O to attack the basket.

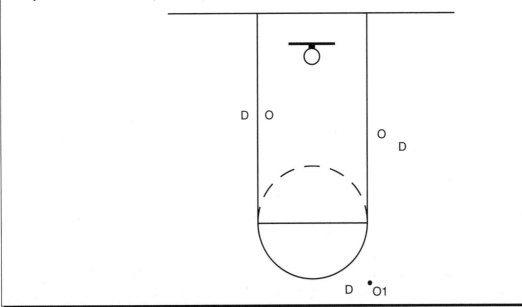

Figure 8.7 Invasion games scenario 2.

From *Sport Foundations for Elementary Physical Education* by Stephen Mitchell, Judith Oslin, and Linda Griffin, 2003, Champaign, IL: Human Kinetics.

you feedback about their own game performance. In addition, they provide you with a permanent product, which does not have to be evaluated immediately.

The following is a way for you to use the self-report journal *so that your students will actually reflect on their understanding of the game.* Students are asked to reflect on game-play data, either at the end of class or as homework. Students are asked to answer the following questions:

- What does the information tell you about your game play?
- How can you improve your play?
- What would you do differently?
- How could you help your team's performance?

The Behavioral and Social Domain

In teaching and learning tactical games, the behavioral and social domain addresses students' socialization into sport. Students need to

be aware that there is not only *in-game* knowledge (e.g., what to do and how to do it) but also knowledge *about* games in general. For example, students need to understand that for competition to be good and appropriate, players need to cooperate with their opponents (each playing their best) as well as with their fellow teammates. The behavioral and social domain parallels the NASPE Content Standard 5, which states: "A physically educated person demonstrates responsible personal and social behavior in physical activity settings" (p. 1). Thus, assessing the behavioral and social domain involves the assessment of rule and procedure adherence, cooperation, etiquette, good sporting behaviors, fair play, and teamwork (including performing assigned or selected roles within teams, such as equipment manager or statistician). We believe that these behaviors are important. They simply do not just happen: They must be planned for and taught, and students must be held accountable for them.

The purpose of this section is twofold. First, we offer two ways to frame your games units to

Net/Wall Games Scenario 1

Solving the tactical problem: Creating space in your opponent's court

Situation: This is a diagram of a court used for a net game. The thinner lines represent the boundaries of the court, and the thick line is the net. In this situation, two players (A and B) are playing a net game. You are player B. Player A hits the ball (or shuttle) to you.

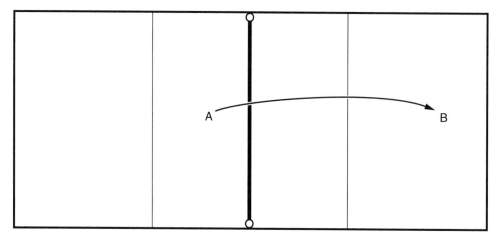

1. Place an X where you want *your* next shot to bounce.
2. Explain why you have placed the X in this position.

3. What type of shot would you need to use?

Figure 8.8 Net/wall games scenario 1.

From *Sport Foundations for Elementary Physical Education* by Stephen Mitchell, Judith Oslin, and Linda Griffin, 2003, Champaign, IL: Human Kinetics.

foster desirable games and sport behaviors and responsibility (i.e., sport citizenship). Second, we offer a few ways to assess your students for appropriate sport citizenship (i.e., behavioral and social domain) in a tactical games approach.

Promoting Appropriate Sport Citizenship

The following are several ways to promote good sport citizenship.

1. *Integrate tactical games with sport education.* Sport education (Siedentop, 1994) has the social and behavioral dimensions of games built right in. Students form teams and take on roles such as coach, equipment manager, and statistician. Teams can be assigned to be special-duty teams during tournaments, to be officials and keep score and game statistics. In sport education, students are placed in teams for the duration of a season, which allows them to get to

Net/Wall Games Scenario 2

Solving the tactical problem: Setting up an attack

Situation: In the figure displayed, team ABC is playing team DEF in a 3 v 3 volleyball game. During a rally, player E sends a free ball over the net to team ABC's player C. What should player C do with the ball?

Draw a line to where player C should put the ball and be ready to explain how player C will do this.

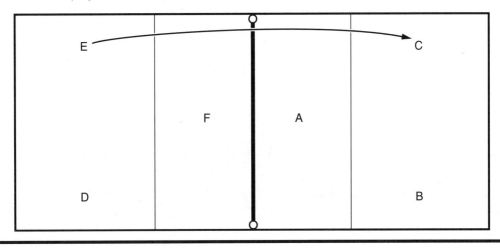

Figure 8.9 Net/wall games scenario 2.

From *Sport Foundations for Elementary Physical Education* by Stephen Mitchell, Judith Oslin, and Linda Griffin, 2003, Champaign, IL: Human Kinetics.

know each other better. This makes it more likely that they can truly work on such things as teamwork and players' roles and responsibilities. Also, question and answer sessions that focus on good sporting behaviors, fair play, and etiquette might be more meaningful when students are affiliated with a team.

2. *Introduce teaching personal and social responsibility (TPSR) levels.* As Hellison (1996) states, responsibility includes both "learning to become more responsible and learning to take responsibility" as a games player. There are five TPSR levels, which can be considered a progression (table 8.8).

We suggest several ways to implement the TPSR levels. Students could report at the end of class by simply raising the number of fingers that corresponds to their perception of the level of their own behavior for the day or week, or they could complete a simple written self-evaluation such as that shown in figure 8.10. Or you could have students complete a journal entry regarding their level with some small reflection. Finally, you, as the teacher, could use this as a way of formative assessment for students (e.g., raising the appropriate number of fingers to a student).

Assessing for Sport Citizenship

Many of the same tools and resources suggested for the cognitive domain can be designed to assess the behavioral and social domain. The following are ideas to get you started with assessment in this domain.

1. *Use a class circle discussion.* The class circle discussion is similar to the question and answer sessions built into every lesson and could be used to discuss the social and behavioral dimensions of games. For example, one of your objectives for the lesson might be for students to demonstrate respect for their peers by making at least two supportive skill- or outcome-related statements to their classmates during a practice task or game. At the end of class (i.e., closure), you could then gather students for a "class circle" to discuss some core values that make for good and appropriate sporting behavior, namely caring, respect, honesty, and responsibility.

2. *Use self-report journals* for students to reflect, or rate using TPSR levels, their sport citizenship for a particular day, event such as a tournament, or overall unit. Students could describe both positive and negative sport behaviors.

3. *Create a good citizenship rubric* (figure 8.11).

Table 8.8 Teaching Personal and Social Responsibility Levels

Level	Personally and socially responsible behavior
I. Respect for the rights and feelings of others	Maintaining self-control Respecting everyone's right to be included Respecting everyone's right to a peaceful conflict resolution
II. Participation and effort	Exploring effort Trying new things Developing a personal definition of success
III. Self-direction	Demonstrating on-task independence Developing a sound knowledge base Developing, carrying out, and evaluating a personal plan Balancing current and future needs Striving against external forces
IV. Sensitivity and responsiveness to the well-being of others	Becoming sensitive and compassionate Contributing to the community and beyond Helping others without rewards
V. Outside the gym	Trying out the levels in the classroom, on the playground and street, and at home Making decisions about the usefulness of the levels outside the gym

Adapted from D. Hellison, 1995.

The Affective Domain

In tactical games teaching and learning, the affective domain addresses the various feelings and emotions students have developed about sport-related games. For example, teachers might ask students how they feel when they win or lose or how they feel about themselves after learning a particular game. A tactical games approach foregrounds students with the underlying goal of appealing to their interest in games playing so that they value (i.e., appreciate) the need to work toward improved game performance. Improving game performance we hope will lead to greater enjoyment, interest, and perceived competence to become lifelong games players.

The affective domain parallels the NASPE Content Standards 6 and 7 (NASPE, 1995), which state that:

Standard 6: A physically educated person demonstrates understanding and respect for differences among people in physical activity settings (p. 1).

Standard 7: A physically educated person understands that physical activity provides

opportunities for enjoyment, challenge, self-expression, and social interaction (p. 1).

As you know, there are many resources to choose from to design your own tools to assess students in the affective domain. Again, many of the ideas and resources in the cognitive and behavioral and social domain sections can be used to assess the affective domain in a tactical games approach. The following are some examples you can use to begin assessing this tricky domain.

1. *Use of self-report journals for students to record:*
   a. How they felt about their particular games units.
   b. How they felt when they scored or made a basket.
   c. How they felt playing against an opponent.
   d. How they felt when they tried a new game.
   e. Successes or challenges in learning a new skill or movement.

Personal and Social Responsibility Evaluation

Name: _____   Class: _____   Team: _____

Answer questions 1 through 9 by circling the most appropriate answer for yourself.
Write down one goal as your answer to number 10.

Levels of responsibility:

I. Respect for the rights and feelings of others

II. Participation and effort

III. Self-direction

IV. Sensitivity and responsiveness to the well-being of others

V. Outside the gym

Evaluation questions: Circle Y (Yes), N (No), or S (Sometimes)

		Yes	No	Sometimes
1.	Did I listen attentively to the teacher today?	Y	N	S
2.	Did I listen to fellow students?	Y	N	S
3.	Did I take on new challenges enthusiastically?	Y	N	S
4.	Did I try hard during the lesson?	Y	N	S
5.	Did I work independently without prompting?	Y	N	S
6.	Did I tune out unnecessary disruptions?	Y	N	S
7.	Did I help others today?	Y	N	S
8.	Have I been doing these things outside the gym?	Y	N	S
9.	At which level did I work today?	I	II	III	IV	V

10. My personal goal for the next lesson is: _____

_____

_____

Figure 8.10 Personal and social responsibility self-evaluation.

From *Sport Foundations for Elementary Physical Education* by Stephen Mitchell, Judith Oslin, and Linda Griffin, 2003, Champaign, IL: Human Kinetics.

Good Sport Citizenship Rubric

Name: _____   Class: _____   Date: _____

Level	Indicators
	Makes no observable errors in interpreting or applying the rules of the game
	Refrains from actions or behaviors that endanger or injure another student
	Recognizes and acknowledges good play by a teammate or opponent

Level 3 = Uses indicators in an extremely consistent manner

Level 2 = Uses indicators with consistency most of the time

Level 1 = Uses indicators with occasional consistency

Figure 8.11 Good sport citizenship rubric.

From *Sport Foundations for Elementary Physical Education* by Stephen Mitchell, Judith Oslin, and Linda Griffin, 2003, Champaign, IL: Human Kinetics.

Name: _____					Class: _____ Date: _____
Positive behavior identified					**Negative behavior identified**
Supports and encourages teammates	5	4	3	2	1 Lacks any show of support or encouragement for teammates
Makes an effort to pass to all members of the team	5	4	3	2	1 Looks for only a select few to pass the Frisbee
Follows all calls without argument	5	4	3	2	1 Argues or breaks rules repeatedly
Returns Frisbee to opposing team in respectful manner	5	4	3	2	1 Makes getting the Frisbee difficult for the opponents when unnecessary
Does not taunt or demean anyone on either team	5	4	3	2	1 Taunts or demeans teammates or opponents
Other	5	4	3	2	1 Other

Figure 8.12 Affective domain rubric.

Adapted, by permission, from V. Melograno, 1996, *Designing the physical education curriculum*, 3rd ed. (Champaign, IL: Human Kinetics), 157.

From *Sport Foundations for Elementary Physical Education* by Stephen Mitchell, Judith Oslin, and Linda Griffin, 2003, Champaign, IL: Human Kinetics.

f. Successes or challenges when playing a particular game.

2. *Role-play.* Ask students to create a play dealing with conflict resolution during a small-sided game that they usually play in class.

3. *Affective domain rubric.* Figure 8.12 provides you with an example of a rubric for assessing the affective domain. For the behaviors listed, keep track of a student during the class (you may track different students for a set interval of time). The example shown uses a scale method of rating; you could adapt the rubric to a simple tally form and record the ratio of acceptable to unacceptable behaviors that you judge as appropriate (e.g., 4:1).

The purpose of affective domain assessment is to keep track of behaviors displayed by students during learning tasks or game play. You need to decide whether to assign a point value to the categories. Keep in mind that the games are self-officiated, so there will be opportunities to witness students taking responsibility for their behavior.

Summary

We have provided you ways to assess your students' games learning through a tactical games approach. We have outlined the potential learning outcomes and aligned a tactical approach to four domains of learning outcomes (i.e., psychomotor, cognitive, behavioral and social, and affective) as well as the NASPE Standards (1995) as guideposts for planning your tactical games unit. Our take-home message is simply that assessment, and particularly authentic assessment, matters. The teaching–learning process is not complete without assessment. By building assessment into your daily teaching, you are making an investment in your students, yourself as a teacher, and physical education as a viable subject.

chapter 9

The Tactical Games Curriculum Model

The tactical approach to games teaching can become, as David Kirk puts it, "mainstream practice" within physical education and youth sports programs (Kirk, 2001). For this possibility to become reality, Kirk suggested that, in addition to a revised research agenda, proponents of tactical games approaches must focus their efforts on conceptualizing a more formalized approach for a tactical games teaching *model* and base instructional materials (e.g., unit and lesson plans, and assessment tools) on this model.

Further, in his book *Instructional Models for Physical Education,* Metzler (2000) issued a call for "model-based instruction" as a means of focusing attention on long-term, holistic learning outcomes. He describes a teaching model as a set of teaching patterns that "ties together theory, planning, classroom management, teaching-learning processes, and assessment" (p. xxiv). In the previous chapters of this book, we have tied together these strands of the curriculum and instruction process. In this concluding chapter, we support Metzler's call for model-based instruction by proposing a conceptual framework for a tactical games model and by linking the elementary and secondary levels to suggest how a tactical games model can span the K–12th grade physical education curriculum. We will revisit the concepts underpinning the original model (simplifying it for the teacher) and re-emphasize the connections among planning, management, teaching-learning processes, and assessment that have been described in the preceding chapters.

Foundations of the Model

We should note that a curriculum model is not value free, and there are several assumptions underpinning the tactical games model. To make our values clear we should identify these assumptions.

Assumptions of the Model

First, we believe that games are an important part of the physical education curriculum because they are potentially enjoyable, lifelong physical activities and because sport itself is a prominent social institution. Clearly, educators who seek to implement games instruction in physical education at all levels value games for their educational benefits, including the emphases on decision making, problem solving, communication, teamwork, and skilled performance.

Second, children can learn to understand and play games at their own individual ability level. Unfortunately, it is common to hear claims that some young children cannot play games because they lack sufficient skill. As proponents of the tactical games model, we argue differently: Young school children can play a game if it is modified to enable meaningful play to occur. Providing meaningful play is exactly the reason for the small-sided nature of game play in the invasion games chapter of this book and for the distinct modifications to net/wall and striking/fielding games provided in chapters 5 and 6.

Third, and related to the previous assumption, games can be modified to be representative of the mature form and conditioned to emphasize tactical problems encountered in the game. Each lesson in chapters 4 through 7 contains examples of games conditioned to place students in problem-solving situations.

Fourth, games have common tactical elements or problems; when students understand these elements, they can transfer learning from one game to another. These tactical problems are the basis of the games classification system presented in table 2.1. Aiming for transfer of learning is well illustrated in chapter 4, where lessons are written in such a way as to provide for transfer of learning across the invasion games category.

Conceptual Framework

A curriculum model is sometimes best understood by referring to a diagram, or conceptual framework, outlining the major components of the model. Figure 9.1 is a conceptual framework for the tactical games model. Central to the model are the tactical problems that various games present that must be overcome in order to *score*, to *prevent scoring*, and to *start* and *restart play*. Having identified the relevant tactical problems a game presents, students will seek to *solve these problems* by making appropriate *decisions* and applying appropriate *movements* and *skills*. Again, many games within each category have similar tactical problems, an understanding of which can assist in transferring performance from one game to another.

We hope we have made clear our belief that it is possible, and desirable, to develop a progressive and sequential tactical games curriculum across the compulsory education spectrum, beginning at about second grade (about age seven). In this text, we have suggested a thematic approach for the elementary grade levels, whereas for the secondary level, our *Teaching Sport Concepts and Skills: A Tactical Games Approach* (Griffin, Mitchell, & Oslin, 1997) uses a more sport specific approach to allow for greater specificity and likely development of performance competence. These approaches raise issues of content development; the conceptual framework (see figure 9.1) can be the foundation for developing tactical frameworks to identify relevant content for learning. These frameworks can then be used to develop levels of game complexity to ensure that content is planned in developmentally appropriate progressions based on the development of game understanding and performance skill. With a tactical approach in use across a whole school district, teachers at the elementary level can begin games teaching by providing younger students with a sound basic understanding of how to play games in general. The

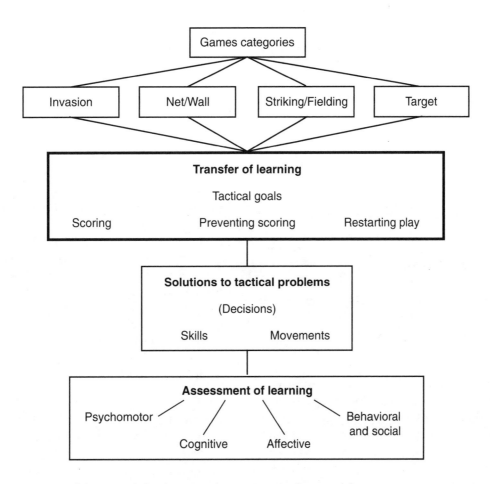

Figure 9.1   A conceptual framework for the tactical games curriculum model.

logical progression at the secondary level would be for instruction to focus on developing greater competence in specific sports by using materials such as those provided in *Teaching Sport Concepts and Skills: A Tactical Games Approach.*

Transfer of Learning

At the elementary level, one of the key theoretical concepts (evident in figure 9.1) underlying the tactical games model is that of transfer. Transfer of learning, a commonly applied principle in education, is well documented in the motor learning literature as providing the basis for the sequencing of skills or concepts to be learned (Magill, 1993). Transfer may be *positive,* when the learning of one skill or concept aids the learning of another. For example, learning to throw a ball overhand will positively affect a child's learning of the tennis service because of the biomechanical similarities of these skills. Or, as another example of positive tactical trans-

fer, remember the young girl we mentioned in the preface whose good understanding of team handball came as a result of her soccer-playing experience.

Conversely, transfer might be *negative,* when the learning of a skill or concept interferes with the learning of another. Such would be the case where a novice performer moved from learning the badminton underhand forehand drive to the tennis forehand drive. In this case, differences in racket weight and technical differences (the wrist is used much more in badminton) might cause negative transfer. Having been accustomed to using wrist action with a badminton racket, young students will have problems with consistency and accuracy if they try to use similar techniques with a (modified) tennis racket.

Support for the principle of transfer in the area of motor skill acquisition is available in the research literature (Dan Ota & Vickers, 1998; Singer, DeFrancesco, & Randall, 1989; Wrisberg & Liu, 1991). Similarly, a study by Mitchell and

Oslin (1999b) has investigated the extent to which knowledge and tactical understanding might transfer from the performance of one game to another. This study found positive transfer of understanding and game performance when novice performers began with badminton and moved to pickleball.

The principle of transfer of learning also applies to teachers. Both preservice teachers and experienced teachers can rely on the principle of learning transfer to overcome their often expressed concern that they don't know games well enough—or, more frequently, do not know a particular game sufficiently—to modify and teach it with any expertise.

Our response to the concern about knowledge of the game is that you probably know a lot more about most games than you realize, particularly if you take what you know about one game and apply it to another. For example, a college basketball player once expressed a concern to one of us that she was not sufficiently comfortable with the game of soccer to develop unit and lesson plans and then teach the game successfully. Our response was to suggest that she might begin by taking her extensive knowledge about basketball and applying it to soccer. Using this approach, she was able to develop lesson content based around deciding when to shoot, pass, or dribble and around defensive aspects of the game, such as marking or guarding. Our point is this: Though it would obviously help, you do not necessarily need to know *all* games well! If you are not familiar with many games, try to learn one game from each category and then apply that knowledge to other games within the same category. Knowledge of one game gives you a good understanding of basic tactical considerations, knowledge of starting and restarting play, and an appreciation for the spirit in which games can and should be played. For those teachers with little or no games experience, resources (including this book) are a good place to begin seeking out lesson ideas.

Aspects of Model-Based Instruction

Metzler (2000) suggests that a curriculum model comprises processes involving planning, class management, teaching and learning, and assessment practices. Here, we address these processes as each relates to a tactical games model.

Planning

Chapters 4 through 7 include numerous lesson outlines using the planning format presented in figure 2.1. This format simplifies the original six-stage Teaching Games for Understanding (TGFU) model presented by Bunker and Thorpe (1982). The original TGFU model (figure 9.2) has six stages for developing decision making and improving performance in game situations. The simplified, three-stage model presented in figure 9.3 focuses on the essential lesson components of the model, namely conditioned game play, development of tactical awareness and decision making through questioning, and development of skill. All parts of the process are important and must be planned so that several requirements are met:

- Games are modified appropriately to encourage student thinking about the tactical problem on which instruction is focused.

- Questions, designed to develop tactical awareness (understanding of what to do to solve a problem), are well thought out.

- Practice tasks teach essential skills to solve problems in as gamelike a manner as possible.

Class Management

Throughout this book, we have acknowledged the time constraints placed on elementary physical educators. These constraints make it necessary to put in place sound and efficient management procedures. Too often in elementary gymnasiums (or on fields or outside courts), we see students enter and sit in squad lines or in a circle, waiting for the teacher to begin the lesson warm-up (which are often stretches and calisthenics). Teachers who adopt these and other time-inefficient procedures are usually the first to raise concerns as to their ability to implement a tactical games lesson within the allocated time. From experience, we can tell you that a tactical games lesson is most effectively implemented when students enter the gymnasium and move straight to equipment setup and

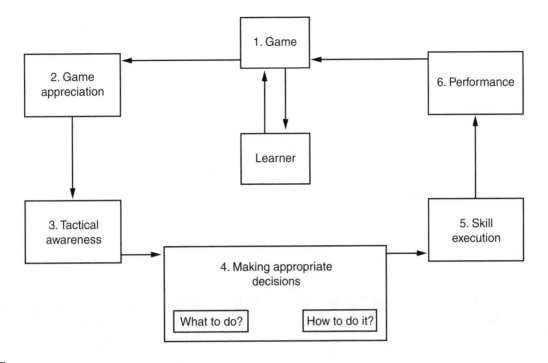

Figure 9.2   Original Teaching Games for Understanding Model.

Adapted, by permission, from R.D. Thorpe and D.J. Bunker, 1986, A model for the teaching of games in secondary schools. In *Rethinking games teaching,* edited by R. Thorpe, D. Bunker, and L. Almond (Loughborough University), 8.

modified or conditioned game play, which is itself appropriate as a warm-up activity. This start-up alleviates the need for transitions between lesson segments and immediately focuses students on the content of the lesson. With students assigned to permanent home courts or fields, the need for attendance squads is alleviated. If required, attendance can simply be taken by observation once students are actively engaged in game play. The entry procedures just described (particularly immediate entry, setup, and game-play routine), and that are an integral facet of the Sport Education model (described in chapter 3), provide an effective framework through which a tactical games model can be implemented in elementary gymnasiums.

Teaching and Learning

Using a tactical games model means the use of mixed teaching strategies, including direct and indirect teaching styles and problem-solving strategies. Teachers trained in movement education, as many elementary physical educators are, should feel a high degree of comfort with this approach. In fact some teachers have first come to understanding tactical games

teaching as being a movement education approach to games instruction. Problems or goals are set, and students are given opportunities to seek solutions to these problems. Solutions to the problems are identified through the questioning process, and these solutions then become the focus of a practice task. Direct instruction might be the preferred teaching style at this point, though this itself may depend on the specificity of the required solution. You should take care to modify practice tasks to help or to challenge students, as the students' abilities require. Lesson outlines in chapters 4 through 7 provide examples of task extensions, but be creative with this aspect of your teaching.

The quality of questions teachers ask is critical, and framing questions should be an integral part of the planning process. Literature on tactical games teaching, whether the original work of Bunker and Thorpe (1982), the Australian concept presented in *Game Sense* (Den Duyn, 1997), or our own work in *Teaching Sport Concepts and Skills,* has been consistent in emphasizing the importance of high-quality questions. Proponents of Game Sense provide good general advice on the types of questions that might

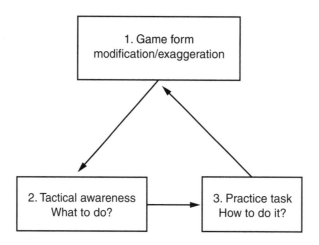

Figure 9.3   Simplified three-stage tactical games model.

be asked of students. These questions fall into three categories:

Time: "When is the best time to . . . ?"

Space: "Where is (can) . . . ?"

Risk: "Which choice . . . ?"

To these three, we can also add questions related to

What: "What skill should you use to . . . ?"

How: "How do you do that?" or "How should that skill look?"

We encourage you to develop your own questions that are meaningful to your students. Bear in mind that you can never anticipate the complete range of answers you might receive from elementary students, so be prepared to probe and perhaps ask a forced choice question ("Do you think this or that?") if greater focus of response is needed. Questioning is not an easy teaching skill to master, and it does not come naturally to everyone. At first it is OK to be "plan dependent" and to rely on writing questions on note cards, if necessary. This may seem a little mechanical, but with practice you will develop more natural questioning skills for the varied situations of your own students and gymnasium.

Assessment

Learner assessment in education is of such importance that assessment concepts are an integral component of the kindergarten through

12th grade National Content Standards for Physical Education (NASPE, 1995) and the focus of the NASPE Assessment Series for Physical Education, which includes practical tools to use for assessing learning in a variety of curriculum areas. Our concerns for learner assessment are threefold:

1. *Assessment should be an ongoing and routine part of instruction.* Assessment of learning takes time. For that reason, assessing learning cannot be left until the end of an instructional unit. Making learner assessment an ongoing and routine process, perhaps assessing one team every lesson, enables you to ensure that the learning of all students is determined and done so on more than one occurrence to account for uncharacteristically good or poor performances. Ongoing assessment is a fairer (for students) and a more accurate means of assessing student learning.

2. *Assessment should be authentic and therefore related to instructional objectives.* Where improvement of game performance is the goal of instruction, then assessment should be conducted within the context of the game. This is particularly important when we consider the wide range of outcomes that are possible in games teaching and learning. More on these outcomes in point 3 below.

3. *Assessment should be completed in all domains, namely the psychomotor, cognitive, behavioral and social, and affective domains.* The original Teaching Games for Understanding model (Bunker & Thorpe, 1982) focused on

outcomes in all domains. Understanding of games was a key cognitive goal as was the motivation to practice and become effective games players. We also attach value to learning in all domains, and we encourage you to remember that what makes physical education unique is its opportunity to achieve learning outcomes in terms of improved performance, which might indicate students' gains in more than one domain. For example, improved support play or marking and guarding might be viewed as an indicator of cognitive learning for which a student should be given credit as well as a psychomotor outcome leading to improved game performance. Game performance assessment tools such as the Games Performance Assessment Instrument described in chapter 8 and the Team Sport Assessment Procedure (Gréhaigne, Godbout, & Bouthier, 1997) have been developed to measure key outcomes during game play.

Summary

In this chapter, we contend it is time to view the tactical games approach as a way of organizing games content in the physical education curriculum in addition to being a teaching method. Games content is a substantial portion of most physical education curricula, even at the elementary level, and the tactical games model (as outlined in this chapter) provides a way of organizing games content so that young students can make conceptual connections between what often seem to be dissimilar games. The model is conceptually grounded in a games classification system that emphasizes tactical similarities among games so that young learners might better understand the common principles of similar games and come to understand games more deeply and play them more effectively.

The model also establishes a planning format that helps students identify the problems of game play, practice the solutions to these problems, and then apply these solutions to test their effectiveness during game play. Teaching styles in the tactical games model might be varied, yet the model predominantly emphasizes indirect, question-driven teaching. Finally, the model emphasizes authentic assessment of learning outcomes related to game play in its broadest sense. The tactical games model emphasizes decision making and movement as valuable aspects of performance that should be recognized, valued, taught, and assessed. Emphasis on these cognitive aspects of game play enables less skilled players to value their own performance even when they are only in a supporting role and, hence, makes learning to play games a worthwhile pursuit for all students. This increased appreciation for the contribution of all players can be, above all, the value of the tactical games model.

final comments

Recall from the preface of this book the concerns of physical educators who wanted to use a tactical games model but were concerned about implementing it at the elementary level. They told us:

- "I really like this method of games teaching, but the beginning lessons seem a bit difficult for my students!"

- "I need to try and adapt this further for my younger students!"

- "Please write a new book to help us make the most out of this approach with elementary students."

In writing this book, we hope to have helped these teachers by providing them guidelines for introducing a tactical games model as well as numerous unit and lesson ideas. The thematic approach we advocate is an effective way of producing knowledgeable and adaptable games players at the elementary level who can then progress to develop greater sport-specific expertise at the middle school and secondary level.

Resources such as our own *Teaching Sport Concepts and Skills: A Tactical Games Approach* (Griffin, Mitchell, & Oslin, 1997) are beginning to provide teachers with tested materials for specific sports. We hope that, in addition to satisfying teacher concerns such as those mentioned above, we have provided a fresh way to view the organization and teaching of games within the elementary physical education curriculum. Both students and teachers will benefit from coming to understand the conceptual similarities among games within the same tactical classification.

Physical education is at a critical crossroads today. Teachers need support and materials to enable them to demonstrate and document student achievement. It is no longer sufficient to suggest a handful of isolated games or lessons to teachers and then expect them to develop them further into developmentally appropriate and sequential curriculum content on their own. We hope to have played a part, along with others, particularly Metzler (2000), in causing a shift from viewing tactical games teaching as simply a teaching method to seeing it as a curriculum model. To aid the teacher in implementing the tactical games model, this book provides organizational frameworks for games content, class management, instruction, and assessment.

We believe that a tactical games model is an alternative, practical, and effective way of thinking about and organizing the games curriculum and games instruction in the context of physical education programs. Through our experience, along with that of our colleagues, and reinforced by our research, we have seen that a tactical games model is preferable for both students and teachers. Both find that increased time spent in meaningful, goal-oriented game play and question-driven skill practice is beneficial to motivation, understanding, and performance. We find that most teachers are astounded that they have not previously thought about games conceptually, and we often get the reaction, "Wow! This makes a lot of sense."

Finally, we find that—almost without exception—teachers who rise to the challenge of thinking differently about games teaching and changing the way they teach have been successful and have not returned to their earlier practices. We hope you will have similarly successful experiences and will let us (and others) know of your success. Good luck!

references

Almond, L. (1986). Reflecting on themes: A games classification. In R. Thorpe, D. Bunker, & L. Almond. *Rethinking games teaching* (pp. 71–72). Loughborough, England: University of Technology.

Bunker, D., & Thorpe, R. (1982). A model for the teaching of games in secondary schools. *Bulletin of Physical Education, 18:* 5–8.

Clement, J. (1993). Using bridging analogies and anchoring intuitions to deal with students' perceptions in physics. *Journal of Research in Science Teaching, 30,* 1241–1257.

Cohen, S.A. (1987). Instructional alignment: Searching for the magic bullet. *Educational Researcher, 16*(8), 16–20.

Dan Ota, K., & Vickers, J.N. (1998). The effects of variable practice on the retention and transfer of two volleyball skills in male club-level athletes. *Journal of Sport and Exercise Psychology, NASPSPA Abstracts, 20*(Suppl.), S121.

Den Duyn, N. (1997). *Game sense: Developing thinking players.* Belconnen, ACT, Australia: Australian Sports Commission.

Dodds, P., Griffin, L.L., & Placek, J.H. (2001). A selected review of the literature on development of learners' domain-specific knowledge. *Journal of Teaching in Physical Education, 20,* 301–313.

French, K.E., Werner, P.H., Rink, J.E., Taylor, K., & Hussey, K. (1996). The effects of a 3-week unit of tactical, skill, or combined tactical and skill instruction on badminton performance of ninth-grade students. *Journal of Teaching in Physical Education, 15,* 418–438.

French, K.E., & Thomas, J.R. (1987). The relation of knowledge development to children's basketball performance. *Journal of Sport Psychology, 9,* 15–32.

Fronske, H., and Wilson, R. (2002). *Teaching cues for basic sport skills for elementary and middle school students.* Boston, MA: Benjamin Cummings.

Gallahue, D.L., & Ozmun, J.C. (1995). *Understanding Motor Development* (3rd ed.). Madison, WI: Brown and Benchmark.

Gentile, A. (1972). A working model for skill acquisition with application to teaching. *Quest, 17,* 3–23.

Graham, G., Holt/Hale, S.A., & Parker, M. (2001). *Children moving: A reflective approach to teaching physical education* (5th ed.). Mountain View, CA: Mayfield.

Gréhaigne, J-F., & Godbout, P. (1995). Tactical knowledge in team sports from a constructivist and cognitivist perspective. *Quest, 47,* 490–505.

Gréhaigne, J-F., Godbout, P., & Bouthier, D. (1997). Performance assessment in team sports. *Journal of Teaching in Physical Education, 16,* 500–516.

Griffin, L., & Oslin, J. (1990). Got a minute: A quick and easy strategy for knowledge testing in physical education. *Strategies: A Journal for Physical and Sport Educators, 4*(2), 6–7, 23.

Griffin, L.L., Dodds, P., & James, A. (1999, April). Game performance assessment in 5th/6th grade tactical badminton curriculum unit. Paper presented at the annual Association Internationale des Écoles Supérieures d'Education Physique World Sport Science Congress, Besançon, France.

Griffin, L.L., Mitchell, S.A., & Oslin, J.L. (1997). *Teaching sport concepts and skills: A tactical games approach.* Champaign, IL: Human Kinetics.

Griffin, L.L., & Placek, J.H. (2001). The understanding and development of learners' domain-specific knowledge [Monograph]. *Journal of Teaching in Physical Education, 20,* 299–419.

Hellison, D. (1996). Teaching personal and social responsibility in physical education. In S.J. Silverman & C.D. Ennis (Eds.), *Student learning in physical education: applying research to enhance* (pp. 269–286). Champaign, IL: Human Kinetics.

Hopple, C. (1995). *Teaching for outcomes in elementary physical education: A guide for curriculum and assessment.* Champaign, IL: Human Kinetics.

James, A., Griffin, L.L., & France, T. (2000, March). Students', teachers', parents', and a principal's perceptions of assessment in elementary physical education. *Research Quarterly for Exercise and Sport, 71*(Suppl.), 73.

Kirk, D. (2001, August 3). Future directions for teaching games for understanding games scene. Keynote address at the International Conference on Teaching

Games for Understanding in Physical Education and Sport, Waterville Valley, NH.

Magill, R.A. (1993). *Motor learning: Concepts and applications.* Madison, WI: Brown and Benchmark.

Melograno, V. (1996). *Designing the physical education curriculum* (3rd ed.). Champaign, IL: Human Kinetics.

Metzler, M.W. (2000). *Instructional models for physical education.* Needham Heights, MA: Allyn and Bacon.

Mitchell, S., & Oslin, J. (1999b). An investigation of tactical understanding in net games. *European Journal of Physical Education, 4,* 162–172.

Mitchell, S., Oslin, J., & Griffin, L. (1995). The effects of two instructional approaches on game performance. *Pedagogy in practice: Teaching and coaching in physical education and sport, 1,* 36–48.

Mitchell, S.A., & Oslin, J.L. (1999a). *Assessment in games teaching. NASPE assessment series.* Reston, VA: National Association of Sport and Physical Education.

Mohnsen, B. (2003). *Teaching middle school physical education: A standards-based approach for grades 5–8* (2nd ed.). Champaign, IL: Human Kinetics.

National Association of Sport and Physical Education (NASPE). (1995). *Moving into the future: National standards for physical education.* Boston, MA: McGraw-Hill.

Nevett, M., Rovengo, I., & Babiarz, M. (2001). Fourth-grade children's knowledge of cutting, passing and tactics in invasion games after a 12-lesson unit of instruction. *Journal of Teaching in Physical Education, 20,* 389–401.

Oslin, J., Collier, C., & Mitchell, S. (2001). Living the curriculum. *Journal of Physical Education, Recreation and Dance, 72*(5), 47–51.

Oslin, J., & Mitchell, S. (1998). Form follows function. *Journal of Physical Education, Recreation and Dance, 69*(6), 46–49.

Oslin, J.L., Mitchell, S.A., & Griffin, L.L. (1998). The Game Performance Assessment Instrument (GPAI): Development and preliminary validation. *Journal of Teaching in Physical Education, 17,* 231–243.

Piaget, J. (1954). *The construction of reality and the child.* New York: Basic Books.

Siedentop, D. (1994). *Sport education.* Champaign, IL: Human Kinetics.

Siedentop, D., Herkowitz, J., & Rink, J. (1984). *Elementary physical education methods.* Inglewood Cliffs, NJ: Prentice Hall.

Siedentop, D., & Tannehill, D. (2000). *Developing teaching skills in physical education* (4th ed.). Mountain View, CA: Mayfield.

Singer, R.N., DeFrancesco, C., & Randall, L.E. (1989). Effectiveness of a global learning strategy practiced in different contexts on primary and transfer self-paced motor tasks. *Journal of Sport and Exercise Psychology, 11,* 290–303.

Tucker, G.R. (1996). Some thoughts concerning innovative language education programmes. *Journal of Multilingual and Multicultural Development, 17,* 315–320.

Turner, A., & Martinek, T. (1992). A comparative analysis of two models for teaching games (technique approach and game-centered (tactical focus) approach). *International Journal of Physical Education, 29*(4), 15–31.

Veal, M.L. (1993). The role of assessment and evaluation in secondary physical education: A pedagogical view. In J.E. Rink (Ed.), *Critical crossroads: Middle and secondary school physical education* (pp. 93–99). Reston, VA: National Association of Sport and Physical Education.

Wandersee, J., Mintzes, J., & Novak, J. (1994). *Handbook of research on science teaching* (pp. 177–210). New York: Macmillan.

Wrisberg, C.A., & Liu, Z. (1991). The effect of contextual variety on the practice, retention, and transfer of an applied motor skill. *Research Quarterly for Exercise and Sport, 62,* 406–412.

Zessoules, T., & Gardner, H. (1991). Authentic assessment: Beyond the buzzword and into the classroom. In V. Perrone (Ed.), *Expanding student assessment* (pp. 47–71). Alexandria, VA: Association for Supervision and Curriculum Development.

about the authors

Stephen Mitchell, PhD, is an associate professor of sport pedagogy at Kent State University. He received his undergraduate and master's degrees from Loughborough University, England, where the tactical approach was first developed; and he earned a PhD in teaching and curriculum at Syracuse University. An avid soccer player and licensed coach, he has employed a tactical approach in teaching and coaching at the elementary, middle school, high school, and college levels since 1982. Dr. Mitchell is a member of the American Alliance for Health, Physical Education, Recreation and Dance (AAHPERD), the Ohio Association for Health, Physical Education, Recreation and Dance (OAHPERD), and the National Association for Physical Education in Higher Education (NAPEHE).

Stephen Mitchell

Judith Oslin, PhD, is a professor of sport pedagogy at Kent State University. She received her undergraduate and master's degrees from Kent State and earned a PhD in sport pedagogy at Ohio State University. She has 28 years of experience as a physical educator and teacher educator. She has used the tactical approach with elementary, middle school, high school, and university students. Dr. Oslin has also presented numerous papers and workshops focusing on implementation of the tactical approach and the Game Performance Assessment Instrument at the international, national, regional, state, and local levels. She is a member of numerous professional organizations, including AAHPERD, NAPEHE, the American Educational Research Association (AERA), and the National Association for Girls and Women in Sport (NAGWS).

Judith Oslin

Linda Griffin, PhD, received her doctorate in physical education and teacher education from Ohio State University. As a physical educator and coach since 1976, Dr. Griffin has conducted extensive research, published nearly 30 articles and book chapters, and given numerous presentations on the tactical approach. She served on the planning committee for the first Teaching Games for Understanding Conference in New Hampshire in 2001. A former college volleyball player and coach, she is an associate professor at the University of Massachusetts at Amherst and a member of AAHPERD and AERA.

Linda Griffin